D0707078

CONTENTS

WORKBOOK 1:
WRITING AND ANALYSIS WORKBOOK TO ACCOMPANY

The
COMPLETE MUSICIAN

AN INTEGRATED APPROACH TO THEORY,
ANALYSIS, AND LISTENING

Fourth Edition

Steven G. Laitz

Eastman School of Music and The Juilliard School

New York   Oxford
OXFORD UNIVERSITY PRESS

Oxford University Press is a department of the University of Oxford.
It furthers the University's objective of excellence in research,
scholarship, and education by publishing worldwide.

Oxford   New York
Auckland   Cape Town   Dar es Salaam   Hong Kong   Karachi
Kuala Lumpur   Madrid   Melbourne   Mexico City   Nairobi
New Delhi   Shanghai   Taipei   Toronto

With offices in
Argentina   Austria   Brazil   Chile   Czech Republic   France   Greece
Guatemala   Hungary   Italy   Japan   Poland   Portugal   Singapore
South Korea   Switzerland   Thailand   Turkey   Ukraine   Vietnam

For titles covered by Section 112 of the US Higher Education Opportunity Act,
please visit www.oup.com/us/he for the latest information about pricing and
alternate formats.

Published by Oxford University Press
198 Madison Avenue, New York, New York 10016
http://www.oup.com

Oxford is a registered trademark of Oxford University Press

ISBN 9780199347100

Printing number: 9

Printed in the United States of America
on acid-free paper

PREFACE

The workbooks accompanying the fourth edition of *The Complete Musician* maintain the same organization as in the previous edition, which was designed specifically for greater flexibility. *Workbook 1: Writing and Analysis* contains all written and analytical activities, including figured bass, melody harmonization, model composition, and analysis. *Workbook Volume 2: Skills and Musicianship* is devoted to musicianship skills with an emphasis on crucial skill development exercises. These include singing model progressions (through arpeggiation), extensive and varied keyboard studies, improvisation, and many types of harmonic dictation (with an emphasis on the music literature). All are performed on the instruments designated by the composers.

Each workbook chapter aligns with the corresponding chapter in the text. The materials are organized into discrete assignments. Exercises are carefully graduated, ranging from basic, introductory tasks (such as identification and comparison), to more-active writing exercises within a highly regulated yet musical context, and finally to elaborate compositions that present students with more creative choices.

Recordings to accompany these exercises—from solo piano to full orchestra—are available on the companion website, www.oup.com/us/laitz. They are played by students and faculty from the Eastman School of Music. Between the two workbooks there are over 3,900 recorded analytical and dictation examples, and more than 15 hours of recorded music, all of which are in high-quality mp3 format. Additional supplementary material is available on the companion website.

Musical Space

ASSIGNMENT 1A.1
EXERCISES FOR SCALES AND KEY SIGNATURES

EXERCISE 1A.1 *Writing Scale Fragments*

Study each of the following scale fragments and determine in which major *and* minor scales the fragments could be members; write out the complete scales and include scale degrees. For example, given the fragment A and C♯ the answer would be:

Major scales: A, D, E
Minor scales: B (natural), C♯ (natural and harmonic), D (melodic and harmonic),
    E (melodic), F♯ (melodic, harmonic, *and* natural). Make sure that you specify the
    form of minor.

1. E♭–F–G	2. F♯–G	3. C–E	4. G–D
5. A–B–C	6. F–G–A♭	7. E–B♭	

WRITING

EXERCISE 1A.2 *Key Signatures, Relative and Parallel Keys*

A. Write the following key signatures from memory: A major, E♭ major, D minor, B major, G minor, F♯ minor, B♭ minor.

B. Name the relative minor keys of E♭ major, A♭ major, B major, and F major; then write their scales using accidentals, not key signatures.

C. Name the relative majors of C minor, F minor, G minor, and A♭ minor; then write their scales using accidentals, not key signatures.

D. Name the parallel minors of A, B, F♯, D, E♭, then write their scales using accidentals, not key signatures.

E. Transpose the given melody as follows:
  1. to the relative minor (use accidentals)
  2. up a fifth (use key signature)
  3. down a whole step (use accidentals)
  4. to the parallel minor (use key signature)

Brahms, "O wüsst' ich doch den Weg zurück"

O wüsst' ich doch den Weg zu-rück, den lie - ben Weg __ zum Kin - der-land!
O   if   I only know the   road back to the dear _ way back _   to   child _   land!

EXERCISE 1A.3 *Intervals*

On a separate sheet of manuscript paper, notate pitches above or below the given pitch name at the required interval and in the appropriate register. Possibilities are diatonic half step, chromatic half step, whole step, fifth, and octave. You may be asked to notate pitches using enharmonic spellings.

Sample solutions:

1. What pitch lies a fifth above A♭4? Answer: E♭5

2. What pitch lies a chromatic half step below C3? Answer: C♭2

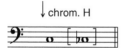

What pitch lies:

A. A whole step above D♭3? _____

B. A diatonic half step below G2? _____

C. An octave above A♭4? (use an enharmonic equivalent) _____

D. A fifth above B♭2? _____

E. A whole step below B5? (use an enharmonic equivalent) _____

F. A chromatic half step above F♯4? _____

G. A fifth below E3? _____

H. A diatonic half step above E6? _____

I. An octave below A4? (use an enharmonic equivalent) _____

J. A whole step above B5? _____

ASSIGNMENT 1A.2
EXERCISES FOR SCALES AND KEY SIGNATURES

EXERCISE 1A.4   *Correction*

A. The key signatures notated do not represent the given keys. Correct the notated key signature, including placement on staff, then provide the correct signature in the clef above or below the one given.

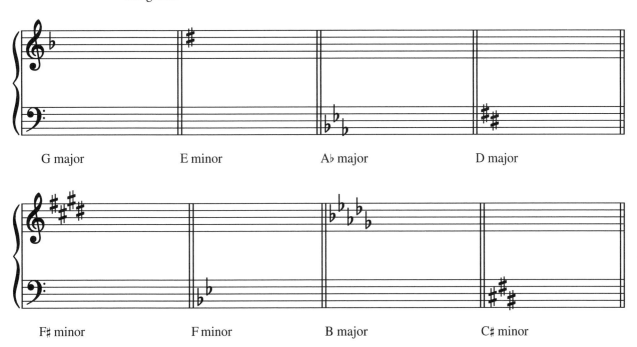

G major   E minor   A♭ major   D major

F♯ minor   F minor   B major   C♯ minor

B. The scales notated do not represent their label. Correct any misspelled or otherwise incorrectly notated pitches in order to agree with the given label.

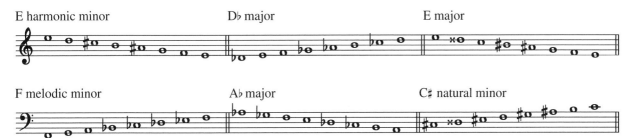

E harmonic minor   D♭ major   E major

F melodic minor   A♭ major   C♯ natural minor

ANALYSIS

EXERCISE 1A.5   *Scale and Key Analysis: Major Mode*

The following examples are taken from the literature. Each fragment is in a major key other than C, lacks a key signature, and may begin and end on a note other than the tonic. Based on the given pitches, determine the key for each example. Place the name of the key at the beginning of each example, and label each pitch by scale degree number.

Sample:

What are the possible keys? E♭ and A♭. Why? Because there are three flats present (which means a key that contains at least three flats is used), indicating E♭ major. Why is A♭ possible? Because there is no D or D♭ in the melody, which would reduce the options to just one. Why couldn't the key be D♭? Because a G♭ would be required, given that D♭ contains five flats, and a G♮ is encountered in the example. What are the clues to narrow it down? E♭ sounds like a resting point more than A♭ does.

A.

What are the possible keys? _____

What are the clues to narrow it down? _____

What key is it? _____

B.

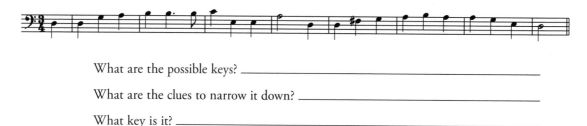

What are the possible keys? _____

What are the clues to narrow it down? _____

What key is it? _____

C.

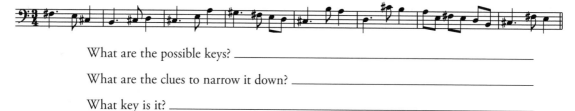

What are the possible keys? _____

What are the clues to narrow it down? _____

What key is it? _____

EXERCISE 1A.6   *Scale Fragments and Transposition*

    A. Transpose each given major-scale opening (Example A) three (3) fifths forward (clockwise) on the circle of fifths. For example, given D–E–F♯ (1̂–2̂–3̂ in D major) you would write B–C♯–D♯, because three fifths up from D is B major (D–A–E–B).

    B. Transpose each natural-minor-scale opening (Example B) three fifths backward (counterclockwise) on the circle of fifths.

A. major: B. minor:

  1.   2.   3.   1.   2.   3.

ASSIGNMENT 1A.3
EXERCISES FOR SCALES AND KEY SIGNATURES

EXERCISE 1A.7   *Brain Twister*

Provided is a series of sharps and flats that will become key signatures. Notate these correctly on staff paper. Then write the following required scales, which bear no relation and often contradict the given key signatures.

Notate the required scales using appropriate accidentals. For example, given the key signature of two sharps (i.e., F♯ and C♯), write a B♭ major scale. You would notate: B♭, C♮, D, E♭, F♮, G, A, B♭. Given the following key signatures:

    A. One sharp, write an E♭ major scale.
    B. Three flats, write a D major scale.
    C. Three sharps, write a C natural minor scale.
    D. Four flats, write a C♯ harmonic minor scale.

ANALYSIS

EXERCISE 1A.8   *Scale Analysis: Minor Keys*

Determine the minor scale/key by considering the following: The key signature for minor scales is derived from the natural minor scale, composers must raise $\hat{7}$ to create a half step between it and $\hat{8}$, the tonic. Thus, you will encounter an added sharp when the key signature contains sharps or an added natural when the key signature contains flats.

For example, in E minor, the relative minor of G major, F♯ appears in the key signature. You will also encounter the chromatic pitch D♯ rather than D♮ on $\hat{7}$, since composers usually use a leading tone. One of the examples ends on its tonic; which one is it?

A. Schumann, "Hör ich das Liedchen klingen" ("When I Hear the Little Song"), *Dichterliebe*, op. 48

B. Schumann, "Wilder Reiter," *Album für die Jugend*, op. 68, no. 8

C. Schumann, "Es leuchtet meine Liebe" ("My Love Gleams"), op. 127, no. 3

D. Mozart, Symphony no. 40 in G minor, K. 550, *Allegro molto*

EXERCISE 1A.9   *Scrambled Major and Minor Scales*

Determine which major and/or minor scale is used in the exercises shown, and notate the ascending form of the scale. Recall that every major scale contains the same pitch classes as its relative natural-minor form. Adhere to the following guidelines:

- Look for accidentals, since their type (sharps or flats) and number will reduce the 12 possible keys to only one or at the most two. For example, given two sharps (F♯ and C♯), the major key would be D and the minor key would be B (natural minor).
- For harmonic and melodic forms of minor: To create ♯$\hat{6}$ and ♯$\hat{7}$ minor keys will add sharps as accidentals or will add naturals as accidentals (which omit flats from the key signature).
- Notate the pitches in ascending order, beginning with $\hat{1}$. Make sure that the key-defining half- and whole-step pattern conforms to one of the patterns that has been discussed. Label the key and the mode, and, when appropriate, specify the type of minor scale used.

The sample solution contains B♭ and E♭, which means that either B♭ major or G minor (natural) could be the scale.

Sample solution:

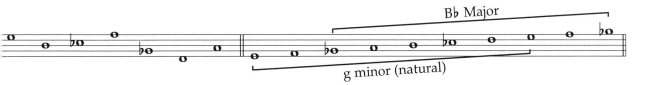

ASSIGNMENT 1A.4   EXERCISES FOR SCALE FORMS: RELATIVE AND PARALLEL RELATIONSHIPS

ANALYSIS

EXERCISE 1A.10   *Minor Scale Forms*

STREAMING AUDIO
www.oup.com/us/laitz

Label the type of minor scale(s) that appear in each of the examples. Circle and identify the following scale degrees using these labels: ♭3̂, ♭6̂, ♯6̂, ♭7̂, ♯7̂. When you encounter the harmonic minor scale, do ♭6̂ and ♯7̂ occur in the same voice? If so, does one lead to the other, or does ♭6̂ arise from and return to 5̂ (i.e., 5̂– ♭6̂–5̂) as ♯7̂ is connected with 8̂?

A. Beethoven, String Quartet in F minor, op. 95, *Allegro con brio*

scale type: _____

B. Bach, "Herr Jesu Christ, du höchstes Gut"

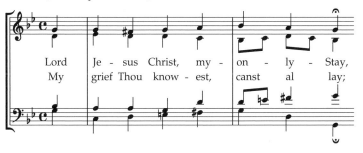

scale type: _____

C. Haydn, Piano Sonata in D major, Hob XVI.33, *Adagio*

scale type: _____

EXERCISE 1A.11   *Scale Analysis: Minor and Major Keys*

Determine the initial key of the excerpt, then bracket new major- and minor-key areas as they occur. Recall the leading tone in minor: $\hat{7}$ will need to be raised, so you will encounter one more accidental than is found in the key signature. For example, the key of B minor contains two sharps, F♯ and C♯, but you will also find A♯, which is not in the key signature but is necessary to create a leading tone.

A. Mozart, Symphony no. 40 in G minor, K. 550

B.

C. Haydn, Piano Sonata in E minor

EXERCISE 1A.12   *Comparing Tonal Relationships: Relative, Parallel, and Dominant*

Each pair of examples shown here is taken from the same piece. Identify their relationship as relative, parallel, or dominant.

- You may encounter parallel relationships in which the enharmonically equivalent key is used for reading ease. For example, a modal shift from A♭ major to its parallel minor would require playing in the seven-flat key of A♭ minor; composers often renotate such a passage in the five-sharp key of G♯ minor.
- Do not assume that the keys implied by the given key signature necessarily apply to the passages.

A. Beethoven Piano Sonata in G major, op. 31/1

B. Haydn, Piano Sonata in F major, Hob XVI.47

C. Haydn, Piano Sonata in F major, Hob XVI.47

D. Schubert, Moments Musicale in C♯ minor, D. 780

ASSIGNMENT 1A.5
EXERCISES FOR SCALES AND INTERVALS

EXERCISE 1A.13   *Analysis and Writing*

Determine the key of each melodic excerpt, then transpose as follows: If the excerpt is in major, transpose to the parallel minor. If the excerpt is in minor, transpose to the relative major.

A. Mozart, Violin Sonata in F major, K. 377, Tema, variation 3

B. "Baa, Baa, Black Sheep"

Baa, baa, black sheep, have you an-y wool? Yes, sir, yes, sir, three bags full.

One for my mas-ter, one for my dame, One for the lit-tle boy who lives down the lane.

C. Mozart, Violin Sonata in G major, K. 379, Tema, Variation 4

D. Mozart Violin Concert no. 3 in G major, K. 216, Rondeau

EXERCISE 1A.14 *Keys and Transpositions*

Determine the possible key(s) for each group of pitches. Then, according to the instructions, transpose each pattern to the empty clef above or below the notated version.

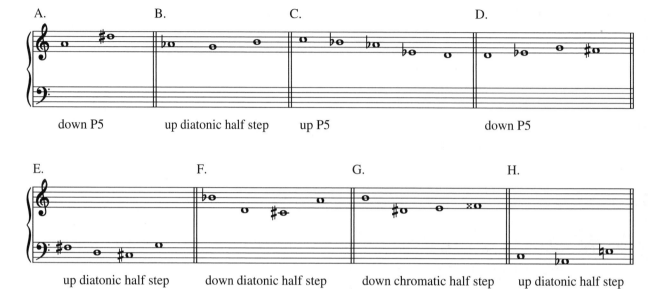

A.	B.	C.	D.
down P5	up diatonic half step	up P5	down P5

E.	F.	G.	H.
up diatonic half step	down diatonic half step	down chromatic half step	up diatonic half step

ASSIGNMENT 1A.6   EXERCISES FOR GENERIC AND DIATONIC INTERVALS

ANALYSIS

EXERCISE 1A.15   *Generic Intervals: Melodic and Harmonic, Simple and Compound*

STREAMING AUDIO
www.oup.com/us/laitz

Fill in all three blanks for A–I:

1. The generic (numerical) size of each interval.
2. Whether the interval occurs melodically (mel) or harmonically (har).
3. Whether the interval is simple (s) or compound (c).

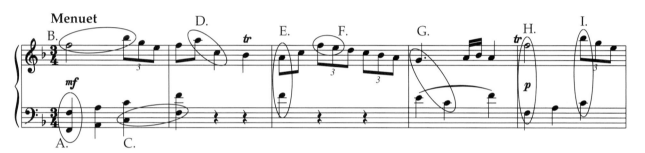

A. 1. _8_	2. _har_	3. _s_	F. 1. ____	2. ____	3. ____
B. 1. ____	2. ____	3. ____	G. 1. ____	2. ____	3. ____
C. 1. ____	2. ____	3. ____	H. 1. ____	2. ____	3. ____
D. 1. ____	2. ____	3. ____	I. 1. ____	2. ____	3. ____
E. 1. ____	2. ____	3. ____			

EXERCISE 1A.16   *Identifying Perfect, Major, and Minor Intervals*

Identify only the perfect, major, and minor intervals; do not label the remaining intervals. Use the analytical technique that views the lower note as the tonic of a scale.

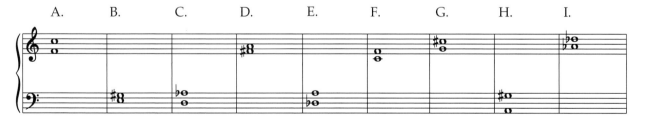

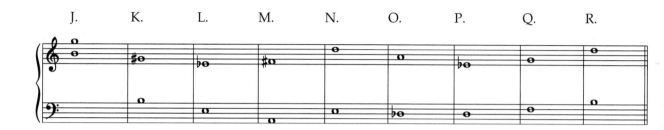

ANALYSIS

EXERCISE 1A.17 *Identifying Descending Melodic Intervals*

Identify the interval notated.

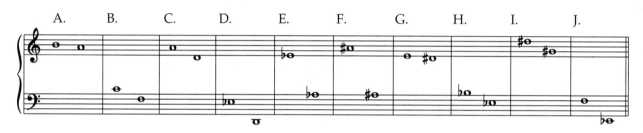

WRITING

EXERCISE 1A.18 *Generating Intervals*

Notate the following intervals above the given pitches.

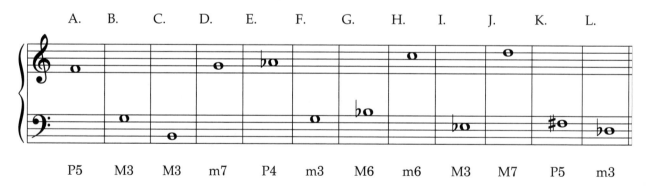

P5   M3   M3   m7   P4   m3   M6   m6   M3   M7   P5   m3

ASSIGNMENT 1A.7
EXERCISES FOR ALL INTERVALS

WRITING

EXERCISE 1A.19   *Generating Intervals*

Notate the following intervals below the given pitches.

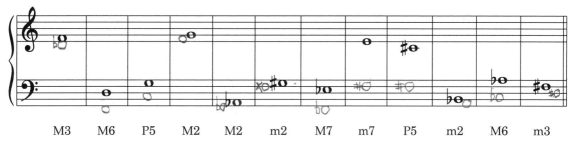

M3   M6   P5   M2   M2   m2   M7   m7   P5   m2   M6   m3

EXERCISE 1A.20   *Notating Intervals*

Notate the intervals in the required clefs:

- A. Treble clef: major seconds above and below:
  F, A, B♭, and F♯
- B. Treble clef: minor thirds above and below:
  G, B, and E♭
- C. Bass clef: perfect fourths above and below:
  F, A♭, and D
- D. Bass clef: minor sevenths above and below:
  D, A, and C♯

WRITING

EXERCISE 1A.21   *Writing Intervals*

Complete the following tasks, making sure that you maintain the generic (numerical) size. For example, increasing the size of a P4 by a half step creates an A4, not a d5.

- A. What would the following intervals become if you increased their size by a half step?
  1. P5 _A5_   2. m3 _M3_   3. M2 _A2_   4. M7 _A7_   5. d3 _m3_
  6. d8 _P8_

- B. What would the following intervals become if you decreased their size by a half step?
  1. m6 _d6_   2. M3 _m3_   3. P4 _d4_   4. A6 _M6_   5. A8 _P8_
  6. M2 _m2_   7. P5 _d5_   8. m3 _d3_

EXERCISE 1A.22   *More Augmented and Diminished Intervals*

Name the pitches that occur above A, C, and E♭ at the intervals shown.

	A	C	E♭
P4			
m3			
M7			
d8			
m2			
A5			

Name the pitches that occur below D, B♭, and F at the intervals shown.

	D	B♭	F
M2			
P5			
m3			
d5			
M7			

ASSIGNMENT 1A.8

WRITING

EXERCISE 1A.23

Name all possible intervals requested in the given key. For example, "In A major, name all possible perfect fifths." *Answer*: A–E, B–F♯, C♯–G♯, D–A, E–B, and F♯–C♯.

A. In F major, name all possible major seconds.

B. In B♭ major, name all possible minor seconds.

C. In the C harmonic minor scale, name all possible major thirds.

D. In F♯ major, name all possible minor sixths.

EXERCISE 1A.24

Notate the requested intervals *below* the given pitch, and label each interval's inversion and whether it is a perfect consonance (PC), an imperfect consonance (IC), or a dissonance (Diss).

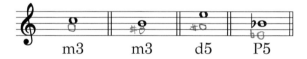

          m3   m3   d5   P5

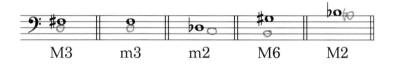

    M3   m3   m2   M6   M2

     d4   A5

ANALYSIS

EXERCISE 1A.25 *Beethoven, String Quartet no. 14 in C♯ minor, op. 131,* **Adagio ma non troppo e molto espresssivo**

Identify the interval of each boxed pair of pitches, label its inversion, and specify whether the interval is a perfect consonance (PC), an imperfect consonance (IC), or a dissonance (DISS).

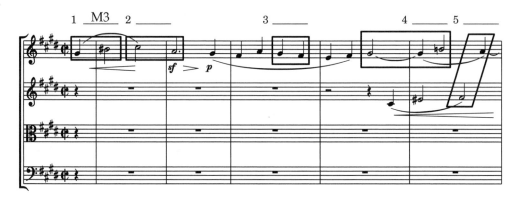

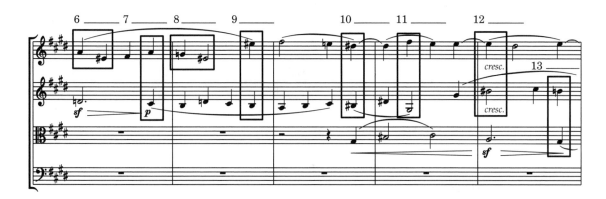

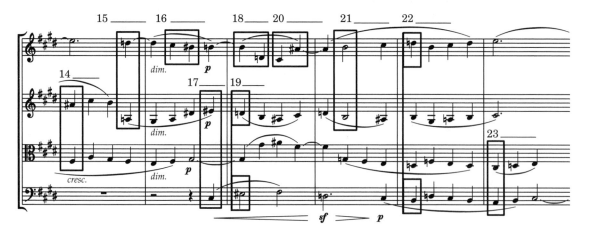

Musical Time: Pulse, Rhythm, and Meter

ASSIGNMENT 1B.1
EXERCISES FOR RHYTHMIC PROCEDURES

EXERCISE 1B.1 *Matching*

Match a rhythm from column X with one in column Y that has the same total duration. Use all options in column Y (i.e., avoid duplicating any answers). The first example in column X is completed for you.

EXERCISE 1B.2   *Pattern Durations*

Write a *single duration* that is equivalent to the notes and/or rests in each of the given patterns. *Be aware*: One answer requires the use of double dots.

Sample: ♪ ♪ ♪ = ♩.

A. =

F. =

B. =

G. =

C. =

H. =

D. =

I. =

E. =

J. =

EXERCISE 1B.3   *Brahms, Intermezzo in F minor, op. 118, no. 4; Ties Versus Phrasing Slurs*

STREAMING AUDIO
www.oup.com/us/laitz

Label ties and phrasing slurs in the given example.

Allegretto un poco agitato

EXERCISE 1B.4   *Rhythmic Proportions*

Perform the following rhythmic passages. Then determine how many of each of the given rhythmic durations would be required to represent the total length of each passage.

Sample solution: = _6_ ♩   _3_ ♩   _4_ ♩.

A. = __ ♩   __ o   __ ♩

ANALYSIS

EXERCISE 1B.5   *Rhythmic Correction*

Except for the first measures of each example, every subsequent measure contains the incorrect number of beats: Some measures have too many beats, while others have too few. You must determine how many beats should be in each measure by studying the correct first measure of each example. Then modify each measure so that it contains the correct number of beats by adding or changing a single rest (R) or note value (N), as requested.

Sample solution:

ASSIGNMENT 1B.2
EXERCISES FOR METER

EXERCISE 1B.6   *Determining Meter*

Supply an appropriate meter signature for each of the following examples. Consider both the number of beats in each measure and their division and subdivision. *Hint*: Consider the beaming patterns.

EXERCISE 1B.7   *Meter Identification and Rhythmic Correction*

Perform each exercise in order to determine the meter. Then supply an appropriate meter signature and bar lines. All examples begin on downbeats, but some of the characteristic metrical groupings (e.g., beams) are missing. Discuss this in a sentence or two. Once you have determined the meter for each example, rewrite it using proper notation. There may be more than one possible meter for some examples.

EXERCISE 1B.8 *Determining Meter in Context*

Determine the most logical meter signature for each of the following examples. Support your answer in a sentence or two.

A. Beethoven, Piano Sonata in E♭ major, op. 7, *Adagio*

B. Brahms, Sonata in F minor for Clarinet and Piano, op. 120, no. 1
   The clarinet sounds a major second lower than written.

C. Haydn, String Quartet in G minor, op. 74, no. 3, *Allegro*

D. Josquin, Credo, from *Missa Pange Lingua*

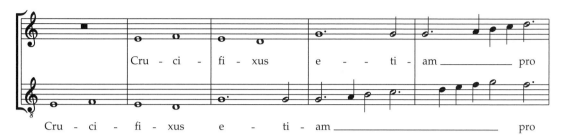

ASSIGNMENT 1B.3
EXERCISE FOR INTERVALS AND RHYTHM

WRITING

EXERCISE 1B.9   *Intervals and Meter Review*

Complete the following melodic intervals. Choose note durations that form a complete measure for the given meter. Ascending and descending intervals are indicated by arrow direction.

Sample solution:

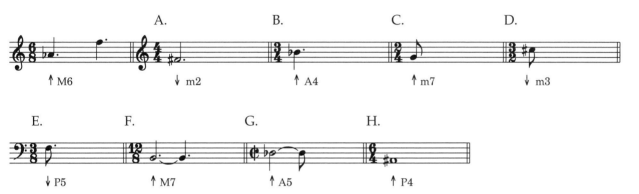

EXERCISE 1B.10   *Analysis: Bach, Gigue, from French Suite in C minor, BWV 813*

STREAMING AUDIO
www.oup.com/us/laitz

Identify each boxed interval in the blanks provided.

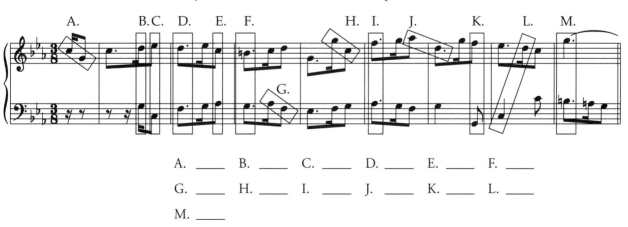

A. ____   B. ____   C. ____   D. ____   E. ____   F. ____

G. ____   H. ____   I. ____   J. ____   K. ____   L. ____

M. ____

EXERCISE 1B.11   *Completing a Mozart Score*

Notate missing pitches based on the requested interval in this excerpt from the *Andante cantabile* of a Mozart string quartet (K. 465). Use a duration that will fill the measure. Consider the musical context to determine the appropriate octave.

A. a P4 above violin 2   F. a d7 above the cello
B. a M10 above the cello   G. a m7 below violin 2
C. a d12 above the viola   H. a M10 above the cello
D. a M6 below violin 1   I. a M6 below violin 1
E. a M3 above violin 2

ASSIGNMENT 1B.4
EXERCISES FOR BAR LINES AND METER

ANALYSIS AND WRITING

EXERCISE 1B.12   *Adding Bar Lines*

Supply bar lines based on the meter signature. Since the rhythmic notation must reflect the meter, you may need to tie rhythms when you insert a bar line. (For example, given the rhythm quarter, quarter, half, in ¾ you would need to tie the half note, which begins on beat 3, to the downbeat of the next measure.) Use beams when possible.

All exercises begin on the downbeat, and the final measure is complete. After adding the bar lines conduct the meter, and either clap or speak the rhythms.

EXERCISE 1B.13   *Determining Meter and Adding Bar Lines*

STREAMING AUDIO
www.oup.com/us/laitz

Determine the meter and add bar lines for each of the following examples; there may be more than one possible answer. Begin by "scanning" the rhythms, noting repetitions that create larger patterns. Recall that accent—and therefore metrical emphasis—is often enhanced by durational accents and by changes of harmony, musical patterning, texture, register, and so on. List at least three criteria that you used to determine each example's meter.

A. Bach, Prelude no. 2 in D minor, *Clavier-büchlein für W. Fr. Bach*, BWV 926

B. Bach, Prelude no. 4 in A minor, from *Sechs kleine Préludien*, BWV 942

C. Grieg, *Lyriske stykker* (*Lyric Pieces*)
1. *Lyriske stykker I* (*Lyric Pieces I*), op. 12, no. 1
   This is the first of Grieg's sixty-six *Lyric Pieces*. The second excerpt, "Remembrances," was written almost a half-century later and is the last *Lyric Piece*. They are obviously contrasting works, but do you notice any similarities?

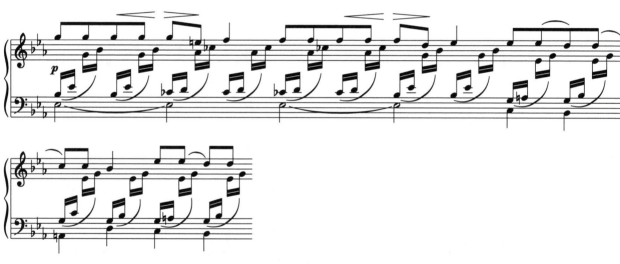

2. "Efterklang" ("Remembrances"), *Lyriske stykker X* (*Lyric Pieces X*), op. 71, no. 7

ASSIGNMENT 1B.5
EXERCISES FOR METER AND RHYTHM

EXERCISE 1B.14   *Determining Meter and Adding Bar Lines*

The following examples are unmetered (some are familiar tunes). Sing through the tunes, trying to determine the best meter according to the following criteria:

- Long notes usually fall on an accented part of the measure. Shorter notes usually follow longer notes and fall on an unaccented part of the measure.
- Changes in melodic contour often coincide with a downbeat or accented beat.
- All examples are in major. Note that $\hat{1}$, $\hat{3}$, and $\hat{5}$ often occur on accented beats.

After you have determined the meter and added bar lines, sing the tune again while conducting. Be aware, as shown in the sample solution, that you may need to omit ties (m. 2) or add ties (m. 6).

Sample solution:

E.

F.

EXERCISE 1B.15 *Single-Measure Completion*

Using either a single rest (R) or a single note (N) complete each measure.

Sample solution:

EXERCISE 1B.16 *Incomplete Measures*

Some measures in the examples that follow do not contain enough beats. Add a single note value that completes any measure with too few beats. Add beams and/or ties when necessary.

REVIEW OF ENHARMONICISM

EXERCISE 1B.17

Identify each of the given intervals. Then, maintaining the tied note, renotate the interval using an enharmonic pitch. Label the new interval. *Note*: The enharmonically renotated interval must retain the same number of half steps as the original interval, and do not use pitches that require double sharps or double flats.

Sample solution:

ASSIGNMENT 1B.6
EXERCISES FOR METER AND RHYTHM

EXERCISE 1B.18   *Matching*

Match a rhythm from column X with one in column Y that has the same total duration. *Note*: There may be more than a single correct answer, and not every letter is matched with a number. The first example in column X is completed for you.

EXERCISE 1B.19   *Rhythmic Correction*

Following are several metered examples, each of which contains numerous rhythmic errors: There are too few or too many beats within most measures. Circle, then change when necessary, one or more given rhythmic values in each measure to make the measure agree with the time signature. Do not change rests or eliminate or add any notes. There may be many ways to correct a measure.

EXERCISE 1B.20 *Beaming*

Following are examples whose rhythmic notation does not reflect the given meter clearly. Clap each rhythm. Then, clarify the meter by renotating each example using the following devices: adding or redistributing beams, adding or deleting ties, combining two or more note values into a single note value, or breaking down a single longer note value into two note values. When you have corrected the notation, conduct the meter and either clap or say the rhythms.

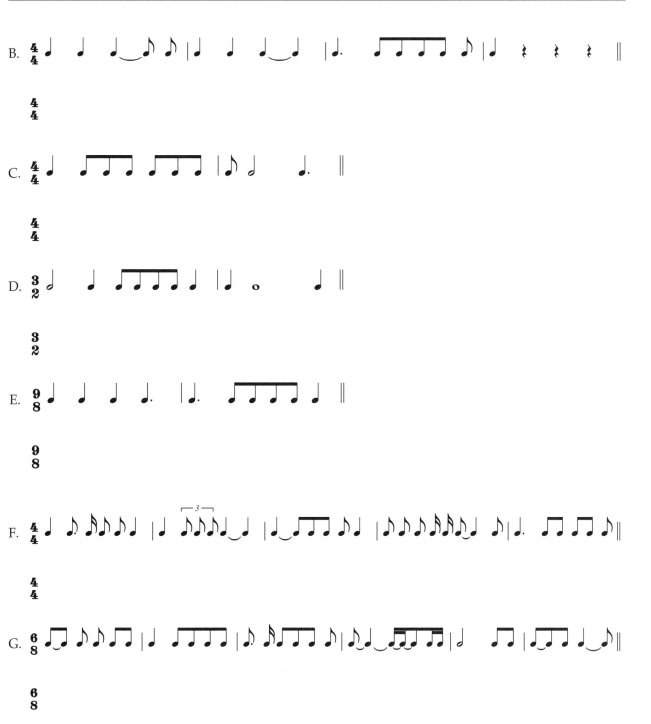

ASSIGNMENT 1B.7   EXERCISES FOR METER AND RHYTHM, SYNCOPATION, AND HEMIOLA

ANALYSIS AND WRITING

EXERCISE 1B.21   *Adding Bar Lines*

Renotate the following rhythms, replacing any note that does not fit in a measure with two smaller notes tied together. Then add beams. *Note*: Examples begin on downbeats but might not end on downbeats. If they do not, add any necessary rests (to complete the final measure). Do not change the given rhythms nor contradict the given meter. For example, given that $\frac{6}{8}$ is generally felt in two large beats, group values around those metrical accents. When you have added the bar lines, conduct the meter and either clap or say the rhythms.

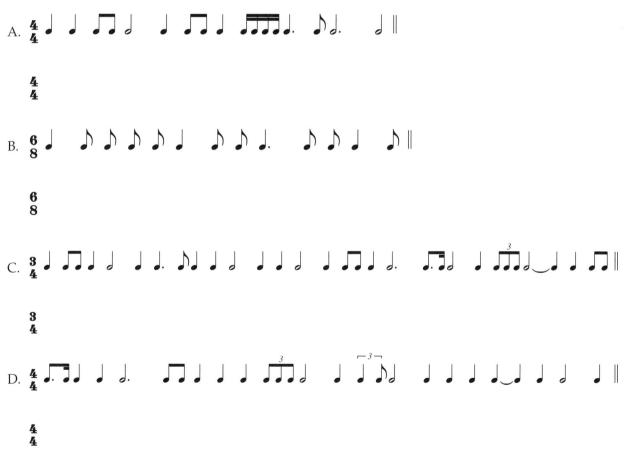

EXERCISE 1B.22   *Determining Meter and Adding Bar Lines*

Determine the best meter for each of the melodies that follow. Then, add a meter signature and bar lines. Tunes may start with an anacrusis.

A.

B.

C.

D.

EXERCISE 1B.23   *Metric Conversion*

Rewrite (on a separate sheet of manuscript paper) the following simple meter examples in the equivalent compound meter and the compound meter examples in simple meter.

Sample solution:

simple triple

compound duple

ASSIGNMENT 1B.8   EXERCISES FOR METER AND RHYTHM, SYNCOPATION, AND HEMIOLA

ANALYSIS

EXERCISE 1B.24   *Syncopation and Hemiola*

STREAMING AUDIO
www.oup.com/us/laitz

Identify instances of syncopation and hemiola in the following excerpts.

A. Brahms, "Wenn du nur zuweilen lächelst," op. 57, no. 2

B. Mozart, Symphony no. 40 in G minor, K. 550, Menuetto and Trio

C. Beethoven, Piano Sonata in E♭ major, op. 31, no. 3, Trio

D. Beethoven, Piano Sonata in A♭ major, op. 110, *Allegro molto*

EXERCISE 1B.25   *Meter Identification and Beaming*

For each example:

1. Determine the most logical meter.
2. Provide a meter signature and bar lines.
3. Add beams to clarify the meter. Remember that notes within one beat should be beamed together. There are no examples of hemiola.

EXERCISE 1B.26 *Analysis of Rhythmic–Metric Disruptions*

STREAMING AUDIO
www.oup.com/us/laitz

Label and bracket examples of syncopation and hemiola in the examples that follow.

A.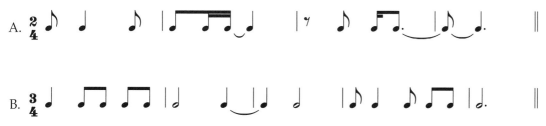

B.

C. Brahms, Violin Concerto, op. 77, *Allegro non troppo*

D. Corelli, Chamber Sonata in E minor, op. 2, no. 4

E. Tchaikovsky, from *Sleeping Beauty*

F. Brahms, Variation 7, *Variations on a Theme by Haydn*, op. 56b

CHAPTER 2

Harnessing Space and Time: Introduction to Melody and Two-Voice Counterpoint

ASSIGNMENT 2.1
EXERCISES FOR MELODY

EXERCISE 2.1 *Melodic Analysis*

Play each melody and briefly address the following questions:

1. Is there an overall shape? Is there a climax?
2. Is there an emphasis on the tonic triad, and is there a cadence?
3. What is the overall range and general tessitura?
4. Describe the primary type of melodic motion (conjunct or disjunct). Are any dissonant intervals involved in the leaps? Does the composer invoke the law of recovery?

A. Mozart, *Die Zauberflöte* (*The Magic Flute*), K. 620

   1. Song, "Der Vogelfänger bin ich ja," act 1

2. Aria, "Zum Leiden bin ich auserkoren," act 1

Zum Lei - den bin ich aus-er-ko-ren, denn mei-ne Toch-ter feh-let
In lone - ly grief I am for-sak-en, For my poor child no more I

mir. _____   Durch sie ging all mein Glück ver - lo - ren
see. _____   With her my hap - pi - ness was tak - en

3. Aria, "Ach, ich fühl's, es ist verschwunden," act 2

Ach, ich _ fühl's, es ist ver - schwunden, e - wig ___ hin mein gan - zes _ Glück,
Ah, I _ feel, to grief and _ sad - ness, Ev - er ___ turned is love's de - light,

B. Beethoven, Piano Sonata in A♭ major, op. 31, no. 3

Allegretto vivace

C. Donizetti, "Regnava nel silenzio" cavatina from *Lucia di Lammermoor*, act 1

Re - gna - va nel ___ si - len - zi - o   al - ta la not - te e bru - na

D. Schumann, "Träumerei," *Kinderszenen* (Scenes from Childhood), op. 15, no. 7

Moderato

E. Chopin, Prelude in D♭ major, "Raindrop," op. 28

EXERCISE 2.2   *Melody Completion*

Study the given pitches' overall contour. Each arrow indicates where you should insert one additional pitch, which will create a smoother, more stepwise line. Be able to sing your completed melody.

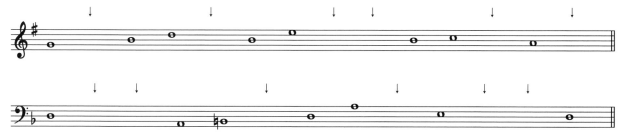

EXERCISE 2.3   *Melody Composition*

Study the given contour patterns. Then, write two 12- to 16-note melodies that begin on the given pitches (and in the keys represented by the key signatures) that generally follow the contour patterns.

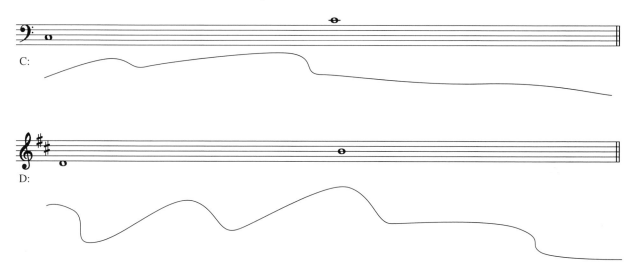

ASSIGNMENT 2.2 EXERCISES FOR COUNTERPOINT: FIRST SPECIES

EXERCISE 2.4 *Adding a Counterpoint to CF Fragments*

Four three-note cantus firmus fragments are given. They are not taken from the beginning or the end of a longer CF but, rather, from the middle. Write four (4) different first-species solutions above and/or below each of the given CFs. Label each interval. A sample solution is given.

Sample solution: given: C D E

Exercises:

A. D F E

B. E A G

C. F D C

EXERCISE 2.5 *Two-Part Writing: Error Detection*

Shown are two first-species, two-voice counterpoints that contain two types of errors: dissonant intervals (2, 4, diminished 5, and 7) and parallel perfect intervals (1, 5, and 8).

1. Label each interval.
2. Circle the errors and specify the type of error ("DISS" for dissonance and "PPI" for parallel perfect intervals).
3. Rewrite each of the counterpoint lines using only consonant intervals (do not change the cantus). *Remember*: (a) Aim for contrary motion, and (b) when writing in parallel motion, use only imperfect intervals. Try to make each line as stepwise (singable) as possible, and restrict nonstepwise motions mostly to skips of a third, with only one leap of a fourth or fifth. Avoid larger leaps completely.

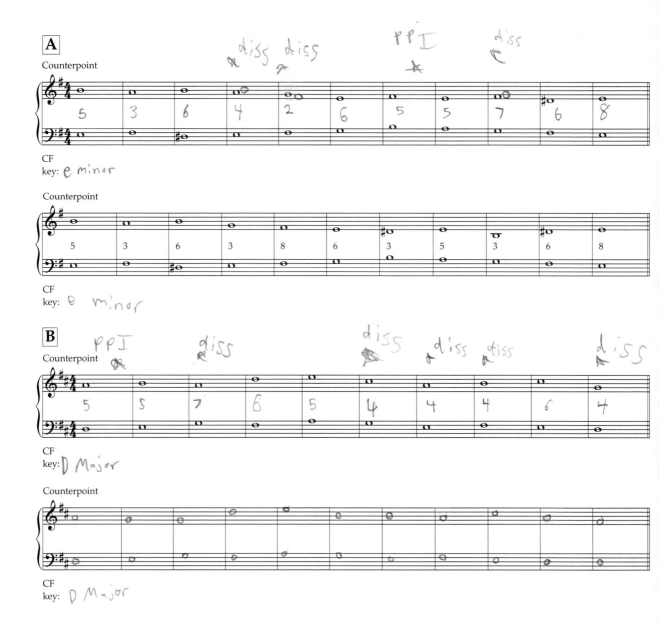

EXERCISE 2.6   *Two-Part Writing: First Species*

Write first-species counterpoint for the examples given.

- The added voice must exhibit a pleasing melodic arch with mostly stepwise motion and should be easy to sing.
- There may be a few leaps, but remember that thirds are the most common, and leaps by a fourth or a fifth may occur no more than once in each exercise.
- Label each vertical interval (between your counterpoint and the cantus firmus), making sure that there are no dissonances and that any parallel intervals are restricted to thirds and sixths.
- Do not change any of the pitches of the cantus firmus.

2.6 on paper
2.7 on flat

Once you have completed writing your counterpoint, try inverting the parts; that is, if you wrote counterpoint above a cantus, place it an octave (or two) below, and vice versa. Does your solution still work (i.e., how are the melodic shapes and vertical intervals between the cantus and the counterpoint)? If it doesn't work, why not? (*Hint*: Consider perfect intervals.)

A.

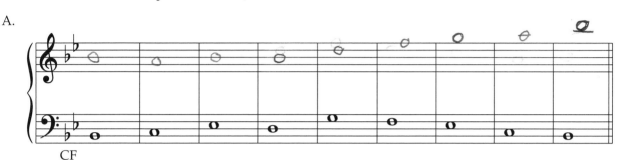

CF

Inversion:

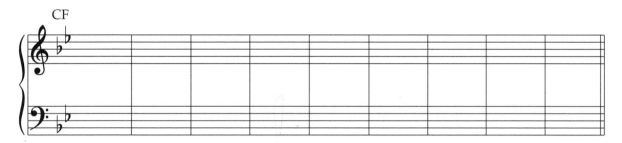

CF

B.

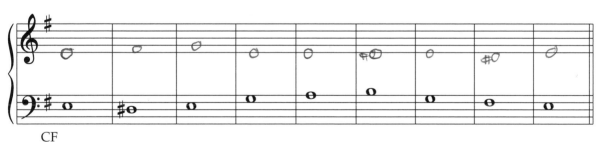

CF

Inversion:

CF

ASSIGNMENT 2.3   EXERCISES FOR COUNTERPOINT: FIRST SPECIES

EXERCISE 2.7   *First Species*

Write first-species counterpoint against the examples of cantus firmus given.

- Your added voice must be a good melody that is mostly stepwise in contour and be easy to sing.
- There may be a few leaps in the counterpoint voice, but remember that thirds are the most common, and leaps by a fourth or a fifth may occur no more than once in each exercise.
- Label each vertical interval (between your counterpoint and the cantus firmus), making sure that there are no dissonances and that any parallel intervals are restricted to thirds and sixths.
- Do not change any of the pitches of the cantus firmus.
- Notate the inversion of each solution below. Label any errors.

A.

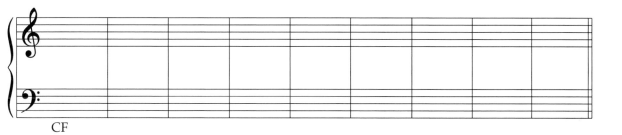

B.

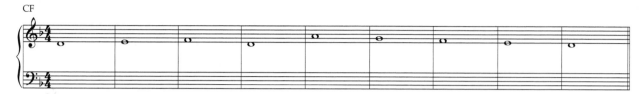

CF

CF:

EXERCISE 2.8   *Analysis of Contrapuntal Motions*

STREAMING AUDIO
www.oup.com/us/laitz

Determine the prevailing contrapuntal motion in each of the two-voice examples that follow. Then, using brackets, label two or more instances of other types of contrapuntal motions. Your choices are parallel (P), similar (S), oblique (O), and contrary (C).

A. Bach, Duetto no. 1 in E minor, BWV 802

B. Grieg, "Gone," *Lyric Pieces*, op. 71

C. Bach, Duetto no. 4 in A minor, BWV 805

D. Haydn, String Quartet in G major, op. 20, no. 4, *Allegretto alla zingarese*

ASSIGNMENT 2.4   EXERCISES FOR COUNTERPOINT: SECOND SPECIES

EXERCISE 2.9   *Adding Second-Species Counterpoint to CF Fragments*

Given are three three-note cantus firmus fragments. They are not taken from the beginning or the end of a longer CF but, rather, from the middle. Write three different second-species solutions above and two below each of the given CFs. Label each interval, and mark passing dissonances with asterisks. Use a whole note in the final measure of each pattern. A sample solution is given.

Sample solution: F D E

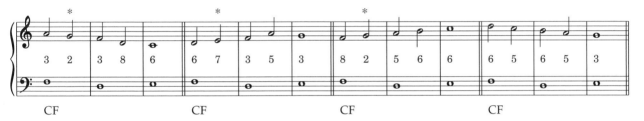

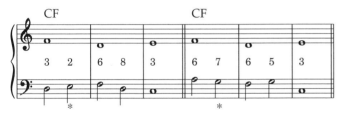

A.

B.

C.

EXERCISE 2.10   *Second Species: Error Detection*

Label each interval and circle and label each error according to the model analysis in Textbook Exercise 2.5.

A.

B.

ASSIGNMENT 2.5   EXERCISES FOR COUNTERPOINT: SECOND SPECIES

EXERCISE 2.11   *Two-Part Writing: Second Species and Consonance*

For this exercise in writing second-species counterpoint, employ only consonance; therefore, you may use steps (but only those involving the interval of a fifth to a sixth or vice versa), consonant skips, or consonant leaps. Label all intervals.

A.

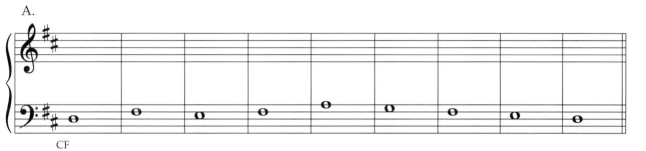

B.

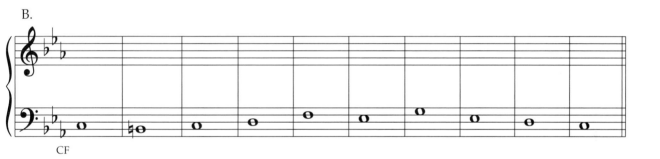

EXERCISE 2.12   *Second-Species Writing: Dissonance and Consonance*

In this exercise you may use consonant skips and leaps and passing dissonance. Remember that all dissonances must:

1. occur only on a weak beat
2. fill the interval of a third that occurs on successive downbeats

A.   Label all intervals.

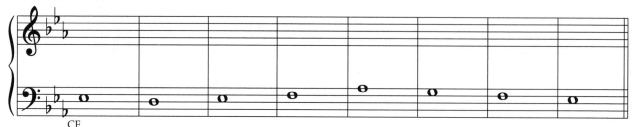

B.

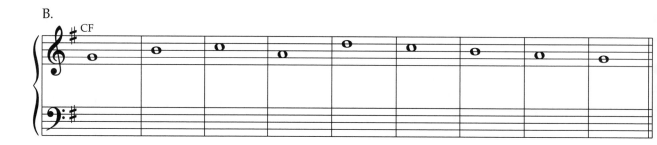

ANALYSIS

EXERCISE 2.13

STREAMING AUDIO
www.oup.com/us/laitz

The examples that follow are, like all tonal examples, held together by outer-voice counterpoint. Circle the structural outer-voice pitches that work together to create first-species counterpoint. Analyze each interval between these outer voices.

A. Schumann, Grosse Sonata in F♯ minor, op. 11, no. 1

B   Bach, Chorale from Cantata no. 5, BWV 5

Soprano.
Where can I flee from grief, Who now will com - fort me?

Alto.
Where can I __ flee from grief, Who now will __ com - fort me?

Tenore.
Where can I flee from grief, Who now will com - fort me?

Basso.
Where can __ I flee __ from grief, Who now will com - fort me?

C. Beethoven, Violin Sonata no. 10 in G major, op. 96, *Adagio espressivo*

D. Schumann, "Humming Song," *Album für die Jugend*, op. 68, no. 3

Nicht schnell

E. Beethoven, Violin Sonata no. 9 in A major, "Kreutzer," op. 47, *Andante con Variazioni*

CHAPTER 3

Musical Density: Triads, Seventh Chords, and Texture

ASSIGNMENT 3.1 EXERCISES FOR ROOT-POSITION TRIADS IN CLOSE AND OPEN POSITIONS

EXERCISE 3.1 *Writing Triads*

Below each requested triad, notate the pitches in the required clef that you will add.

1. D major: bass   2. B minor: treble   3. F♯ minor: treble   4. A major: bass

5. E♭ minor: bass   6. C♯ major: treble   7. D♯ major: treble   8. E♯ major: bass

EXERCISE 3.2 *Error Detection*

Incorrectly spelled root-position major, minor, and diminished triads are shown. On the given staff, notate the corrected triad and label the triad type. The errors include enharmonic spelling (e.g., a C-major triad must be spelled in thirds: C–E–G, not C–F♭–G) and wrong-note spelling (e.g., a G-minor triad is spelled G–B♭–D, not G–B♭–E♭). There may be two possible answers in some cases. *Assume that the root is correct. Label the triad type beneath your answer.*

Sample solution:

F–G♯–C

1. D–G♭–A   2. C–D♯–G   3. F–A–C♭

4. A–C–D♯   5. D–F–G♯   6. E–A♭–B

EXERCISE 3.3   *Writing Root-Position Triads in Close and Open Positions*

STREAMING AUDIO
www.oup.com/us/laitz

The roots of various major, minor, and diminished triads are provided.

1. Notate in close position the missing pitches of the required triad type.
2. Renotate each triad in open position (three voices; there are several arrangements possible).
3. On a separate sheet of manuscript paper, renotate each triad in four voices (two voices in the treble and two in the bass staves); double the root (there are several arrangements possible).

Sample solution:

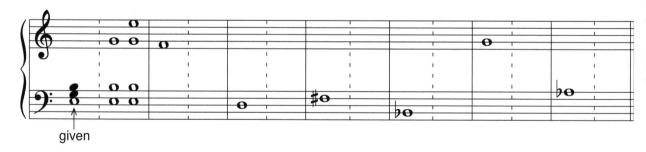

EXERCISE 3.4   *Writing Triads*

Complete the following tasks in the clef and position (open or close) required.

Line A: Notate root-position major triads.
Line B: Notate root-position minor triads (all open position).
Line C: Notate root-position diminished triads (all close position).

Sample solution:

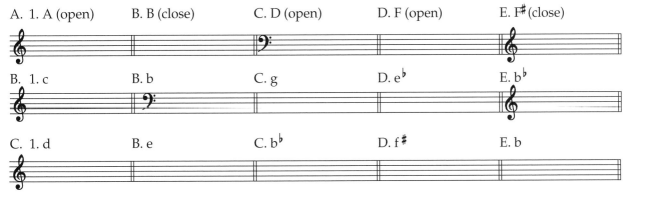

ASSIGNMENT 3.2
EXERCISES FOR TRIADS IN INVERSION

EXERCISE 3.5   *Chordal Membership*

Given the triad quality and one member of the triad (root, triad, or fifth), determine the triad type.

1. C is the third of what major triad? __A♭__   the fifth of what minor triad? __F__

2. A♭ is the third of what major triad? __F♭__   the fifth of what diminished triad? __D__

3. E is the third of what minor triad? __C#__   the fifth of what major triad? __A__

4. G is the third of what diminished triad? __E__   the fifth of what diminished triad? __C#__

WRITING

EXERCISE 3.6   *Writing Triads in Inversion and Other Triadic Manipulations*

The given pitch is the bass note. Build triads above the given pitch according to the instructions. Label each triad by letter name. Refer to the sample solution.

Sample solution:

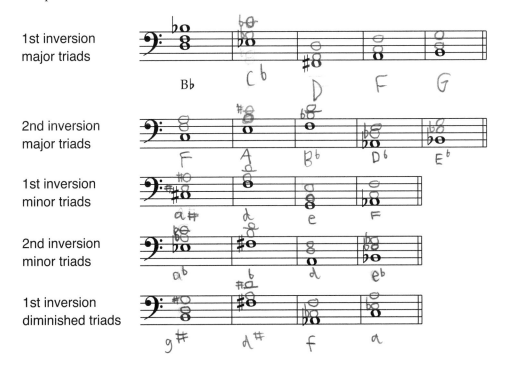

EXERCISE 3.7 *Completing Triads*

Fill in the blanks from the information given.

Sample solution:

fifth	A	C	B♭	F	D#	G♭	A	E	C♭	G#	B
third	(F#)	A	Gb	D	B	E♭	F#	C#	A♭	E	G#
root	(D)	F	E♭	B	G#	Cb	D#	A	F	C#	E
type	M	M	m	d	m	M	d	M	d	m	M

EXERCISE 3.8 *Pitch and Triad Membership*

Each pitch given is a potential member of nine triads (we will consider major, minor, and diminished triads only). For example, given the pitch D, it could be the:

1. root of a D major, D minor, or D diminished triad;
2. third of a B♭ major, B minor, or B diminished triad;
3. fifth of a G major, G minor, or G# diminished triad.

Determine the nine possible major, minor, and diminished triads of which each of the following pitches could be members:

	Root:	Third:	Fifth:
A. C:	C M, C m, C dim	A♭ M, a m, a dim	F M, f m, f# dim
B. F:	F M, f m, f dim	D♭ M, d m, d dim	B♭ M, b♭ m, b dim
C. B♭:	B♭ M, B♭ m, B♭ dim	G♭ M, g m, g dim	E M, E♭ m, e dim
D. C#:	C# M, C# m, C# dim	A M, a# m, a# dim	F# M, f# m, f× dim
E. F#:	F# M, F# m, f# dim	D M, d# m, d# dim	B M, b m, b# dim

EXERCISE 3.9 *Brain Twister*

From each of the following pairs, make as many different types of triads as possible. (Use a separate sheet of manuscript paper.) We will consider all four triad types (major, minor, diminished, and augmented). For example, given the pair of pitches G and B, you can make four different triads: G–B–D (major), G–B–D# (augmented), E–G–B (minor), and E♭–G–B (augmented).

A. A and C   B. D and F#   C. B♭ and D♭
D. F and C   E. C and A#   F. C# and E

EXERCISE 3.10   *Analysis of and Writing Triads*

Analyze using roman numerals, and provide a figured bass for each boxed chord.

Mozart, from *The Magic Flute*:

A. "Drei Knäbchen"

B. "Wie? Wie? Wie?"

C. Mozart, String Quartet in B♭ major, K. 458, *Allegro vivace assai*

ASSIGNMENT 3.3   EXERCISE FOR TRIADS: ANALYSIS AND WRITING

EXERCISE 3.11   *Completing Triads*

Add a third pitch to each pair of pitches to form the specified triad as shown for the first case. Label the root name of each triad in the space provided. Do *not* alter any of the given pitches.

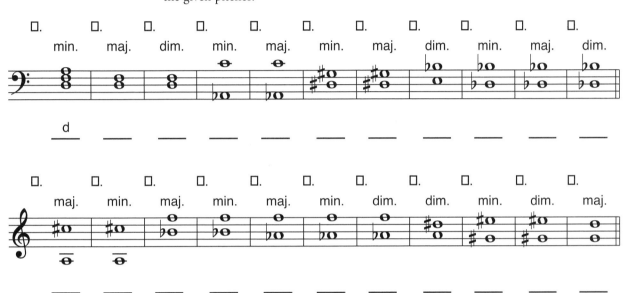

EXERCISE 3.12   *Figured Bass Realization*

Create triads by adding the two missing pitches above the bass. Use open position. Play your solutions as written and then in a different open position.

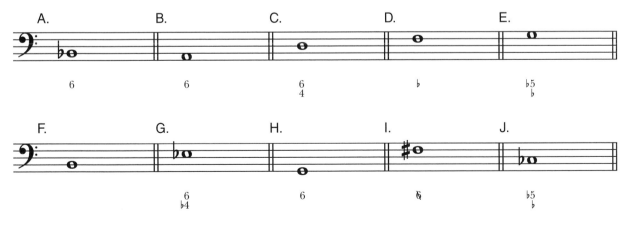

EXERCISE 3.13   *Figured Bass Construction*

Construct chords above each bass note observing the figured bass. There is no underlying key in this exercise, thus no key signature, so add any necessary accidentals. Provide root and quality for each. There is more than one possible solution for each exercise. After playing the series of chords, return to the beginning of the exercise and play only the given bass pitch, singing the intervals above as required.

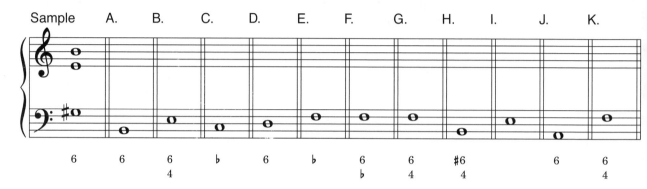

ANALYSIS

EXERCISE 3.14   *Triads in Four Voices and in Various Spacings*

1. Determine the root and quality of the triad.
2. Determine which member of the chord is in the bass: root (1), third (3), or fifth (5).
3. Determine which member of the triad is doubled: root (1), third (3), or fifth (5).
4. Provide a full (i.e., no shorthand) figured bass analysis that shows accidentals (i.e., consider the exercise to be in C major).

	A.	B.	C.	D.	E.	F.	G.	H.	I.	J.	K.	L.
root	A♭											
chord quality	M											
chord member in bass	1											
doubled note	1											
figured bass	♭5 3											

ASSIGNMENT 3.4
EXERCISES FOR FIGURED BASS

EXERCISE 3.15   *Analysis*

For each of the following, label the *major* key, the roman numeral, and the full figured bass of the given chord within that key.

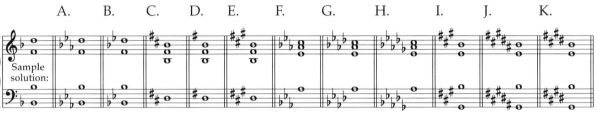

F: IV

WRITING

EXERCISE 3.16

Notate triads based on the given key and the roman numeral. Use accidentals, not key signatures. Voice chords in close or open spacing as required. Create a four-voice setting by doubling the root for open-spacing chords. Exercise A is solved for you.

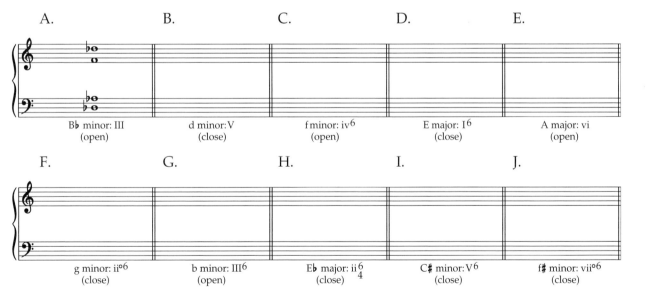

EXERCISE 3.17   *Illustrations*

Complete the given writing tasks, and analyze your work.

A. In D minor, write the following root-position triads in four voices, close position (tightly compressed), doubling the bass: i, III, V, VI.

B. In B♭ major, write the following root-position triads in four voices, using a wide spacing and doubling the bass note: ii, IV, vi, vii°.

C. In C minor, write the following root-position and inverted triads in a spacing of your choice, doubling the root: i⁶, ii°, III, iv⁶, V, V⁶, VI, vii°⁶. For vii° and ii°, double the chordal third.

A.

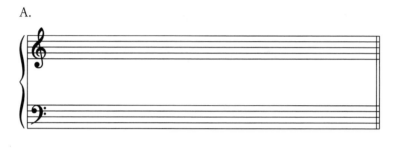

B.

C.

ASSIGNMENT 3.5   EXERCISES FOR TRIADS IN FOUR VOICES AND GENERATING TRIADS FROM SCALE DEGREES

EXERCISE 3.18   *Triads in Four Voices and in Various Spacings*

1. Determine the root and quality of the triad.
2. Determine which member of the chord is in the bass: root (R), third (3rd), or fifth (5th).
3. Determine which member of the triad is doubled: root (R), third (3rd), or fifth (5th).
4. Provide a full (i.e., no shorthand) figured bass analysis that shows accidentals (i.e., consider the exercise to be in C major).

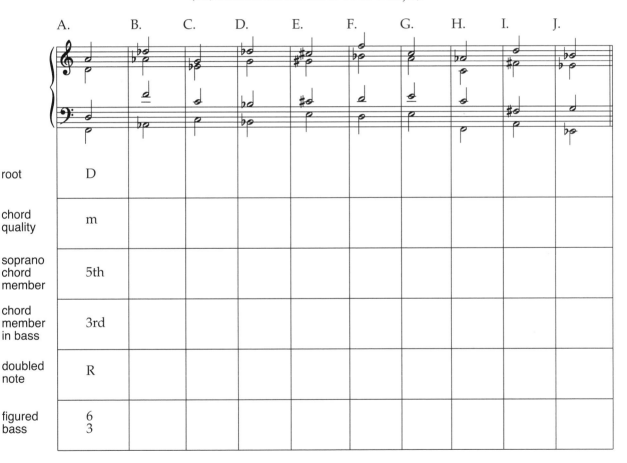

	A.	B.	C.	D.	E.	F.	G.	H.	I.	J.
root		D								
chord quality		m								
soprano chord member		5th								
chord member in bass		3rd								
doubled note		R								
figured bass		6 3								

EXERCISE 3.19   *Figured Bass Realization*

Given the following bass notes and figures, identify the key, and add the missing two voices above each bass note in close position. Write the root of each chord beneath the figures and identify the triad quality.

Sample solution:

EXERCISE 3.20   *Writing Triads Generated from Various Scale Degrees*

The given pitches represent the chordal roots of triads within a given key. However, no key signature is provided, nor required accidentals for any of the given pitches. Complete each triad in close position by adding two pitches and any necessary accidentals (based on the given key) and roman numerals.

For example, given the key of A major and the pitch C, you must first sharp the C, since C♯, not C♮, occurs in A major. Then add two pitches—a third and a fifth above the C♯. Given that the key of A major contains three sharps, you will also need to sharp the G. Add the roman numeral "iii," since a triad built on C♯ in A major is built on 3̂. You can check your work: iii in major should be a minor triad; sure enough, C♯–E–G♯ is a minor triad.

A. Given the key of D major and the following scale degrees:

B. Given the key of B♭ major and the following scale degrees:

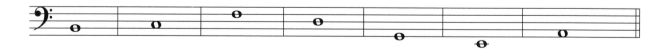

C. Given the key of G minor and the following scale degrees:

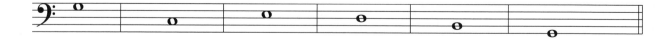

EXERCISE 3.21   *Notating Triads in Root Position and Inversion Within a Key*

Notate triads in close position as requested; use accidentals rather than key signatures. Then revoice each triad in four voices, chorale style, and open position. Double the root.

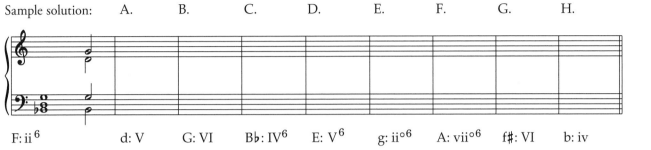

Sample solution: A.   B.   C.   D.   E.   F.   G.   H.

F: ii^6 d: V   G: VI   B♭: IV^6 E: V^6 g: ii^{o6} A: vii^{o6} f♯: VI   b: iv

EXERCISE 3.22   *Brain Twister*

Complete the following. Name three major and three minor keys in which each of the following triads appear. Use roman numerals for your answers. For example, A major: I in A major, IV in E major; V in D major, III in F♯ minor, V in D minor, and IV in E minor.

	Major keys			Minor keys		
1. D major:	___	___	___	___	___	___
2. A minor:	___	___	___	___	___	___
3. F major:	___	___	___	___	___	___
4. B♭ major:	___	___	___	___	___	___

ASSIGNMENT 3.6
EXERCISES FOR HARMONIC ANALYSIS

EXERCISE 3.23   *Preparation and Review for Analysis*

A complete harmonic analysis combines roman numerals and figured bass:

- The roman numeral identifies the root (by scale degree) and the quality of a chord.
- The figure from the figured bass identifies the inversion of the chord and the melodic motion (such as 5–6 or 4–3).

Here is a step-by-step analytical procedure:

1. Determine the key of the example, because the key signature alone implies two possible keys: either the major or the relative minor. Chromatic alterations of pitches provide a helpful hint because this often indicates leading tones in minor.
2. Write out the letter name of the keys followed by a colon at the beginning of the exercise, under the bass staff. Use uppercase letters to represent a major key and lowercase letters to represent a minor key.
3. Identify triad roots, and write the appropriate roman numeral under each harmony.
4. If the triad is in root position, you're done. However, if the triad is inverted, you must supply a figured bass. The following example shows a sample harmonic analysis.

EXERCISE 3.24   *Harmonic Analysis*

The following triads appear in four voices and in various inversions.

1. Label the key.
2. Identify triad roots with roman numerals.
3. Include a figured bass for inverted triads.

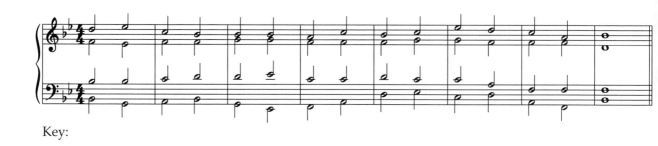

Key:

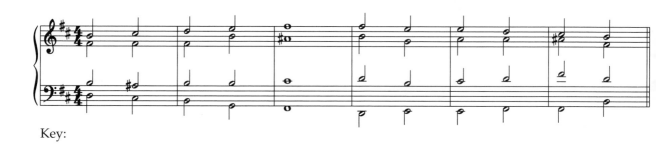

Key:

EXERCISE 3.25 *Contextual Analysis*

STREAMING AUDIO
www.oup.com/us/laitz

Using roman numerals and figured bass, analyze each of the following bracketed harmonies. The notes in parentheses are nonchord tones and should not be considered. Expect to encounter both triads and seventh chords in root position and inversion. For Exercise C, no harmonies are bracketed; you must determine the chord changes yourself.

A. Bellini, "Ah! Si, fa core, abbraciami," from *Norma,* act 1

B. Mozart, Violin Sonata in B♭, K. 379

C. Mozart, Violin Sonata in D minor, K. 421

Ty Brown

ASSIGNMENT 3.7   EXERCISES FOR ROOT-POSITION AND INVERTED SEVENTH CHORDS

EXERCISE 3.26   *Identification of Root-Position Seventh Chords*

STREAMING AUDIO
www.oup.com/us/laitz

Listen to the following series of root-position seventh chords that are written in close position.

1. Identify the type of seventh chord by choosing among Mm (major-minor), MM (major), mm (minor), dm (half diminished, ⌀7), and dd (diminished, °7).
2. Transform each seventh chord as follows: Mm ↔ dd, MM ↔ dm, transpose mm up a minor third.

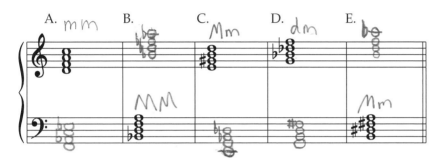

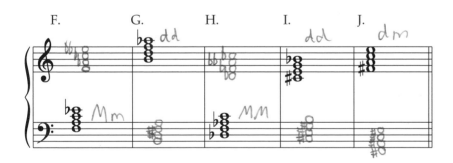

EXERCISE 3.27   *Writing More Seventh Chords*

A. Spell the seventh chords given the following:
   1. C is the third of a Mm seventh chord: A♭, C, E♭, G♭
   2. A♭ is the third of a MM seventh chord: F♭, A♭, C♭, E♭
   3. B♭ is the fifth of a mm seventh chord: E♭, G♭, B♭, D♭
   4. D is the seventh of a dm seventh chord: E, G, B♭, D
   5. E is the fifth of a dd seventh chord: A#, C#, E, G

B. Write the seventh chord in which both given pitches are the specified members:

Sample solution:

Given: F and D of Mm sevenths
Answer: B♭: B♭–D–F–A♭   and   G: G–B–D–F

This answer is deduced as follows: F and D form the interval of a minor third, and in a Mm seventh chord, there is a minor third between the third and the fifth of the chord (i.e., B♭–D–F–A♭) and between the fifth and the seventh of the chord (i.e., G–B–D–F). One of the exercises has only one solution, rather than two. Which one is it, and why?

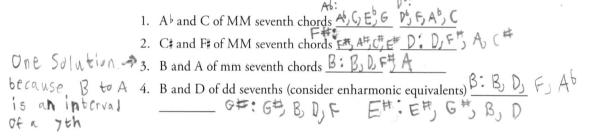

1. A♭ and C of MM seventh chords   A♭: A♭, C, E♭, G   D♭: D♭, F, A♭, C
2. C♯ and F♯ of MM seventh chords   F♯: F♯, A♯, C♯, E♯   D: D, F♯, A, C♯
One Solution → 3. B and A of mm seventh chords   B: B, D, F♯, A
because B to A 4. B and D of dd sevenths (consider enharmonic equivalents)   B: B, D, F, A♭
is an interval   G♯: G♯, B, D, F   E♯: E♯, G♯, B, D
of a 7th

EXERCISE 3.28   *Constructing Seventh Chords*

1. Notate pitches based on the given intervals and contour (arrow directions indicate whether the interval is to be reckoned above or below the given pitch).
2. Vertically stack the given pitches and determine the root, type of seventh chord, and inversion. (A sample solution is given.)

Sample solution:

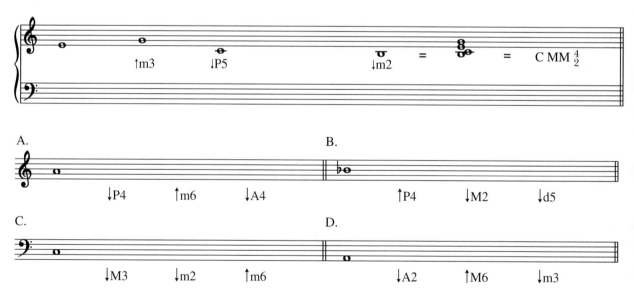

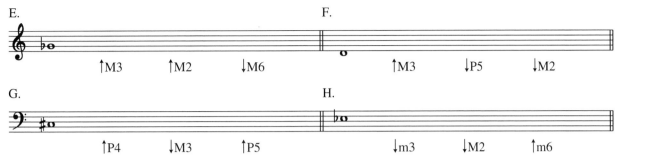

E.

↑M3   ↑M2   ↓M6

F.

↑M3   ↓P5   ↓M2

G.

↑P4   ↓M3   ↑P5

H.

↓m3   ↓M2   ↑m6

ASSIGNMENT 3.8   EXERCISES FOR FIGURED BASS AND SEVENTH CHORDS

EXERCISE 3.29   *Distinction Between Scale Degrees, Figured Bass, and Chordal Members*

In this example, determine the following:

1. full figured bass
2. type of seventh chord
3. member of chord that is circled
4. member of chord in the bass
5. scale degree in the bass

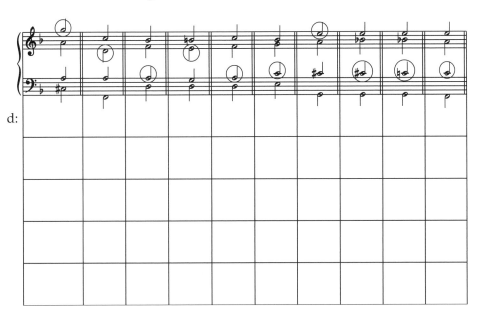

EXERCISE 3.30   *Functional Analysis of Seventh Chords*

STREAMING AUDIO
www.oup.com/us/laitz

1. Identify the key of each exercise and provide a harmonic analysis (using roman numerals and figured bass). (Recall that root-position seventh chords need not contain a fifth.)
2. Circle and label the root (1) and the seventh (7) in each chord.

A.

B.

ANALYSIS

EXERCISE 3.31   *Figured Bass Analysis*

Determine the quality of the following seventh chords occurring in root position and inversion and then supply the appropriate full figured bass (don't forget to include accidentals).

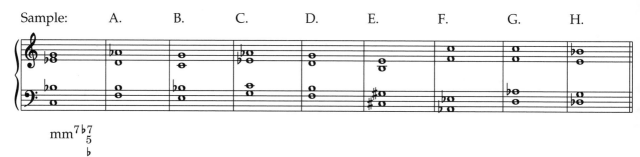

WRITING

EXERCISE 3.32   *Figured Bass: Construction*

Realize each of the following figured basses by writing in four voices. Remember that there are no doublings for seventh chords because they contain four different pitches. Label each type of seventh chord according to its quality (Mm, MM, mm, dm, or dd). Assume that there are no sharps or flats in the key signature.

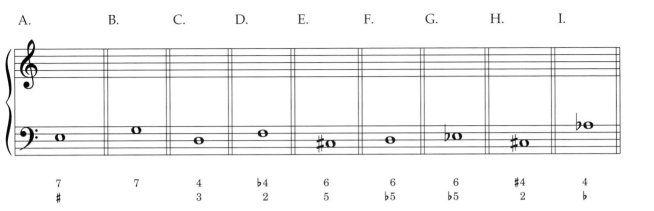

ASSIGNMENT 3.9   EXERCISES FOR TRIADS AND SEVENTH CHORDS IN THE LITERATURE

WRITING

EXERCISE 3.33   *Seventh Chords Through the Octave*

On a separate sheet of manuscript paper, write the specified root-position seventh chord. Then, renotate the chord at the interval specified. When you begin to encounter double flats and sharps, use enharmonic equivalents for easier notation.

1. Major-major seventh chord that begins on F and ascends through major thirds until the return to F.
2. Major-minor seventh chord that begins on G and ascends through major seconds until the return to G.
3. Minor-minor seventh chord that begins on A and descends through minor thirds until the return to A.

EXERCISE 3.34   *Figured Bass: Construction*

Given is a figured bass that incorporates triads and seventh chords in root position and inversion. Realize each chord according to the figured bass by writing in four voices (thus, for triads you will double the root; there are no doublings for seventh chords, since they contain four different pitches). Then label triad and seventh-chord types. Since there is no underlying key in this exercise, therefore no key signature, you must add any necessary accidentals.

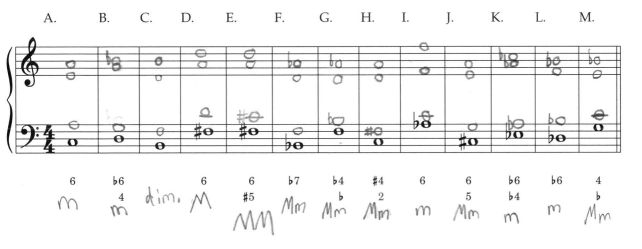

WRITING

EXERCISE 3.35   *Writing Seventh Chords Generated from Scale Degrees*

Complete the required tasks (including roman numeral analysis and construction of chords) from the information provided.

	A.	B.	C.	D.	E.	F.	G.
key:	F Maj		g		e	Maj	Maj
RN:	IV^7	7	ii$^{\varnothing 6}_{5}$			V$^6_5$	ii$^6_5$

EXERCISE 3.36   *Analysis*

STREAMING AUDIO
www.oup.com/us/laitz

This exercise develops immediate comprehension of triads and seventh chords in various textures. Listen to each example and determine:

1. Size (triad, seventh chord).
2. Root name and quality (for triads: major, minor and diminished; for seventh chords: Mm, MM, mm, dm, and dd). *Do not use roman numerals in your analysis.*
3. Member of chord in the bass (R, 3rd, 5th, 7th).

A. Bach, Christ ist erstanden," Cantata no. 66, *Erfreut euch, ihr Herzen*, BWV 66

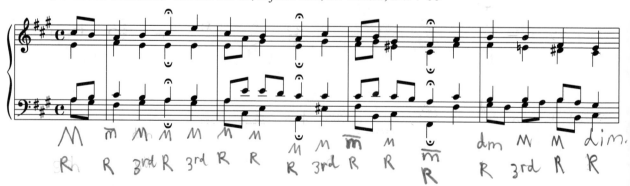

B. Schumann, "Anfangs wollt' ich fast verzagen" ("At First I Almost Despaired"), *Liederkreis*, op. 24, no. 8

C. Debussy, *Canope*, *Preludes*, book 2, no. 10
   Identify only the sonorities enclosed in boxes.

EXERCISE 3.37   *Contextual Analysis*

STREAMING AUDIO
www.oup.com/us/laitz

This exercise develops immediate comprehension of triads and seventh chords in various textures. Notes in parentheses are nonchord tones. Listen to each example and determine:

1. Size (triad, seventh chord).
2. Root name and quality (for triads: major, minor and diminished; beware, there is one instance of an augmented triad; for seventh chords: Mm, MM, mm, dm, dd). *Do not use roman numerals in your analysis.*
3. Member of chord in the bass (R, 3rd, 5th, 7th).

A. Tchaikovsky, "Morning Prayer," *Children's Album*, op. 39, no. 1

B. Corelli, Concerto Grosso no. 9 in F major, op. 6, *Adagio*

C. Brahms, "Ich stund an einem Morgen" ("One Morning I Stood"), *Deutsche Volkslieder*,
WoO 32, no. 9

1. Ich stund an ei - nem Mor - gen heim - lich an ei - nem Ort
   da hätt ich mich ver - bor - gen, ich hört kläg - li - che Wort
2. Herz - lieb, ich hab ver - nom - men, du wollst von hin - nen schier,
   wenn willst u wie - der - kom - men, das sollst du sa - gen mir;

EXERCISE 3.38 *Functional Analysis*

STREAMING AUDIO
www.oup.com/us/laitz

Determine the key and provide a roman numeral analysis.

A. Bellini, "Sola, furtiva, al tempio" ("Alone, Furtive, to the Temple"), from *Norma*, act I, scene vii.
Consider the left-hand bass notes to occupy two beats of each measure because they continue
to "ring."

B. Mozart, Sonata for Piano and Violin in F major, K. 377, *Tema*

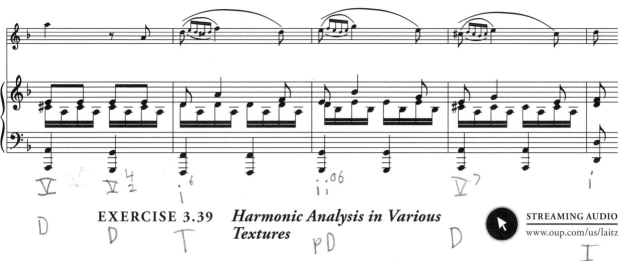

EXERCISE 3.39 *Harmonic Analysis in Various Textures*

STREAMING AUDIO
www.oup.com/us/laitz

Provided are short excerpts in various textures. Complete the following tasks:

1. Circle each harmony and label root, type of harmony (for triads: Maj, min, dim; for seventh chords: Mm, MM, mm, dm, dd) and inversion, if any (for triads: $\frac{6}{3}$, $\frac{6}{4}$; for seventh chords $\frac{6}{5}$, $\frac{4}{3}$, $\frac{4}{2}$).

2. Describe the harmonic rhythm in terms of its rate of change (fast or slow), and whether or not it is regular.

3. Make a reduction on manuscript paper that includes the following:
   a. a bass note (which may or may not be the root, depending on whether the chord is inverted)
   b. two upper voices, added to complete triads, and three upper voices, added to complete seventh chords. Use close position, with the highest note of the texture functioning as the soprano.

A. Corelli, Concerto Grosso no. 2 in F major, *Allegro*

B. Beethoven, Piano Trio in E♭, op. 1, no. 1, Finale

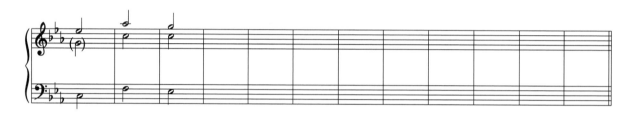

C. Haydn, String Quartet op. 20, no. 5, III, *Adagio*
   Include a roman numeral analysis.

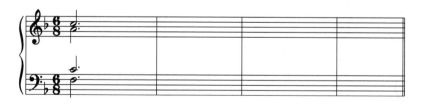

D. Bach, Prelude in C major, BWV 846, from *Well-Tempered Clavier*, Book 1

Include a roman numeral analysis. Compare this example with the preceding example by Haydn.

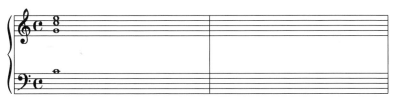

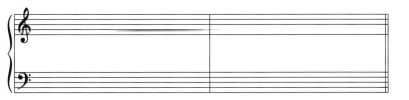

CHAPTER 4

When Harmony, Melody, and Rhythm Converge

ASSIGNMENT 4.1 EXERCISES FOR EMBELLISHING TONES AND HARMONIC ANALYSIS

EXERCISE 4.1 *Harmonic and Melodic Analysis*

STREAMING AUDIO
www.oup.com/us/laitz

Analyze, marking the following on the scores. Do not analyze with roman numerals.

1. Size of chord (triad or seventh chord)
2. Root name and quality (triad: M, m, d; seventh: Mm, MM, mm, dm, dd)
3. Member of the chord that is in the bass and soprano (e.g., root, third, etc.)
4. Label the following embellishing tones in the upper-voice melodies according to these types:
   a. passing tones and whether they are consonant or dissonant: "CPT" or "DPT"
   b. neighboring tones and whether they are upper or lower types: "UN" or "LN"
   c. chordal leaps: "CL"

A. Mozart, *Variations on "Ah vous dirais-je, Maman,"* K. 265, Variation 6

Both the "Twinkle tune" and the harmony appear in the right hand, while the faster embellishing tones appear in the left hand. Thus, you will need to consider the right-hand chords as you distinguish between chord tones and nonchord tones in the left hand (ignore the G⁵ and F⁵ in the right hand of mm. 3 and 4, enclosed in parentheses). Circle and label all nonchord tones in the bass.

VAR. VI.

B. Beethoven, Violin Sonata no. 3 in E♭ major, op. 12, no. 3, Rondo

EXERCISE 4.2 *Verticalization*

STREAMING AUDIO
www.oup.com/us/laitz

The examples that follow are written in a florid style. However, each depends on the flow of harmonies. Rewrite each example in chorale (vertical) style (four voices: soprano, alto, tenor, and bass) and provide an analysis that includes chord type and inversion. Do not use roman numerals unless specified in the example.

A. Schumann, "Wiegenliedchen," *Kinderszenen*, op. 124, No. 6
  Analyze mm. 1–6 using roman numerals.

Nicht schnell

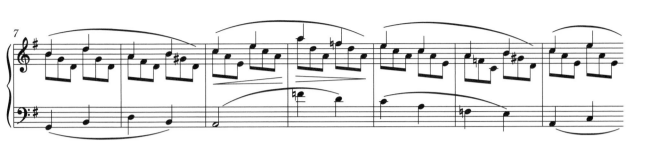

B. Beethoven, Piano Sonata in C major, op. 2, no. 3, Trio

ASSIGNMENT 4.2   EXERCISES FOR EMBELLISHING TONES AND HARMONIC ANALYSIS

ANALYSIS

EXERCISE 4.3   *Harmonic and Melodic Analysis*

STREAMING AUDIO
www.oup.com/us/laitz

Analyze, marking the following items on the scores. Do *not* analyze with roman numerals. Ignore all pitches in parentheses.

1. Size of chord (triad or seventh chord)
2. Root name and quality (triad: M, m, d; seventh: Mm, MM, mm, dm, dd)
3. Member of the chord that is in the bass and soprano (e.g., root, third, etc.)
4. Label the following embellishing tones in the upper-voice melodies according to these types:
   a. passing tones and whether they are consonant or dissonant ("CPT" or "DPT")
   b. neighboring tones and whether they are upper or lower types ("UN" or "LN")
   c. chordal leaps ("CL")

A. Schubert, Waltz in A♭ major, *36 Originaltänze*, op. 9a, D. 365

Like many waltzes, the left-hand downbeat note controls the harmony throughout the measure; consider it sounding even though Schubert has not specified that it be sustained.

B. Haydn, String Quartet in C major, op. 20, no. 2, *Adagio*

C. Schumann, "Ich will meine Seele tauchen," from *Dichterliebe*
   Arrows indicate embellishing tones; label each.

Kelch   der Li - lie hin - ein;   die Li - lie soll klin   -   gend

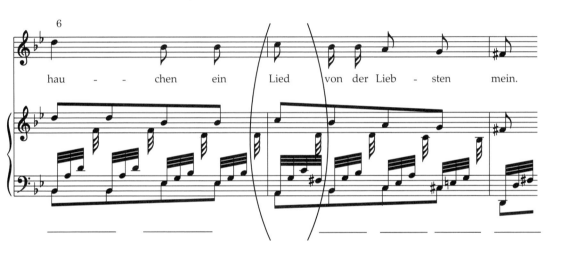

hau - - chen ein   Lied   von der Lieb - sten   mein.

ASSIGNMENT 4.3   EXERCISES FOR MELODIC FLUENCY: ANALYSIS AND COMPOSITION

EXERCISE 4.4   *Melodic Fluency*

STREAMING AUDIO
www.oup.com/us/laitz

Circle the pitches that participate in the structural melodic line.

1. The pitches that you choose must be:

   - consonant with the bass (or chord tones, which include the chordal seventh), and
   - must be accented in some way (e.g., metrically, rhythmically).

2. Look for parallel musical relationships to support your connections.
3. Notice in the sample solution that an overall stepwise descent of a fifth occurs from C^6 to F^5.

Beethoven clearly marks the stepwise descent in the following ways:

1. The descent from C to B♭ in mm. 1–4 occurs in parallel melodic/rhythmic contexts (see mm. 1–2 and 5–6).
2. Measures 5–8 and 9–12 are near repetitions of each another. However, note that the abrupt leap of B♭ down an octave (m. 5), the sudden shift to *piano* and *dolce*, and the incomplete descent only to A ($\hat{3}$) reveals that mm. 5–8 are subordinate to 9–12, where the original register is recaptured as is the dynamic level, and the structural melodic line completes its descent from B♭^{5} to F^5.

Sample solution:
Beethoven, Symphony no. 8 in F major, op. 93, *Allegro vivace con brio*

A. Mozart, "Notte e giorno faticar," from *Don Giovanni*, K. 527, act 1, scene 1

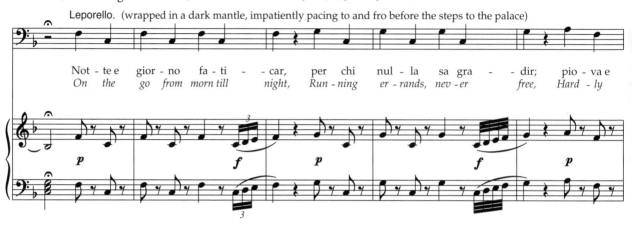

Leporello. (wrapped in a dark mantle, impatiently pacing to and fro before the steps to the palace)

Not - te e gior - no fa - ti - - car, per chi nul - la sa gra - - dir; pio - va e
On the go from morn till night, Run - ning er - rands, nev -er free, Hard - ly

ven - to sop - por - - tar, man - giar ma - le, e mal dor - - mir! _____
time to snatch a bite; This is not the life for me. _____

Vo - - glio far il gen - til - uo - mo,
I would like to play the mas - ter,

B. Schumann, "Winterszeit II," *Album für die Jugend*, op. 68, no. 39

C. Haydn, String Quartet in F minor, op. 20, no. 5, *Allegro moderato*

D. Mozart, Rondo in F major, K. 494

EXERCISE 4.5   *Melodic Fluency, Harmony, and Embellishing Tones*

The florid soprano melody of each example that follows depends upon more slowly moving stepwise lines. Complete the following tasks.

1. Circle and stem each note of the structural stepwise line, then beam them together.
2. In example E, identify harmonies; use roman numerals for the bass notes with horizontal dashes beneath them.
3. Label the type of embellishing tone for each soprano pitch beneath an arrow.

A. Arlen, "Over the Rainbow"

B. Rodgers and Hammerstein, "Do-Re-Mi," from *The Sound of Music*

C. Beethoven, German Dance

D. Verdi, "La donna è mobile," from *Rigoletto*, act 3

E. Albinoni, Sonata in C for Oboe and Basso Continuo, *Menuet*

F. Beethoven, Symphony no. 6 in F major, *Allegretto*

EXERCISE 4.6   *Embellishment*

The first-species counterpoints given here are composed of slow-moving, primarily stepwise melodies, along with their implied harmonies (in parentheses). You are to add embellishing tones to the upper voice to create a florid melody that provides ornamentation for the given underlying, melodically fluent line. You may add the following embellishing tones: passing tones, neighbors (both upper and lower), and chordal skips and leaps. You may also combine two or more of these embellishing tones. An example and solution are also presented.

Given is a 1:1 counterpoint in D minor, with implied chords in parentheses. You are to do the following:

1. a. If the implied missing chordal members are given (in parentheses, as in the sample solution), then analyze each chord with roman numerals (so that you will have a clear idea of the types of embellishing tones you can add and how they will function in the given harmonic environment).
    b. If the roman numerals are given (below the bass staff), then notate the missing pitch (or pitches) of the chord above the given bass pitch in the bass clef so that you can see all of the chordal members, and enclose within parentheses (as in the sample solution).
2. Add embellishing tones. The sample shows how one can add specific types of embellishing tones to each measure (e.g., m. 1 = passing tones, m. 2 = a combination of neighbor tones and chordal leaps, etc.). Here are guidelines for adding embellishing tones.
    a. Use a primary rhythmic value in your solution along with those values that are at the next-faster and next-slower levels. For example, the eighth note is the basic rhythmic value in the given solution, along with quarter and sixteenth values (the quarter note is the next-longer value and the sixteenth note is the next-shorter value).
    b. Create a logical and unified embellished melody by using only two or three rhythmic and melodic ideas. For example, the sample solution uses primarily eighth notes and the melodic ideas are mostly passing tones and chordal skips that fill in the interval of the third.
    c. Don't forget the contrapuntal rules and guidelines you learned in Chapter 2. These include melodic principles (e.g., no dissonant leaps) and the way the voices combine (e.g., parallels).

Sample solution:

ASSIGNMENT 4.4
EXERCISES FOR MELODIC FLUENCY

ANALYSIS

EXERCISE 4.7 *Melodic Fluency*

STREAMING AUDIO
www.oup.com/us/laitz

Circle the pitches that participate in the structural melodic line. The pitches that you choose must be consonant with the bass and must be accented in some way (e.g., metrically, rhythmically). Look for parallel musical relationships to support your connections.

A. Mozart, "Porgi, amor, qualche ristoro," from *Le Nozze di Figaro (The Marriage of Figaro)*, K. 492, act 2, scene 1

B. Mozart, String Quartet in E♭ major, K. 171, *Adagio*
   Compare this excerpt with the one from *Figaro*.

C. Bach, Prelude in C minor, BWV 871, *Well-Tempered Clavier*, Book 2

EXERCISE 4.8   *Composition: Melodic Fluency and Embellishment*

Consider the unmetered, arhythmic melodic fragments that follow to be the structural pitches of a melodically fluent melody that you will embellish. Your embellishments may take any number of forms (see the two sample solutions: the first shows how a single pitch [E] might be embellished by various chordal leaps, neighbors, passing motions, and combinations of those figures, and the second shows how the two-pitch fragment E–F♯ can be embellished). Set each melodic fragment in two *different* meters. Strive for the following:

1. an integrated four- to eight-measure melody that relies on only two or three different types of embellishing tones;
2. that the structural, melodically fluent, pitches are aurally prominent (e.g., place them on metrically accented beats or parts of beats, extend their duration, etc.).

Sample solution:

CHAPTER 5

Tonic and Dominant as Tonal Pillars and Introduction to Voice Leading

ASSIGNMENT 5.1   EXERCISES FOR TONIC AND DOMINANT HARMONIES

EXERCISE 5.1   *Analysis*

STREAMING AUDIO
www.oup.com/us/laitz

Using roman numerals, analyze each harmony in the following examples.

A. Vivaldi, Violin Sonata in A major, *Allegro*

B. Beethoven, Violin Sonata in G major, op. 30, no. 3, *Allegro assai*
The sixteenth-note embellishment is governed by the implied harmony that is represented by the metrically accented notes (i.e., those notes that occur every half measure).

EXERCISE 5.2   *Review: Spelling Tonic and Dominant*

Complete the following table by spelling the required tonic and dominant triads and the dominant seventh chord. Remember, V and V^7 are Mm seventh chords in minor keys, which will require raising $\hat{7}$ to create a leading tone.

KEY:	D major	e minor	A major	g minor	b minor	A♭ major	f minor
I/i	D–F♯–A						
V							
V^7							C♯–E♯–G♯–B

EXERCISE 5.3   *Correction*

1. Identify the key of each four-voice authentic cadence.
2. Identify each spelling and doubling error. Assume that each chord should be in root position, complete, and with a doubled root.
3. Rewrite a corrected version immediately below in the space provided.

ASSIGNMENT 5.2
EXERCISES FOR TONIC AND DOMINANT

ANALYSIS

EXERCISE 5.4

Determine the following for the chord progressions given:

1. Whether the harmony is tonic or dominant (use roman numerals)
2. Whether close (c) or open position (o) is used
3. Which note is doubled—circle the doubled pitch class and indicate whether it is the root, third, or fifth (R, 3, 5)

A.

B.

EXERCISE 5.5   *Writing Cadences*

Write cadences using only I and V in root position. Begin with a key signature and the outer voices; then fill in alto and tenor lines. Analyze each chord with roman numerals.

A. Imperfect authentic cadences (IAC) in B♭ major and F♯ minor
B. Half cadences (HC) in G minor and E♭ major
C. Perfect authentic cadences (PAC) in C minor and A major

A.   B.

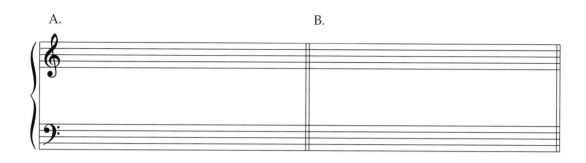

C.

ANALYSIS

EXERCISE 5.6   *Error Detection Involving I and V*

Each example contains one or two errors, including errors in construction (e.g., missing chordal member, poor spacing, incorrect doubling, etc.) and voice leading (e.g., parallels, direct intervals, nonresolution vof tendency tones, etc.). Identify and label the key; label and circle each error. Rewrite the corrected versions on the manuscript paper provided.

A.   B.   C.

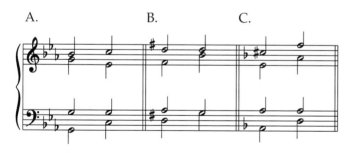

A.   B.   C.

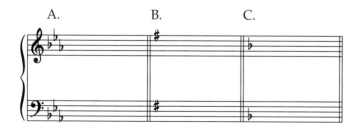

D.   E.   F.

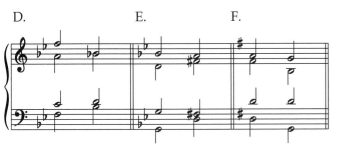

D.   E.   F.

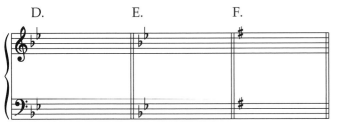

ASSIGNMENT 5.3   ERROR DETECTION AND WRITING OF TONIC AND DOMINANT

EXERCISE 5.7   *Extended Error Detection*

Analyze the key and roman numerals. Then label chord construction and voice-leading errors. Only tonic and dominant occur. The sample solution includes a shorthand labeling system you may wish to use (or, just describe each error).

Sample solution:

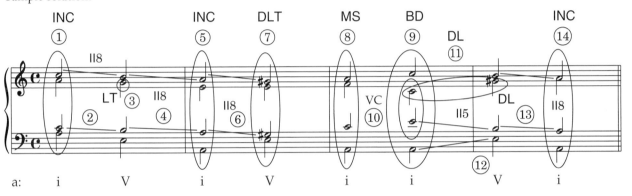

1. An incomplete chord (INC) is a poor way to begin. (Although the fifth is the only chordal member that can be omitted, its absence is justified only if it makes the voice leading smoother. At the beginning of an exercise, where many options are possible, there is no reason to omit it.)
2. Tenor–soprano parallel octaves (P8, with parallel lines showing which voices are involved and the pitches that create the parallels).
3. The $\hat{7}$ must be raised to create a leading tone (LT). In minor, you must add this chromaticism to the pitch.
4. Tenor–soprano parallel octaves.
5. No third in the tonic chord (INC). Remember, only the fifth may be absent in a chord.
6. The parallel octaves continue in tenor and soprano.
7. Double leading tone (DLT).
8. Misspelled tonic harmony: F is not a member of the chord (MS).
9. Doubled third for no reason; in fact, it creates problems (see item 10). Remember, you may double anything (except for dissonant notes or the leading tone), since smooth voice leading is the goal, but keep in mind that doubled roots are most common. *Note*: "BD" means bad doubling.
10. Voice crossing (VC).
11. Difficult, dissonant leap in alto (DL).
12. Contrary ("antiparallel") fifths (C5, with contrary-motion lines showing voices involved).
13. Parallels between soprano and tenor.
14. Four roots and no third or fifth.

WRITING

EXERCISE 5.8   *Completion of Missing Voices*

Determine the key and add roman numerals to the incomplete root-position tonic and
dominant vtriads. Then, decide which voice(s) is/are missing (based on stem direction)
and the appropriate chordal member needed to create an SATB texture.

EXERCISE 5.9 *Figured Bass*

Realize the following figured basses in four voices (SATB), including roman numerals. Change the upper-voice spacings for any repeated bass notes.

A.   B.

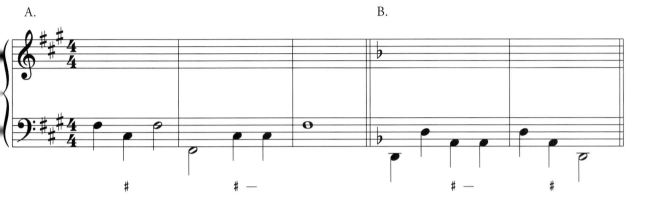

ASSIGNMENT 5.4 EXERCISES FOR WRITING TONIC AND DOMINANT

EXERCISE 5.10 *Completion of Missing Voices*

Determine the key and add roman numerals to the incomplete tonic and dominant triads. Add the appropriate pitches to create a four-voice (SATB) texture. Double the chord's root and use only root-position tonic and dominant triads.

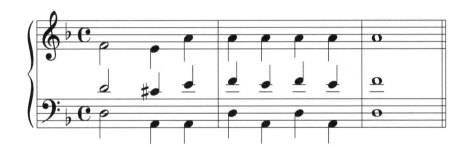

EXERCISE 5.11 *Part Writing Tonic and Dominant in Major*

1. Notate in a meter of your choice the following soprano scale degrees:
   a. In D major, $\hat{1}$–$\hat{7}$–$\hat{1}$
   b. In A minor, $\hat{1}$–$\hat{2}$–$\hat{3}$
   c. In E♭ major, $\hat{3}$–$\hat{2}$–$\hat{1}$
2. Add a bass line that implies only tonic and dominant harmonies in root position.
3. Fill in the alto and tenor voices to create a four-voice chorale texture. Remember that stems go up for soprano and tenor and down for alto and bass.
4. Analyze and then transpose to the key of A minor.

A.

B.

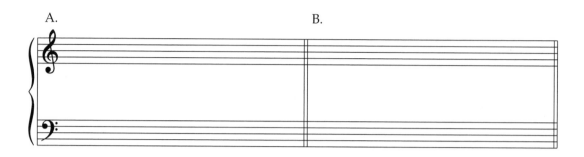

C.

EXERCISE 5.12   *Analysis of Tonic and Dominant: Review*

Analyze the following examples.

A. Corelli, Concerto Grosso in G minor, "Christmas Concerto," op. 6, no. 8, *Vivace*

key: ___   ___   ___   ___

B. Corelli, Sonata, op. 1, no. 9, *Allegro*

key: ____   ____   ____   ____   ____   ____   ____   ____   ____

EXERCISE 5.13   *Unfigured Bass and Soprano*

Figured basses are the first steps in understanding harmony because they prescribe harmonic content precisely, leaving you no choice in what chords to use. Unfigured basses are more challenging, since a given bass note can be harmonized by more than one harmony (e.g., any bass note could be the root, third, or fifth of a triad). Thus, unfigured basses require mastery of the most typical and logical harmonic progressions.

An intermediate step between figured bass and unfigured bass is the unfigured bass with a given soprano, since the addition of the soprano voice restricts your chord choice considerably. Look for cadences and short melodic patterns that have harmonic settings you have learned. Avoid vertical "third stacking" in which you haphazardly choose harmonies based on individual bass pitches. Only after you have grouped bass and soprano pitches into logical musical units should you begin to add inner voices and roman numerals. This exercise contains a few passing tones indicated by parentheses.

ASSIGNMENT 5.5   EXERCISES FOR WRITING TONIC AND DOMINANT

WRITING

EXERCISE 5.14   *Potpourri of Activities*

Complete the following tasks in four voices as required. Use only root-position tonic and dominants. Chromatically raise $\hat{7}$ in minor. Label key, add key signatures, and roman numerals.

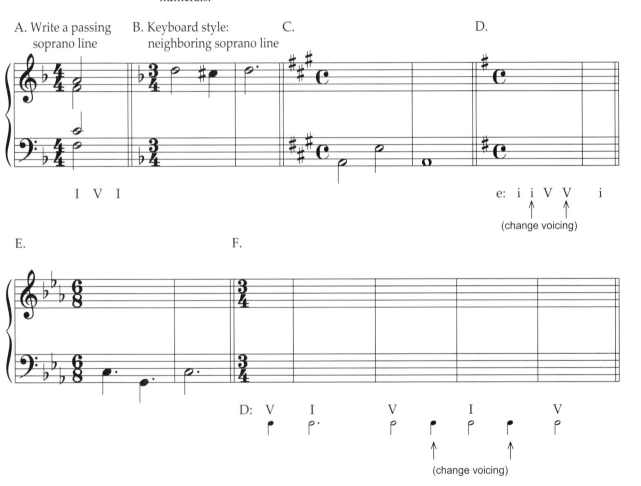

EXERCISE 5.15 *Harmonizing Cadential Soprano Progressions*

Choose a meter, then write four-voice cadential progressions using only root-position tonic and dominant harmonies based on these soprano fragments. Your order of composition should be bass line, then alto and tenor lines. Analyze with roman numerals and label the cadence.

A. $\hat{3}$ $\hat{2}$ $\hat{1}$ $\hat{7}$ $\hat{1}$ (D minor, B minor)
B. $\hat{1}$ $\hat{7}$ $\hat{1}$ $\hat{2}$ $\hat{3}$ (E major, C minor)
C. $\hat{1}$ $\hat{2}$ $\hat{3}$ $\hat{5}$ $\hat{5}$ (B♭ major, E minor)

A.

B.

C.

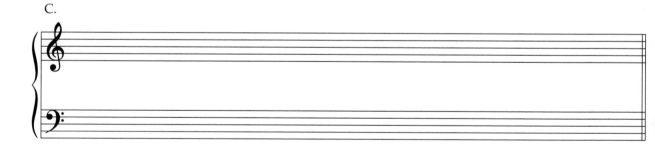

CHAPTER 6

The Impact of Melody, Rhythm, and Meter on Harmony; Introduction to V^7; and Harmonizing Florid Melodies

ASSIGNMENT 6.1
EXERCISES FOR ANALYSIS AND WRITING V^7

EXERCISE 6.1 *Analysis of I, V, and V^7*

STREAMING AUDIO
www.oup.com/us/laitz

1. Label each tonic and dominant harmony. Distinguish between V and V^7.
2. Specify whether each seventh is prepared (not a requirement) and indicate resolution by an arrow (a requirement).

   - If the seventh appears in the top voice, consider the possibility that it might be part of a longer, more slowly moving structural line that spans the entire melody, in which case it occurs at the supermetrical level (recall our studies of melodic fluency).
   - Remember, the seventh is resolved only by a change of harmony.
   - In freer textures, the resolution may occur in a different voice or even a different register.

A. Handel, Violin Sonata in F major, no. 3, *Allegro*

B. Weber, "German Dance"

C. Schubert, "Wiegenlied," op. 98, no. 2

EXERCISE 6.2   *Error Detection*

The following four-voice progressions that include root-position I, V, and V⁷ contain one or two part-writing errors, including construction (spelling, spacing, doubling, etc.) and voice-leading problems (parallels, improper resolution of seventh, etc.). Label the key of each example, then identify and label each type of error. Focus especially on errors of the following types:

1. Incorrect treatment of tendency tones:
   a. The chordal seventh ($\hat{4}$) must resolve down by step.
   b. The leading tone ($\hat{7}$) must ascend, unless it occurs in an inner voice.

2. V^7 follows V; the use of V after V^7 is not allowed, given that V^7 intensifies V.

Sample solution:

EXERCISE 6.3   *V^7 in Three Voices*

Identify the key and complete the following V^7 chords in three voices. Thus, the V^7 chords will necessarily be incomplete (lacking the fifth). Resolve each V^7 to its tonic.

Sample solution:

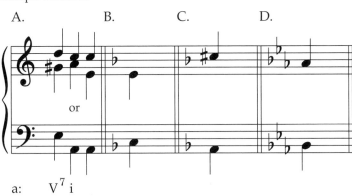

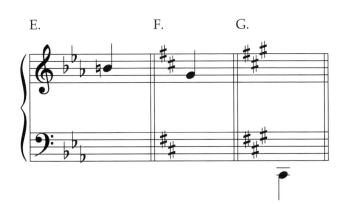

ASSIGNMENT 6.2
ANALYSIS AND WRITING V⁷

EXERCISE 6.4   *Analysis of I, V, and V⁷*

Label each tonic and dominant harmony, distinguishing between V and V⁷.

A. Schumann, "In der Fremde" ("In Foreign Lands"), *Liederkreis*, op. 39, no. 1
The seventh of V⁷ appears prominently in the vocal line of m. 4. Does it resolve to the immediately following A in the vocal line? The seventh also appears in the right hand of the accompaniment. Which appearance of the seventh seems more structural, and why?

B. Mozart, Serenade in D major, "Posthorn," K. 320, *Andante grazioso*

EXERCISE 6.5

Write V⁷ chords in four voices and resolve each to the tonic. In these examples, there may be an opportunity to either double the root (and omit the fifth) or write a complete seventh chord. Indicate whether your chord is complete (C) or incomplete (I). Letter A is completed for you.

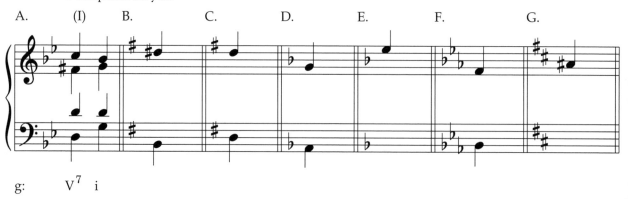

EXERCISE 6.6   *Writing Root-Position V^7*

Complete the following tasks in four voices. Begin by writing note-against-note outer voices, then, fill in tenor and alto.

    A. Using a passing soprano line, write I–V^7–I in D major and G minor.
    B. Using a neighboring soprano line, write I–V^7–I in E major and C minor.

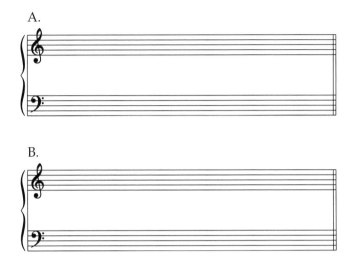

EXERCISE 6.7   *Figured Bass*

Realize the following two figured basses in four voices. Write the soprano first, then add tenor and alto. Do a two-level analysis: The first level should include every harmonic change, and the second level should prioritize harmonies based on their metrical placement and on the subordinate passing and neighboring motions of the soprano.

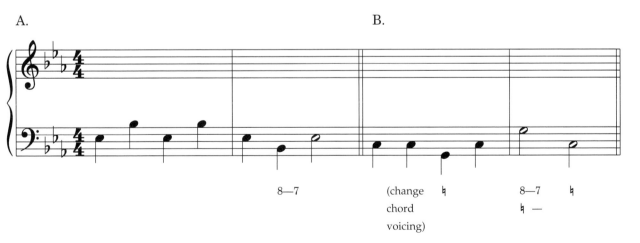

ASSIGNMENT 6.3
EXERCISES FOR ANALYSIS AND WRITING V⁷

EXERCISE 6.8 *Analysis of I, V, and V⁷*

STREAMING AUDIO
www.oup.com/us/laitz

1. Label each tonic and dominant harmony. Distinguish between V and V⁷.
2. Specify whether each seventh is prepared (not a requirement) and indicate resolution by an arrow (a requirement).
   a. If the seventh appears in the top voice, consider the possibility that it might be part of a longer, slower-moving structural line that spans the entire melody, in which case it occurs at the supermetrical level (recall our studies of melodic fluency).
   b. Remember, the seventh is resolved only by a change of harmony.
   c. In freer textures the resolution may occur in a different voice or even a different register.

This is the first of several orchestral scores that you will need to negotiate in this book. Don't panic; you can employ certain strategies when first encountering a full orchestral score. Focus on the instruments that are easiest to read and carry the most important harmonic and contrapuntal materials. Begin by looking at the strings, which are the backbone of the orchestra and are laid out in string-quartet style: Cello and double bass carry the bass and therefore the harmonic underpinning, while the first violin carries the contrapuntal melody. The viola part is written in the alto clef.

You can then look to the woodwinds, which very often double the strings. High woodwinds (flutes and oboes) share material with the first and second violin parts, and the bassoon is aligned with the cellos and double basses. Occasionally the high woodwinds may have a separate melody from the upper strings, so examine these parts carefully. Remember, all the strings and many of the winds sound as written (though there are exceptions, such as B♭ clarinet and oboe d'amore in A). Most of the brass instruments are transposing (horns in F sound down a perfect fifth from the notated pitch, and trumpets in B♭ sound a major second lower than written); it was not until the nineteenth century that the brass arose as an independent force in the orchestra. In the 1700s and in the first half of the nineteenth century, brass instruments generally doubled other instruments. In this excerpt, Mozart is using brass instruments in C, therefore, the pitches you see are the pitches that sound (though horn in C actually sounds one octave lower than written).

A. Mozart, Symphony no. 22 in C major, K. 162, *Allegro assai*

This next example contains a supermetrical passing seventh—the passing motion takes place over several measures. Label only root-position tonic and dominant harmonies. Then, trace the three-note melodic line that comprises the preparation of the seventh, the dissonant seventh, and its resolution.

B. Mozart, String Quartet in A major, K. 464, *Allegro*

EXERCISE 6.9   *Error Detection*

The following four-voice progressions that include root-position I, V, and V⁷ contain one or more part-writing errors, including construction (spelling, spacing, doubling, etc.) and voice-leading problems (parallels, improper resolution of seventh, etc.). Label the key of each example, then identify and label each type of error. Focus especially on the following types of errors:

1. Incorrect treatment of tendency tones:
   a. The chordal seventh ($\hat{4}$) must resolve down by step.
   b. The leading tone ($\hat{7}$) must ascend, unless it occurs in an inner voice.
2. V⁷ follows V; the use of V after V⁷ is not allowed, given that V⁷ intensifies V.

WRITING

EXERCISE 6.10   *Authentic Cadences and Figured Bass*

Identify the key for each example, then write authentic cadences in four voices. You may write perfect or imperfect cadences. Specify the type of cadence and analyze with roman numerals. Be sure to obey the voice leading if given by a horizontal dash in the figured bass. Letter A is completed for you.

Sample solution:

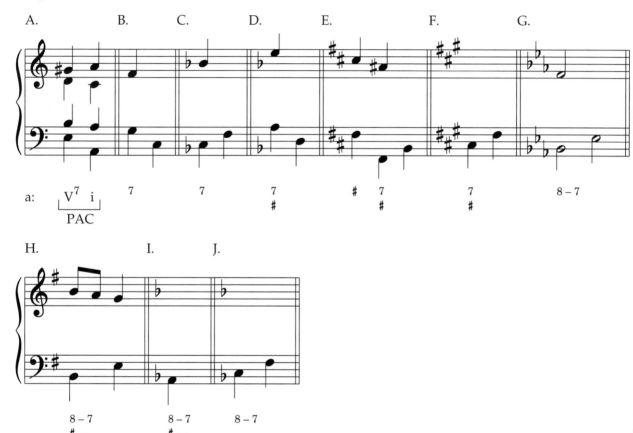

ASSIGNMENT 6.4
MORE EXERCISES FOR WRITING V⁷

WRITING

EXERCISE 6.11   *Authentic Cadences and Figured Bass*

Identify the key for each example, then write authentic cadences in four voices. You may write perfect or imperfect cadences. Specify the type of cadence and analyze with roman numerals. Be sure to obey the voice leading if given by a horizontal dash in the figured bass.

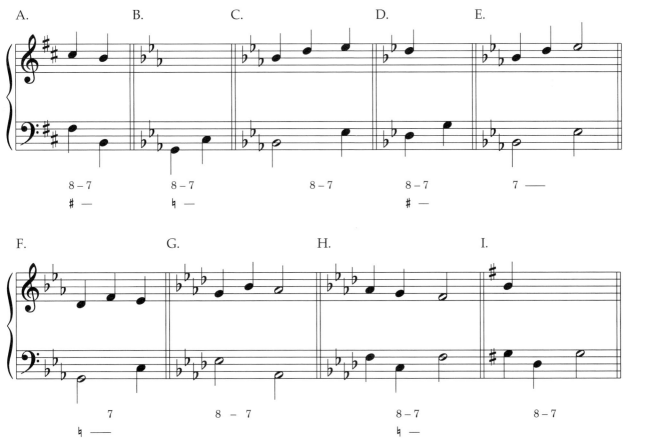

EXERCISE 6.12   *Soprano Harmonization*

1. Determine the key and whether root-position I, V, or V[7] chords are implied by the soprano lines; add roman numerals.
2. Harmonize each soprano pitch with a single bass note to create note-against-note counterpoint.
3. Finally, fill in the alto and tenor voices.

ASSIGNMENT 6.5   EXERCISES FOR MELODY HARMONIZATION USING I, V, AND V^7

EXERCISE 6.13   *Harmonization Using V and V^7*

After choosing a meter, use I, V, and V^7 for the following soprano fragments. Remember, the chord progression V to V^7 is not reversible. Write each exercise in a different major key and its relative-minor key.

A. $\hat{3}$–$\hat{4}$–$\hat{3}$ B. $\hat{5}$–$\hat{4}$–$\hat{3}$–$\hat{2}$–$\hat{1}$ C. $\hat{1}$–$\hat{7}$–$\hat{1}$–$\hat{2}$–$\hat{4}$–$\hat{3}$
D. $\hat{3}$–$\hat{2}$–$\hat{1}$–$\hat{7}$–$\hat{1}$ E. $\hat{2}$–$\hat{7}$–$\hat{1}$–$\hat{2}$–$\hat{3}$

EXERCISE 6.14   *Harmonization of Florid Melodies*

Harmonize any two of the following tunes using usually one chord per measure. However, some tunes may permit the same harmony to continue for two or more measures, while others may require two chords within a single measure. Use only root-position I, V, and V^7. Apply the following method:

1. Determine the key.
2. Sing or play the tune.
3. Find cadences.
4. Determine the harmonic rhythm.
5. Determine individual harmonies by looking at accented pitches. Remember, $\hat{1}$–$\hat{3}$–$\hat{5}$ implies a I chord and $\hat{5}$–$\hat{7}$–$\hat{2}$ (and often $\hat{4}$) imply a V$^{(7)}$ harmony. Arpeggiations and chordal skips imply a single harmony.
6. Add roman numerals below the melody (see Letter A).

Note: Most embellishing tones occur on weak beats or weak parts of beats.

A. Mozart, "Longing for Spring," K. 596, *Giocoso*

B. Mozart, Symphony no. 39, K. 543, *Allegretto*

C. Haydn, "Surprise" Symphony in G major, no. 94, *Allegro*

D. Russian folk tune, *Andante grazioso*

CHAPTER 7

Contrapuntal Expansions of Tonic and Dominant: Six-Three Chords

ASSIGNMENT 7.1   EXERCISES FOR TONIC AND DOMINANT SIX-THREE CHORDS

ANALYSIS

EXERCISE 7.1

STREAMING AUDIO
www.oup.com/us/laitz

Use two levels to analyze the following examples that contain $\frac{5}{3}$ and $\frac{6}{3}$ tonic and dominant triads. (Recall that level one is descriptive and provides an analysis of every chord, using roman numerals and figured bass. Level two is interpretive, and identifies what chords are more important than others by using roman numerals for structural chords, and contrapuntal functions [P, N, CL], for expanding harmonies.) Shown is a sample solution.

Sample solution:

Hasse, Trio Sonata no. 1 in E minor for Two Flutes and Basso Continuo, *Largo*

A.

B. Schubert, "Auf dem Flusse," *Winterreise*, D. 911

The E in the right hand of m. 3 is a nonchord tone that postpones the D♯ that follows.

EXERCISE 7.2 *Figured Bass*

1. Determine the key.
2. Study the figured bass, adding a soprano that moves primarily by step and creates mostly imperfect consonances with the bass (i.e., thirds and sixths).
3. Analyze, including a second-level analysis.
4. Fill in inner voices.

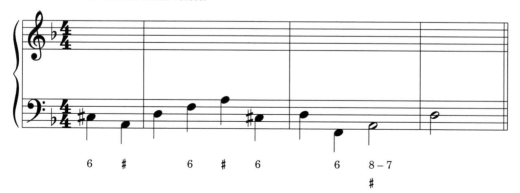

EXERCISE 7.3   *Analysis*

STREAMING AUDIO
www.oup.com/us/laitz

On the surface, this excerpt appears quite complex. First, complete your two-level analysis. Then, dismantle the surface and reduce it to a chorale-like texture in the empty staves provided by identifying and removing gestures and figurations that embellish a single tone (changes of direction in each line indicate these). The first measure is completed for you. Take care with the entry of Violin 2: Is this a new voice? Or a doubling of a previously existing one? Stem the larger passing motion that is revealed by this reduction in the score.

A. Vivaldi, Concerto Grosso in G major, op. 9, no. 10, Ryom 300, Ricordi 125, *Allegro molto*

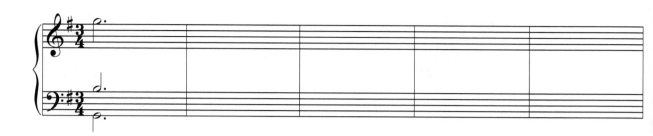

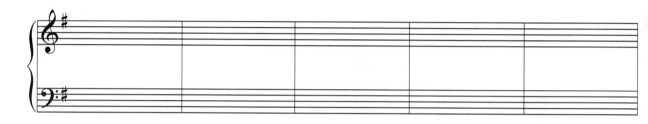

B. Beethoven, "Freudvoll und leidvoll" ("Joyful and Sorrowful"), op. 84, no. 4

Accented embellishing tones occur on beat two of each measure; you need not analyze these for now.

C. Mozart, Piano Sonata in F major, K. 280, *Allegro assai*

D. Bach, "Das neugeborne Kindelein," BWV 122

The bracketed tone is an accented passing tone, which you need not analyze for now. Note how Bach has the alto imitate the bass in the first measure, carrying it above the soprano and avoiding the monotony of three Gs at the top of such a clear and simple texture.

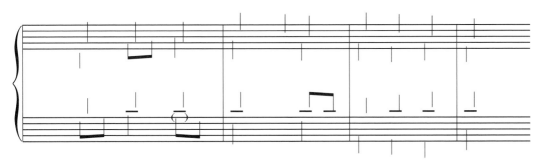

EXERCISE 7.4 *Analysis*

Complete the following tasks in four-voice chorale style. Analyze, using first- and second-level analysis.

A. In D major, set I–vii°⁶–I⁶ three times. Each time use a different soprano melody.

B. In D minor, set the following progression in $\frac{3}{4}$ meter, remembering that structural chords tend to be on stronger beats and subordinate chords tend to be on weaker beats: i–vii°⁶–i⁶–V⁶–i–V⁷–i.

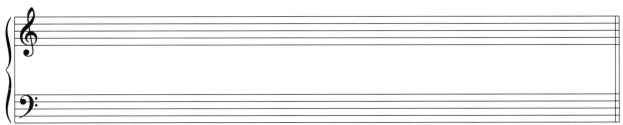

C. Set the progression from letter B in $\frac{4}{4}$ meter.

ASSIGNMENT 7.3   EXERCISES FOR IV⁶
(ALSO vii°⁶, I, I⁶, V, V⁶, AND V⁷)

EXERCISE 7.5   *Analysis*

STREAMING AUDIO
www.oup.com/us/laitz

Using two levels, analyze the following examples.

A. Verdi, "Au sein de la puissance," from *Les Vêpres Siciliennes* (*Sicilian Vespers*), act 3

B. C. P. E. Bach, Sonata no. 5 in A minor for Flute and Keyboard, Wq 128, H.555

C. Bach, "Du Friedefürst, Herr Jesu Christ," BWV 116

WRITING

EXERCISE 7.6   *Matching and Composition*

In the left-hand column, labeled "Bass Harmonies," is a summary of the progressions and prolongations that we have encountered. In the right-hand column is a series of soprano scale-degree patterns. Match the soprano patterns with the appropriate bass progression (there will be some multiple solutions). Then, in B minor, choose a meter and string together three of the patterns to create a convincing progression. Close with an authentic cadence. Add alto and tenor. Analyze using roman numerals and include a second-level analysis.

Bass Harmonies	Soprano Scale Degrees
1. I–V^7–I	A. $\hat{3}$–$\hat{4}$–$\hat{5}$–$\hat{4}$–$\hat{3}$
2. I–V^6–V^7–I	B. $\hat{5}$–$\hat{5}$–$\hat{4}$–$\hat{2}$–$\hat{1}$
3. I–V–V^6–I	C. $\hat{3}$–$\hat{2}$–$\hat{1}$–$\hat{7}$–$\hat{1}$
4. I–V^6–I–I^6–V^7–I	D. $\hat{1}$–$\hat{2}$–$\hat{3}$
5. I–vii$^{\circ 6}$–I^6–V^7–I	E. $\hat{3}$–$\hat{2}$–$\hat{5}$–$\hat{3}$
6. I–IV^6–I^6–V^7–I	F. $\hat{3}$–$\hat{1}$–$\hat{7}$–$\hat{1}$
7. I–V–IV^6–V^6–I	G. $\hat{1}$–$\hat{2}$–$\hat{3}$–$\hat{1}$–$\hat{2}$–$\hat{1}$
8. I^6–V^6–I	H. $\hat{1}$–$\hat{7}$–$\hat{1}$

ASSIGNMENT 7.4
COMPOSITION USING ⁵₃ AND ⁶₃ CHORDS

EXERCISE 7.7   *Figured Bass*

Realize the following figured bass by adding a soprano melody, analyzing, and adding inner voices.

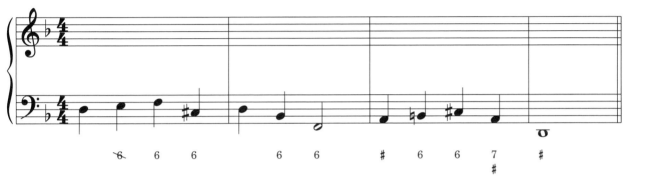

EXERCISE 7.8   *Melody Writing over an Accompaniment*

1. Analyze the implied harmonies of the accompaniment.
2. Continue the accompaniment based on the harmonic implications of the given bass.
3. Write a florid melody.

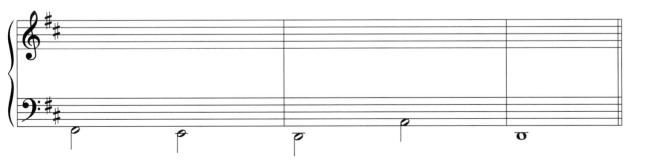

ASSIGNMENT 7.5
COMPOSITION USING $^6_3$ AND $^6_8$ CHORDS

EXERCISE 7.9   *Soprano Harmonization*

Harmonize each pitch of the following melody using the chords we have studied. Analyze using two levels.

EXERCISE 7.10   *Melody Harmonization*

Harmonize the given melody using a single harmony per measure, except in mm. 5 and 7, where you will write two harmonies in each measure. You need add only a single bass note, but make sure you include a complete roman numeral and figured bass analysis.

CHAPTER 8

More Contrapuntal Expansions: Inversions of V^7, Introduction to Leading-Tone Seventh Chords, and Reduction and Elaboration

ASSIGNMENT 8.1   EXERCISES FOR INVERSIONS OF V^7 (AND SIX-THREE CHORDS)

ANALYSIS

EXERCISE 8.1

STREAMING AUDIO
www.oup.com/us/laitz

In the following excerpts from Mozart piano sonatas, the tonic is expanded with inversions of V^7. Provide a first- and second-level analysis. Some chords may be incomplete, but it is possible to determine their identity from the context.

A. Sonata in C major, K. 279, *Andante*

B. Sonata in F major, K. 547a, *Allegretto*

C. Sonata in C major, K. 279, *Andante*

D. Sonata in D major, K. 576, *Adagio*

E. Sonata in G major, K. 283, *Allegro*

F. Sonata in B♭ major, K. 281, *Allegro*

G. Sonata in C major, K. 309, *Allegro*

EXERCISE 8.2 *Inversions of V⁷ and Figured Bass*

Realize the following figured bass in four voices and provide a two-level harmonic analysis.

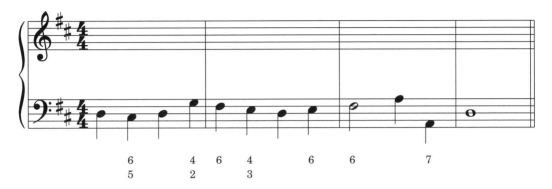

ASSIGNMENT 8.2   EXERCISES FOR INVERSIONS OF V⁷ (AND SIX-THREE CHORDS)

EXERCISE 8.3   *Writing Inversions of V⁷*

Complete the following tasks in four voices and add an appropriate meter. Play your solutions, being able to sing the bass voice while playing the upper voices.

A. In D major, expand tonic using V$^6_5$ as a neighbor.
B. In D minor, expand tonic using a passing V$^4_3$; close with a PAC.
C. In F♯ minor, expand tonic using an incomplete neighboring V$^4_2$; close with a HC.

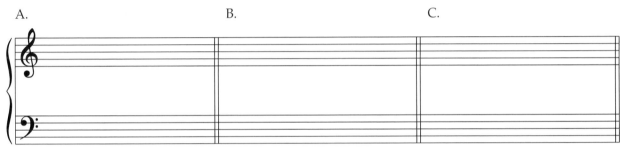

EXERCISE 8.4   *Figured Bass*

Realize the following figured bass in four voices and provide a two-level harmonic analysis.

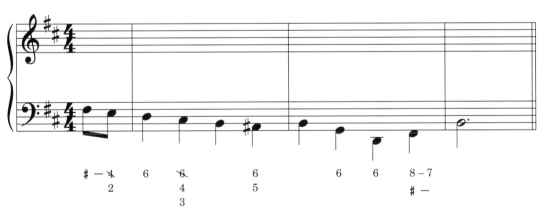

EXERCISE 8.5   *Analysis*

STREAMING AUDIO
www.oup.com/us/laitz

In the following excerpts, the tonic is expanded with inversions of V⁷. Provide first- and second-level analyses. Some chords may be incomplete, but it is possible to determine their identity from the context.

A. Loeillet, Sonata for Oboe in A minor, op. 5, no. 2, *Allegro*

B. Tchaikovsky, "The Sick Doll," *Children's Pieces*, op. 39

C. Beethoven, Piano Sonata no. 2 in A major, op. 2, no. 2, *Largo appassionato*

When you do your second-level analysis, focus on m. 3, because it is possible to interpret it as dominant or tonic. Your choice will affect its performance considerably. For example, if you view the dominant to control the measure, the tonic will not be played in a way as to indicate a return to that function; rather, it will sound as if it is harmonizing a soprano passing tone that links statements of the dominant. If you view the tonic as in control, then you might slightly delay and/or intensify its return through dynamics, therefore breaking any connection between the preceding and following dominant.

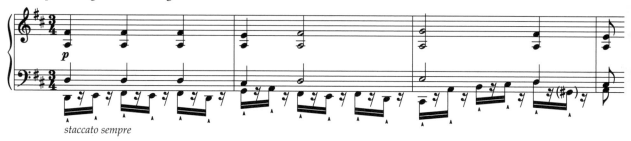

D. Beethoven, Rondo, Violin Sonata in D major, op. 12, no. 1

As in Exercise C, m. 3 may be variously interpreted as a dominant or tonic in your second-level analysis.

ASSIGNMENT 8.3   EXERCISES FOR INVERSIONS OF V⁷ (AND SIX-THREE CHORDS)

EXERCISE 8.6   *Writing*

Complete the tasks as required:

A. Add roman numerals and inner voices based on outer-voice implications.   B. Add SATB.

C. Harmonize in three different ways; consider the possibility of relative key harmonizations. Provide a two-level analysis.

EXERCISE 8.7   WRITING INVERSIONS OF V⁷

Using only inversions of V⁷ to expand the tonic, continue the following progressions according to the textural patterns laid out in the first measures of letters A and B. You might, before you begin, sketch the progressions and voice leading out in chorale style on a separate sheet of manuscript paper. As usual, pay particular attention to the outer-voice counterpoint. Add roman numerals and include a second-level analysis.

A. Given the following soprano line in A major: $\hat{3}$–$\hat{4}$–$\hat{3}$–$\hat{2}$–$\hat{3}$–$\hat{5}$–$\hat{4}$–$\hat{3}$–$\hat{2}$–$\hat{1}$
B. Given the following bass line in B minor: $\hat{1}$– #$\hat{7}$–$\hat{1}$–$\hat{4}$–$\hat{3}$–$\hat{2}$– #$\hat{7}$–$\hat{1}$

A. Keep the voices reasonably close together to avoid discontinuity in the texture. A gap should not be created in the middle, nor should one of the voices (including the bass) be separated off, registrally, from the other three.

B. You might add variety by using the quarter note on the third beat in the left hand, from time to time and where appropriate, to embellish the bass with a consonant leap.

EXERCISE 8.8 *Analytical Snapshots*

STREAMING AUDIO
www.oup.com/us/laitz

Each of the following short excerpts contains expansions of the tonic and the dominant using inversions of V^7. Expect to encounter vii^{o6}, IV^6, and V^6 as well. Analyze each using two levels.

A. Schumann, "An meinem Herzen, an meiner Brust" ("At My Heart, at My Breast"), *Frauenliebe und Leben* ("A Woman's Life and Love"), op. 42, no. 7

B. Beethoven, Piano Sonata in G major, op. 31, no. 1, *Adagio grazioso*

C. Beethoven, Piano Sonata in G major, op. 49, no. 2, *Allegro ma non troppo*

In what key is this passage?

ASSIGNMENT 8.4   EXERCISES FOR vii°⁷ AND vii°⁷ IN ROOT POSITION AND INVERSIONS

ANALYSIS

EXERCISE 8.9

STREAMING AUDIO
www.oup.com/us/laitz

Analyze the following excerpts using two levels. Label preparation and resolution of sevenths.

A. Haydn, String Quartet, op. 17, no. 5, Hob III.29, *Adagio*

B. Haydn, String Quartet, op. 9, no. 4, Hob III.22, Menuet

C. Mozart, Piano Sonata in F major, K. 332, *Allegro*
   In what key is this passage?

D. Mozart, Piano Sonata in F major, K. 332, *Allegro assai*
   In what key is this passage?

E. J. Strauss, Overture, *Die Fledermaus*

EXERCISE 8.10   *Figured Bass*

Realize the following figured bass and analyze. Then add and label unaccented embellishing tones in the upper voices that include passing tones, neighboring notes, and chordal skips and leaps. Make use of the dissonant intervals called for by the figures when writing neighboring figures in the soprano (the dissonance pulls the two voices towards each other on the next beat). Analyze using two levels.

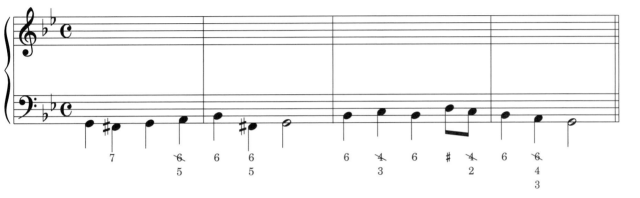

ASSIGNMENT 8.5
EXERCISES FOR vii°⁷

EXERCISE 8.11   *Analysis*

Analyze the following excerpts using two levels.

A. C. P. E. Bach, Sonata no. 5 in A minor for Flute and Continuo, Wq 128 H.555

B. Beethoven, Piano Sonata no. 5 in C minor, op. 10, no. 1, *Allegro*
The metrically accented dissonances that occur in the right hand in mm. 14–16 are called "suspensions" and are addressed in Chapter 10.

C. Gluck, "Pantomime," from *Alceste*

EXERCISE 8.12   *Figured Bass and Contrapuntal Expansions*

1. Realize the figured bass in keyboard style.
2. Analyze, then sing either outer voice while playing the other three voices.

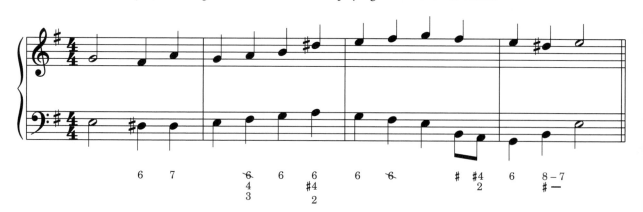

EXERCISE 8.13   *Writing Complete Progressions*

Write the following progressions in four-part chorale style.

- Use any meter, remembering to place contrapuntal harmonies on weak beats.
- You may use a variety of rhythmic values.
- Provide a second-level analysis.

A. Write in D minor:

Soprano scale degrees:	$\hat{3}$	$\hat{4}$	$\hat{5}$	$\hat{4}$	$\hat{3}$	$\hat{4}$	$\hat{3}$
Roman numeral:	I	V$^4_3$	I^6	vii$^{\circ 7}$	I	vii$^{\circ 6}_5$	I

B. Write in G minor (remember to raise $\hat{7}$ for the leading tone):

Soprano scale degrees:	$\hat{1}$	$\hat{7}$	$\hat{1}$	$\hat{2}$	$\hat{4}$	$\hat{3}$	$\hat{2}$	$\hat{1}$	$\hat{7}$	$\hat{1}$
Roman numeral:	i	V$^4_3$	i^6	vii$^{\circ 6}_5$	vii$^{\circ 7}$	i	V$^4_2$	i^6	vii$^{\circ 6}$	i

A.

B.

The Pre-Dominant Function and the Phrase Model

EXERCISE 9.1 *Analysis*

STREAMING AUDIO
www.oup.com/us/laitz

Analyze the following examples using two levels.

A. Verdi, "Anch' io dischiuso un giorno," from *Nabucco*, act 2

B. Mozart, Symphony in D, K. 81, *Andante*

C. Corelli, Chamber Sonata in E♭, op. 2, no. 11, Giga

Be aware of the key signature since it represents the key of this inner movement, but not the piece as a whole.

WRITING

EXERCISE 9.2   *Error Detection*

The following exercise contains a number of voice-leading errors. After providing a roman numeral analysis (two levels), circle and label voice-leading and spelling problems.

EXERCISE 9.3

Complete the following tasks in four voices. Add missing roman numerals.

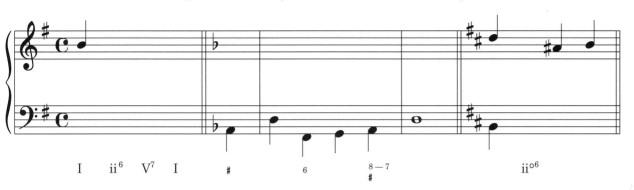

I   ii⁶   V⁷   I   #   6   8 — 7   ii°⁶
                                                         #

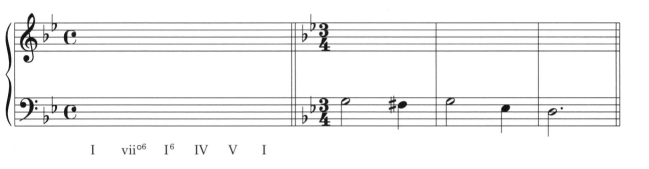

I   vii°⁶   I⁶   IV   V   I

ASSIGNMENT 9.2
MORE EXERCISES FOR ii AND IV

WRITING

EXERCISE 9.4   *Figured Bass*

Realize the following figured bass, first composing the soprano in good counterpoint with the bass, and then adding inner voices. Analyze with two levels.

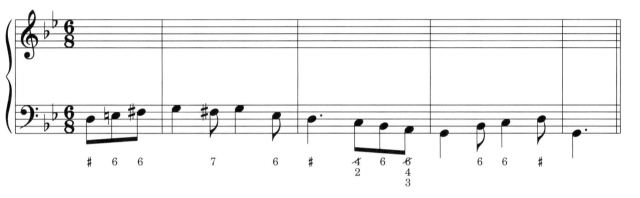

EXERCISE 9.5   *Analysis*

Analyze the following examples using two levels.

A. Haydn, Symphony no. 88 in G major, Hob I.88, *Allegro*

B. Mozart, "Wer ein Liebchen hat gefunden," from *Die Entführung aus dem Serail* ("The Abduction from the Seraglio"), K. 384

C. Corelli, Violin Sonata in A major, op. 5, no. 6, *Largo*

Although there are numerous incomplete chords, the context and figured bass will provide chordal implications. The slurs indicate two harmonic motions (i.e., two T–PD–D motions).

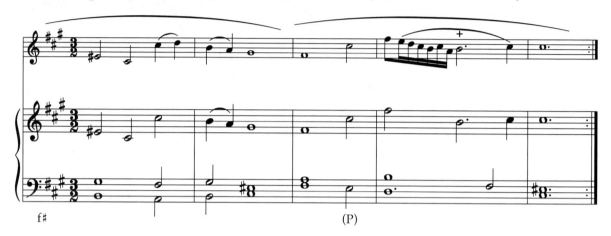

ASSIGNMENT 9.3   COMPOSITION AND ANALYSIS INVOLVING ii AND IV

WRITING

EXERCISE 9.6   *Pre-Dominants and Figured Bass*

Realize the figured bass as follows:

1. Compose a soprano that works in good counterpoint with the bass (consider, e.g., what a good soprano line would be for the opening paradigm $\hat{1}$–$\hat{7}$–$\hat{1}$, or the $\hat{3}$–$\hat{2}$–$\hat{1}$ in m. 3, or the $\hat{1}$–$\hat{2}$–$\hat{3}$ in mm. 5 and 7).
2. Add inner voices.
3. Analyze with two levels.

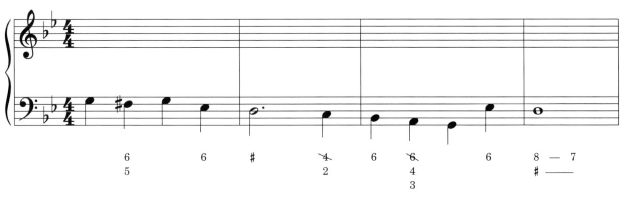

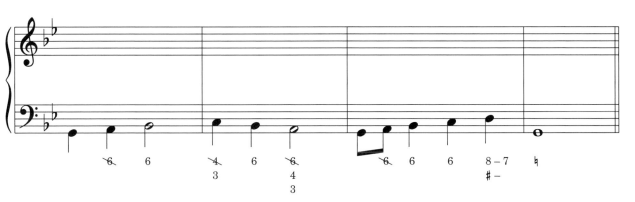

EXERCISE 9.7   *Recipes*

The following lists of "ingredients" and steps are for "recipes" that incorporate pre-dominants. The lists do not appear in a logical order; if you carry out the instructions in the order in which they appear, the progressions will not work. First, arrange the instructions in logical order, then write the progressions in four-voice chorale style. Choose an appropriate meter for each progression.

A. Write a progression in D minor that:

- includes the pre-dominant ii°⁶
- expands tonic with a form of vii°⁷
- includes a perfect authentic cadence

B. Write a progression in F major that:

- includes a half cadence
- includes a form of vii°⁷ in a tonic expansion
- includes the pre-dominant IV
- includes the following bass in the tonic expansion: $\hat{1}$–$\hat{7}$–$\hat{1}$–$\hat{2}$–$\hat{3}$–$\hat{4}$–$\hat{3}$

C. Write a progression in B minor that:

- includes a phrygian cadence
- expands the tonic with a voice exchange

A.

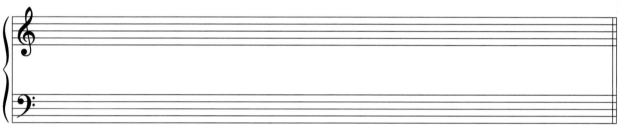

B.

C.

ANALYSIS

EXERCISE 9.8

Analyze the following excerpts with two levels of roman numerals.

A. Mozart, "Das Kinderspiel," K. 598

B. Haydn, String Quartet in D major, op. 20, no. 4, Hob III.34

C. Haydn, String Quartet in E♭ major, "The Joke," op. 33, no. 2, Hob III.38

ASSIGNMENT 9.4   MORE COMPOSITION AND ANALYSIS INVOLVING ii AND IV

EXERCISE 9.9   *Multiple Settings of a Soprano Melody*

Write three different, logical bass lines for the soprano melody. Analyze.

EXERCISE 9.10   *Composition*

Each phrase in the following excerpts closes with a half cadence. For each excerpt, write a phrase that closes on tonic and matches the basic style, character, general harmonic rhythm, and figuration of the given phrase. (*Hint*: Most of the material in the first phrase can return in the second phrase. Consult the list of phrase models to see what part of the first phrase must be rewritten to end with an authentic cadence.)

A.

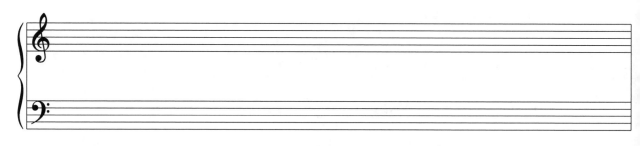

B. Vivaldi, Violin Concerto in C major, Ryom 176, *Largo*

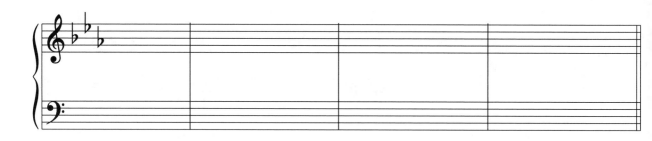

EXERCISE 9.11

Analyze the following examples with two levels. In a couple of sentences, discuss the possibility that Example A is a single phrase, while Example B contains two distinct phrases, in spite of the fact that the first example is longer than the second example.

A. Haydn, String Quartet in E♭ major, "The Joke," op. 33, no. 2, Hob III.38

B. Haydn, String Quartet in G major, op. 64, no. 4, Hob III.66

CHAPTER 10

Accented and Chromatic Embellishing Tones

ASSIGNMENT 10.1 ANALYSIS OF ACCENTED AND UNACCENTED EMBELLISHING TONES AND WRITING SUSPENSIONS

EXERCISE 10.1

STREAMING AUDIO
www.oup.com/us/laitz

The following examples contain both accented and unaccented embellishing tones, which may occur in any voice. Begin by providing roman numerals. Then use the shorthand method presented in the text to label all embellishing tones. The chords employed are restricted to those we have already encountered (except in examples of suspension chains. For these, simply provide figured bass labels of type [9–8 and 7–6]). Label the components of suspensions (preparation "P," suspension "S," and resolution "R"). The sample solution has been solved for you.

Sample solution:

Haydn, Piano Sonata no. 50 in D major, Hob XVI.37, *Presto non troppo*

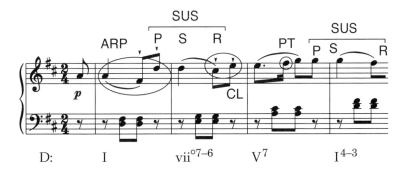

A. Bach, Chorale, "Ermuntre dich, mein schwacher Geist," BWV 454

B. Bach, Chorale, "Christe, du Beistand deiner Kreuzgemeine," BWV 275

C. Beethoven, Piano Sonata in B♭, op. 22, Menuetto

D. Brahms, "Du mein einzig Licht," *Deutsches Volkslieder*, WoO 33, no. 37

Du mein ein - zig   Licht,

EXERCISE 10.2

Label errors in suspension writing and in other accented and unaccented embellishments as well as errors in chord spelling and voice leading. *Note*: Assume that there are no appoggiaturas or anticipations in this exercise. Analyze using two levels of roman numerals.

A.

B.

C.

D.

EXERCISE 10.3 *Writing*

Complete the figured basses in Exercises A and B. For Exercise C, add the upper voices to the unfigured bass and add at least four suspensions. Analyze each example using two levels.

A.

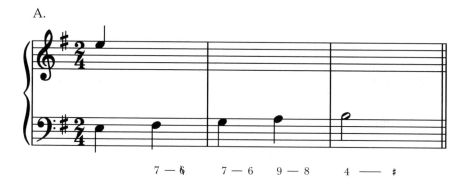

B.

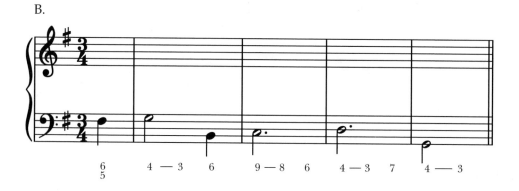

C.

ASSIGNMENT 10.2 ANALYSIS OF ALL EMBELLISHING TONES AND WRITING SUSPENSIONS

EXERCISE 10.4 *Analysis*

STREAMING AUDIO
www.oup.com/us/laitz

The following examples employ both accented and unaccented embellishing tones, which may occur in any voice. Begin by providing roman numerals. Then use the short-hand method presented in the text to label all embellishing tones. The chords employed are restricted to those we have already encountered (except in the cases of suspension chains. For these, simply provide figured bass labels of type [9–8 and 7–6]). Label the components of suspensions (preparation "P," suspension "S," and resolution "R").

A. Beethoven, Piano Sonata in C minor, op. 10, no. 1, *Adagio molto*

B. Haydn, Piano Sonata no. 39, in D major, Hob XVI.24, *Adagio*

C. Roseingrave, Gavotte in D major for Flute and Continuo

Note: Do not supply Roman numerals for this example.

EXERCISE 10.5   *Writing Suspensions: Realignment*

Analyze the following progressions using two levels. Then, on a separate sheet of manuscript paper, add suspensions to the progressions. Measures 1–2 of Exercise A are completed for you. Given that the resolutions will occur on the weak second and fourth beats, the note values will need to change from half notes to primarily quarter notes. Add one or two suspensions per measure. *Hint*: Look for descending stepwise motion, then suspend the upper note to create an accented dissonance that will naturally descend. You may also add chordal leaps to prepare suspensions. These faster notes create another submetrical level of activity, so use them sparingly.

EXERCISE 10.6   *Figured Bass*

Realize in four voices the suspension-filled figured basses that follow. Analyze using two levels.

A.

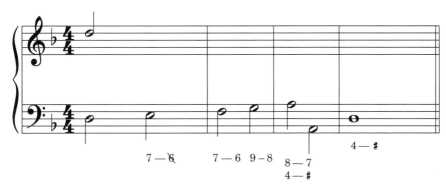

B.

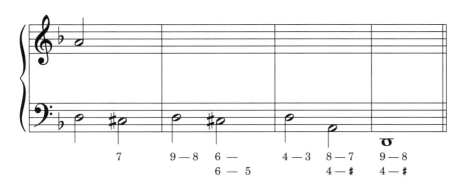

ASSIGNMENT 10.3 MORE EXERCISES FOR ALL EMBELLISHING TONES

ANALYSIS

EXERCISE 10.7

STREAMING AUDIO
www.oup.com/us/laitz

The following examples employ both accented and unaccented embellishing tones, which may occur in any voice. Begin by providing roman numerals. Then label all embellishing tones using the shorthand method presented in the text. For all examples, label the components of suspensions (preparation "P," suspension "S," and resolution "R").

A. Mozart, Sonatina in C major, K. 545, Menuetto

B. Haydn, Piano Sonata no. 11 in B♭ major, Hob XVI.2, *Largo*

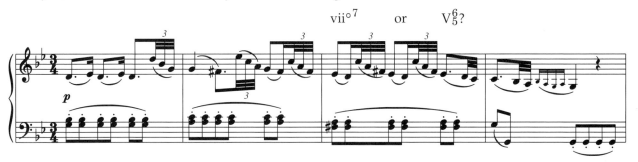

C. Beethoven, Piano Sonata in A♭ major, op. 26, *Andante*

WRITING

EXERCISE 10.8   *Writing Suspensions*

Add suspensions according to the given figured bass. When suspensions occur in an outer voice, you must realign the given pitch, since it will be displaced by the suspension. Fill in the inner voices and analyze.

A.   B.

WRITING

EXERCISE 10.9   *Corelli, Trio Sonata in G minor, op. 1, no. 10*

Add as many of the following embellishing tones as possible to Corelli's trio sonata: PT, APT, S. Label and analyze using figures (no roman numerals).

A.

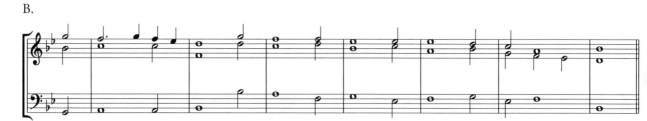

B.

ASSIGNMENT 10.4   MORE EXERCISES FOR ALL EMBELLISHING TONES

EXERCISE 10.10   *Analysis*

STREAMING AUDIO
www.oup.com/us/laitz

Analyze the following excerpts.

A. Schumann, "Chiarina," *Carnaval,* op. 9

Stem the ascending structural line in the top voice of the right hand; note that each tone of the structural line will be part of the underlying harmony and not an embellishing tone. Observe the bass's descent, which is shadowed in tenths by the right hand's lower voice. What do you notice about the placement of each of these lines in the measure? What effect does this have?

B. Mozart, String Quartet in G major, K. 156, *Tempo di Menuetto*

C. Tchaikovsky, Symphony no. 4, op. 36, *Andantino in modo di canzona*

How does the eighth-note rest affect the metrical placement of the melodic tones?

(VI)

D. Loeillet, Sonata in G major for Two Flutes and Basso Continuo, op. 1, no. 2, *Grave*

6

EXERCISE 10.11   *Elaborating Homophonic Textures*

The following excerpts from Bach's chorales have been stripped of their embellishing tones. Each excerpt appears twice. Add *unaccented* embellishing tones in the first appearance. (These include PT [single and double], NT, CL, ANT, and ARP.) Add only *accented* embellishing tones in the chorale's second appearance. These include APT, S (single, double, and figurated), and APP. Label each type of embellishing tone. Adhere to the following guidelines:

1. One or two embellishments per measure is enough; it is easy to overload the voices with tones that obscure or even contradict the harmony. Since leaping dissonances in the inner voices confuse the harmony, it is generally safest to avoid them. Reserve such incomplete neighbors, including the appoggiatura, for the soprano, and even then use them sparingly. The best way to make sure that you have not produced a garish mess is to play your solutions at the piano.
2. It is easy to create problematic parallels when adding passing tones and chordal leaps. Check to make sure you have not fallen into this trap.

A. "Dies sing die heil'gen zehn Gebot," BWV 298

1. Unaccented

2. Accented

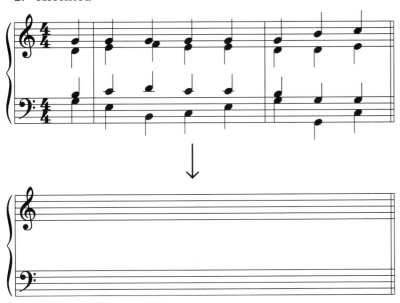

B. "Für Freuden lasst uns springen," BWV 313

1. Unaccented

2. Accented

WRITING

EXERCISE 10.12   *Adding Suspensions*

Each of the following examples will, for the most part, *not* permit the addition of suspensions because the majority of the voices in the subsequent chords are higher than those of the preceding chord.

Rewrite each example by inserting revoiced chords that are higher than the preceding chord and will therefore prepare a suspension. Notice that not only will such revoicings permit suspensions, but, also, as in the case of Exercise D, will help to avoid the marked parallel fifths.

Sample solutions:

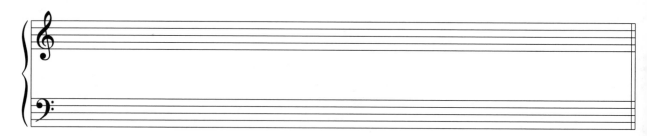

CHAPTER 11

Six-Four Chords, Revisiting the Subdominant, and Summary of Contrapuntal Expansions

ASSIGNMENT 11.1
EXERCISES FOR SIX-FOUR CHORDS

EXERCISE 11.1 *Analysis*

STREAMING AUDIO
www.oup.com/us/laitz

Listen to each of the following homophonic examples. Provide a two-level roman numeral analysis. Your expanded harmonic vocabulary now includes:

In major keys	Function(s)	In minor keys
I, I⁶	Tonic	i, i⁶
ii, ii⁶	PD	ii°⁶
IV, IV⁶	PD, or expand tonic	iv, iv⁶
V, V⁶, V⁷	D, or expand tonic	V, V⁶, V⁷
V⁶₅, V⁴₃, V⁴₂	D, or expand tonic	V⁶₅, V⁴₃, V⁴₂
vii°⁶	expand tonic	vii°⁶, vii°⁷, vii°⁶₅, vii°⁴₃
⁶₄ chords	Passing, pedal, cadential, arpeggiating	⁶₄ chords

A.

B.

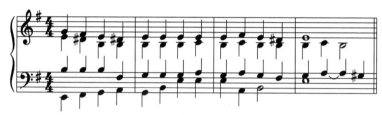

C.

D. "Amazing Grace"

I   once was   lost, but   now am   found, Was   blind, but __   now I   see. _____
How   pre - cious   did   that   grace ap -   pear The   hour I __   first   be -   lieved. _____

E. Mozart, Piano Sonata in B♭ major, K. 570, *Adagio*

WRITING

EXERCISE 11.2

Complete the following tasks in four voices (SATB).

A. In D major, write I–P$^6_4$–I^6–IV–V$^6_4$–$^5_3$–I.
B. In F minor, set the melody $\hat{5}$–$\hat{6}$–$\hat{5}$–$\hat{4}$–$\hat{3}$–$\hat{2}$–$\hat{1}$. Include two six-four chords.
C. In A major, write a progression that expands tonic with a six-four chord. Close your progression with a PAC that includes a cadential six-four chord.

A.

B.

C.

EXERCISE 11.3 *Unfigured Bass*

Study the outer-voice counterpoint and, based on harmonic implications, analyze and add inner voices. Add as many six-four chords as possible.

ASSIGNMENT 11.2
EXERCISES FOR SIX-FOUR CHORDS

EXERCISE 11.4   *Analysis*

STREAMING AUDIO
www.oup.com/us/laitz

Listen to each of the following homophonic examples. Provide a two-level roman numeral analysis.

A. Schubert, "Der Lindenbaum," *Winterreise*, op. 89, no. 5, D. 911

B. Schumann, "Der Himmel hat eine Träne geweint," op. 37, no. 1
Where do the circled B♭s in measure 3 resolve?

C. Brahms, Symphony no. 1 in C minor, op. 68, *Allegro non troppo*

WRITING

EXERCISE 11.5   *Harmonic Filling*

The pitches given for each exercise represent beginning and ending points of contrapuntal expansions and harmonic progressions. You are to insert one chord or no more than two chords between the given pitches (marked with brackets). The resulting progression must be logical. Find at least three solutions for each exercise. For example, in the sample solution, the pitches G and B are given, implying a tonic expansion of I–I⁶. Seven different solutions are given. Analyze each of your solutions.

Add soprano scale degree numbers above letters A–D and bass scale degree numbers below E–H.

Sample solution:

A.

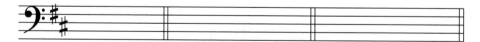

B.

C.

D.

E.

F.

G.

H.

EXERCISE 11.6 *Harmonizing Florid Melodies*

Study the given folk and classical tunes; harmonize them with one to two chords per measure by adding roman numerals.

A. Henry Bishop and John Payne, "Home Sweet Home"

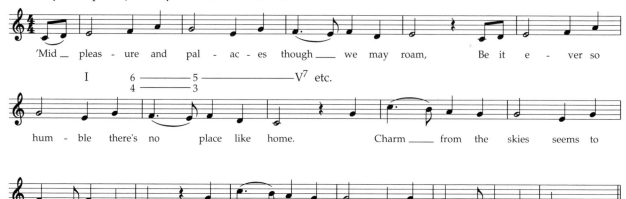

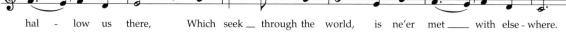

B. "Baa, Baa, Black Sheep"

C. Mozart, Violin Concerto no. 2 in D major, K. 211, Rondeau

ASSIGNMENT 11.3
EXERCISES FOR SIX-FOUR CHORDS

EXERCISE 11.7   *Figured Bass*

Realize the following figured bass in four voices. The exercise contains numerous six-four chords as well as other new devices. Analyze and be able to sing either outer voice while playing the other voices. *Note*: Measure 1 contains a triple suspension. You are used to the $\frac{5}{2}$ bass suspension that resolves to V6; here the added figure, 4, indicates resolution to a V$_3^6$ chord.

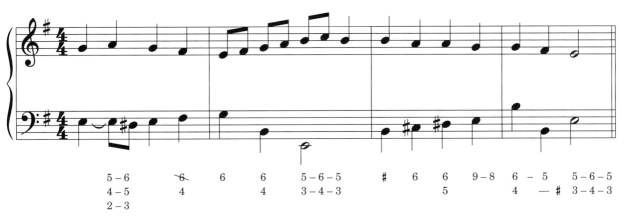

EXERCISE 11.8

Study each of the following tunes; harmonize each one with one to two chords per measure by adding roman numerals.

A. "Flow Gently, Sweet Afton"

1. Flow   gen - tly   sweet __   Af - ton,   a - mong   thy   green   braes;   Flow
2. Thy   crys - tal   stream __   Af - ton,   how   love - ly   it   glides,   And

gen - tly,   I'll   sing   thee   a   song   in   thy   praise;
winds   by   the   cot   where   my   Ma - ry   re - sides.

B. Beethoven, "Ich liebe dich," WoO 123

Ich lie - be dich, so wie du mich, am A - bend und am Mor - gen, noch _ war kein Tag, wo

du und ich nicht theil - ten uns' - re _ Sor - gen.

C. Mozart, Violin Concerto no. 3 in G major, K. 216, Rondeau

EXERCISE 11.9 *Analysis*

STREAMING AUDIO
www.oup.com/us/laitz

Given are excerpts from the literature. Analyze with two levels.

A. Beethoven, Symphony no. 9, in D minor, op. 125, *Adagio molto e cantabile*

B. Verdi, "Anchi' io dischiuso un giorno," *Nabucco*, act 2

C. Mozart, Piano Sonata in C major, K. 309, *Allegretto*

Rondo

D. Tchaikovsky, "Old French Song," *Children's Album*, op. 3, no. 16

ASSIGNMENT 11.4
EXERCISES FOR SIX-FOUR CHORDS

EXERCISE 11.10

Cad $^6_4$ = Double $\hat{5}$

Ped $^6_4$ = Double Pedal

Complete the following exercises to create four voices in chorale style accompanied by a complete roman numeral analysis. Label each key. You must determine an appropriate meter signature and rhythmic setting, given the presence of six-four chords. You should change the rhythmic value of the given voices.

A.   B.   C.

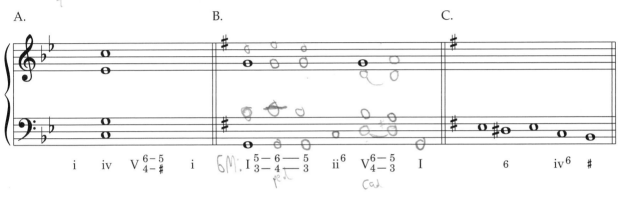

i   iv   V$^{6-5}_{4-\sharp}$ i   Gm: I$^{5-6-5}_{3-4-3}$ ii^6 V$^{6-5}_{4-3}$ I   6   iv^6 $\sharp$

D.   E.

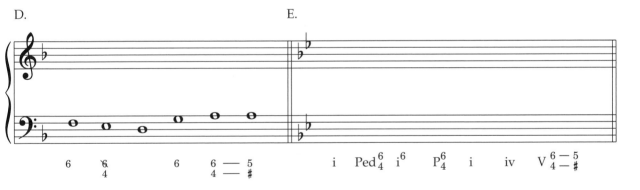

6   6̇$_4$ 6   6—5$_4$—$\sharp$ i   Ped$^6_4$ i^6 P$^6_4$ i   iv   V$^{6-5}_{4-\sharp}$

EXERCISE 11.11 *Analysis*

Analyze the following excerpts with two levels of roman numerals.

A. Leclair, Trio Sonata in D major, op. 2, no. 8, *Allegro assai*

B. Mozart, Piano Sonata in C major, K. 330/i, *Allegro moderato*

C. Mozart, "Lacrimosa," *Requiem*, K. 626, *Larghetto*

D. Schubert, "Gesang des Harfners III," D. 480, no. 3

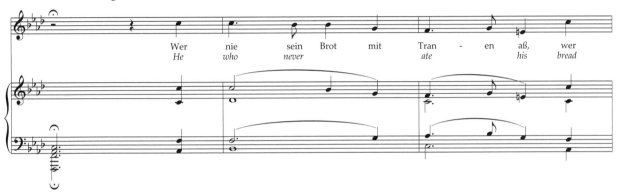

Wer nie sein Brot mit Tran - en aß, wer
He who never ate his bread

nie die kum - mer vol - len Nach - - te
with tears, he who never through miserable nights

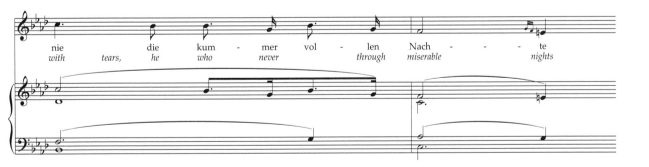

CHAPTER 12

The Pre-Dominant Refines the Phrase Model

ASSIGNMENT 12.1 EXERCISES FOR PRE-DOMINANT SEVENTH HARMONIES

WRITING

EXERCISE 12.1

Complete the following exercises in four-voice chorale style. Circle all chordal sevenths, making sure that each is prepared and resolved.

A.

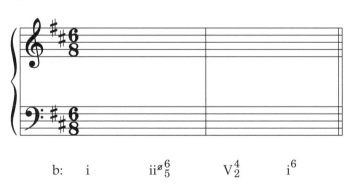

b: i   ii^ø$^6_5$ V$^4_2$ i^6

B. Note: You should use an incomplete seventh chord for either the ii^7 or the V^7 harmonies.

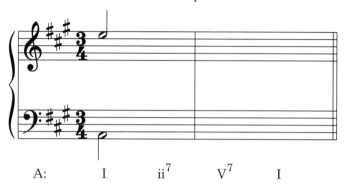

A: I   ii^7 V^7 I

C.

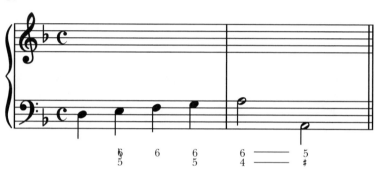

D.

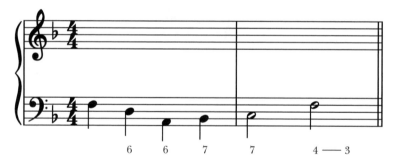

EXERCISE 12.2   *Analysis of Pre-Dominant Harmonies*

Analyze each example using two levels. Circle and label the preparation, dissonance, and resolution of all sevenths.

A. Corelli, Concerto Grosso in F major, op. 6, no. 6, *Adagio*

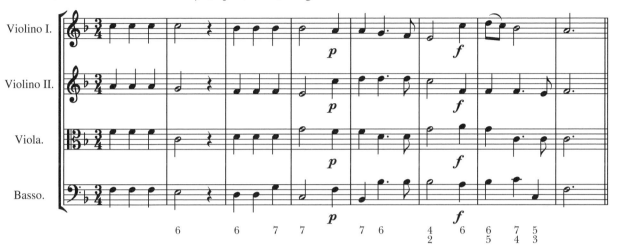

B. Beethoven, Minuet for Piano in E♭ major, WoO 82

Is the chord in m. 3 a IV^7 or ii$^6_5$? Your decision rests on the function of the G^4 in the soprano.

C. Mahler, Symphony no. 4 in G major, *Bedächtig, Nicht eilen*

D. Handel, "Lascia ch'io pianga," from *Rinaldo*, act 2

E. Bach, *Geistliche Lied*

ASSIGNMENT 12.2 EXERCISES FOR PRE-DOMINANT SEVENTH HARMONIES

WRITING

EXERCISE 12.3 *Pre-Dominant Seventh Chords in Context*

Complete the following progressions in four voices. Circle any chordal sevenths and check for proper resolutions and, for pre-dominant sevenths, preparations.

A.

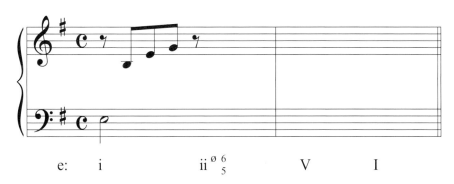

e: i   ii$^{\varnothing}{}^{6}_{5}$ V   I

B.

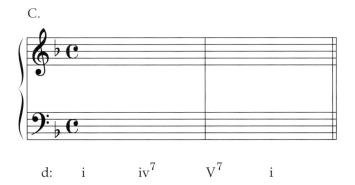

E♭:   I   ii$^{6}_{5}$ V   I

C.

d: i   iv^{7} V^{7} i

EXERCISE 12.4 *Analysis*

STREAMING AUDIO
www.oup.com/us/laitz

Create a two-level harmonic analysis for the following excerpts that contain predominant seventh chords.

A. Bach, *Geistliche Lied*

Two excerpts follow from Mozart's first symphony, written at the age of 8. The first excerpt comes from the opening of the piece and contains a single progression. The second excerpt is drawn from later material and contains two complete harmonic progressions in two different keys. Determine the key for each progression; analyze using roman numerals; then, in a sentence or two, compare the three progressions.

B. Mozart, Symphony no. 1 in E♭ major, K. 16, *Allegro molto*. Corni in Mi♭: Sound a minor third above notated pitches.

1.

2.

ASSIGNMENT 12.3   EXERCISES FOR EMBEDDED PHRASE MODELS AND EXPANDED PRE-DOMINANT HARMONIES

ANALYSIS

EXERCISE 12.5   *Analysis of Embedded Phrase Models and Expanded Pre-Dominant Functions*

STREAMING AUDIO
www.oup.com/us/laitz

1. Label tonic, pre-dominant, and dominant functions, focusing on expanded pre-dominants.
2. Next, determine how each expanded function is accomplished. For example, do you find literal repetition, change of inversion, passing or neighboring chords, or EPMs? Label the chords and summarize what occurs in the pre-dominant area.
3. Finally, provide roman numerals for the entire passage.

A.

B. Mozart, Symphony in C major, "Linz," K. 425, *Presto*

C. Bach, Siciliana from Flute Sonata in E♭ major, BWV 1031

D. Mozart, Symphony no. 30 in D major, K. 202, Menuetto

WRITING

EXERCISE 12.6 FIGURED BASS

Realize the following figured bass example in four-voice keyboard style. Provide a two-level analysis.

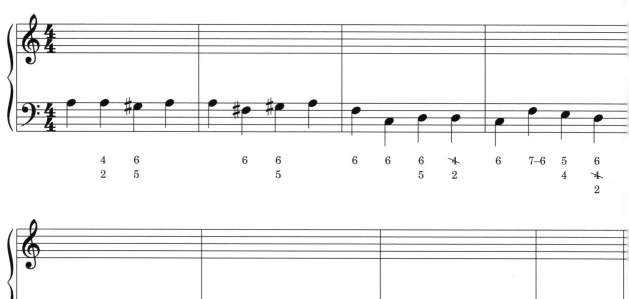

ASSIGNMENT 12.4   WRITING PRE-DOMINANT HARMONIES AND ANALYZING PHRASES AND SUBPHRASES

EXERCISE 12.7   *Unfigured Bass and Melody Harmonization*

Determine the best harmonizations for the following examples using only the chords we have studied. Add the missing outer voice first. Include a two-level analysis. Add inner voices. Finally, add embellishing tones as required (you may alter the rhythms in the given voices to add suspensions and other metrically accented embellishing tones). In each exercise, include and label the following:

1. Two different suspensions
2. Two unaccented passing tones
3. One accented passing tone
4. One neighbor or appoggiatura

A.

B.

EXERCISE 12.8   *Phrases and Subphrases*

STREAMING AUDIO
www.oup.com/us/laitz

Determine whether the following examples contain single phrases with one or more sub-phrases, or if there are multiple phrases. Support your answer in one or two sentences. Bracket phrases beneath the bass clef and subphrases above the treble clef.

Here are some considerations:

1. Remember, phrases are self-standing musical units that contain harmonic motion (i.e., a traversing of tonic and dominant functions) and end with a cadence.
2. Subphrases combine to create phrases (usually in proportional pairs) and therefore are components of phrases. Yet subphrases are in many ways self-standing, given that they may contain miniature harmonic motions (e.g., EPMs) and even weak cadential gestures (e.g., contrapuntal cadences).
3. Be aware that musical flow may come to a stop because of a caesura, but does not necessarily mean that you have encountered a subphrase.

Notice there will often be more than one possible interpretation in these examples.

A. Haydn, Piano Sonata no. 19 in E minor, Hob XVI.47, *Allegro*

B. Mozart, "Bei Männern," from *The Magic Flute*, K. 620, act 1, scene 7

C. Haydn, Piano Sonata no. 35 in A♭ major, Hob XVI. 43, *Moderato*

ASSIGNMENT 12.5   WRITING PRE-DOMINANT HARMONIES, EPMs, EXPANDED PRE-DOMINANTS, AND ANALYSIS OF SUBPHRASES AND COMPOSITE PHRASES

EXERCISE 12.9   *Figured Bass*

Realize the following figured bass, first composing the soprano and then adding inner voices. Analyze with two levels.

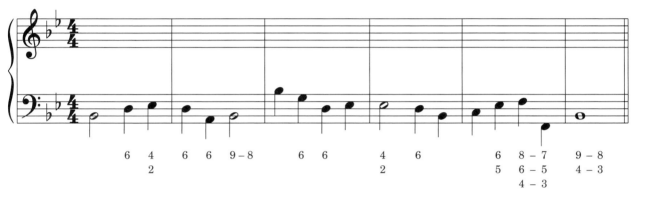

EXERCISE 12.10   *Writing*

A. Write the given progressions that contain EPMs or expanded pre-dominants in the key of A major and a meter and texture of your choice.

EPMS: $I–ii^4_2–V^6_5–I–IV–V^7–I$
              T————PD D T

or

$i–IV^6–V^6_5–i–ii^{o6}_5–cad^6_4–^5_3–i$
T————PD—D——T

B. Expanded PD: $I–V^6_5–I–ii^6–I^6–ii–cad^6_4–^5_3–I$
                        T——PD———D——T

or

$i–i^6–V^4_3–i–iv^6–i –ii^{o6}_5–cad^6_4–^5_3–i$
T———PD————D——T

A.

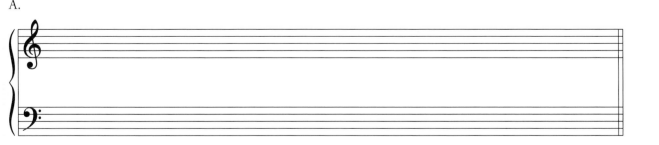

B.

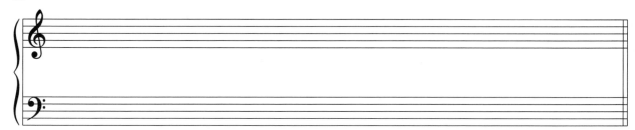

ANALYSIS

EXERCISE 12.11   *Subphrases and Composite Phrases*

STREAMING AUDIO
www.oup.com/us/laitz

Analyze each example, determining whether the composer has created extended phrases through a single large-scale progression or through a series of linked subordinate harmonic motions.

A. Haydn, Piano Sonata no. 32 in G minor, Hob XVI.44, *Allegretto*

B. Schubert, "Die Sterne"

bin   oft   schon dar - ü - ber vom Schlum -mer er - wacht .

C. Haydn, Piano Sonata in E♭ major, Hob XVI.52, *Presto*

CHAPTER 13

The Submediant: A New Diatonic Harmony, and Further Extensions of the Phrase Model

ASSIGNMENT 13.1
EXERCISES FOR THE SUBMEDIANT HARMONY

EXERCISE 13.1 *Analysis*

STREAMING AUDIO
www.oup.com/us/laitz

Analyze the following excerpts, each of which contains the submediant harmony.

A. Mozart, "Rex tremendae majestatis," *Requiem*, K. 626

B. Chopin, Nocturne in C minor, op. 48, no. 1

WRITING

EXERCISE 13.2

The following progressions incorporate vi and include a few guiding soprano scale degrees. Select an appropriate meter and rhythm based on the progression (for example, cadential six-four chords must be placed on strong beats). Write the bass and then the soprano, and fill in the inner voices. Provide a two-level analysis, marking the function of vi (e.g., tonic substitute, harmonic bass arpeggiation, etc.). In many cases, this step will involve an interpretive decision with two or more possible answers.

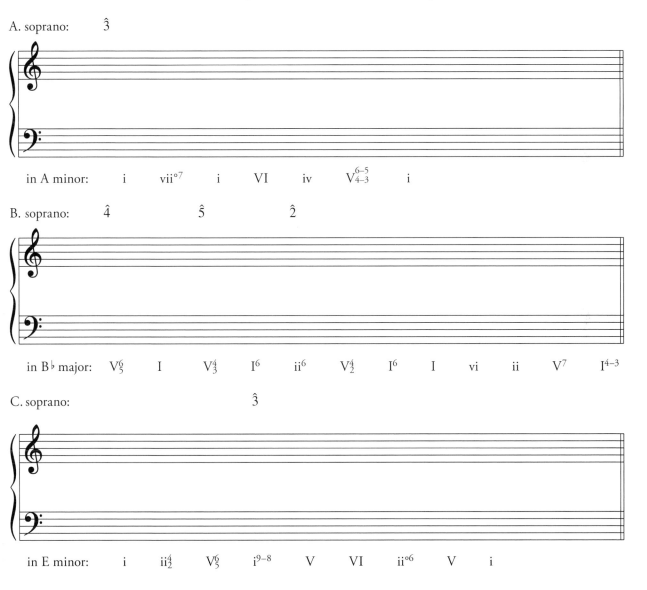

A. soprano: $\hat{3}$

in A minor: i   vii°⁷   i   VI   iv   V⁶⁻⁵₄₋₃   i

B. soprano: $\hat{4}$ $\hat{5}$ $\hat{2}$

in B♭ major: V⁶₅   I   V⁴₃   I⁶   ii⁶   V⁴₂   I⁶   I   vi   ii   V⁷   I⁴⁻³

C. soprano: $\hat{3}$

in E minor: i   ii⁴₂   V⁶₅   i⁹⁻⁸   V   VI   ii°⁶   V   i

ASSIGNMENT 13.2
EXERCISES FOR THE SUBMEDIANT HARMONY

ANALYSIS

EXERCISE 13.3

Here are three different harmonizations by Bach of the opening of the chorale tune "Jesu meine Freude" from his *St. Matthew Passion* (BWV 244). Analyze each setting, then write a paragraph comparing and contrasting them. Which do you like best and why?

A.

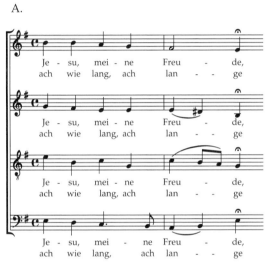

B.

C.

EXERCISE 13.4 *Illustration*

In any minor key, write a progression that includes the following tasks, which appear in order of composition:

1. A tonic prolongation that includes one suspension figure
2. A descending bass arpeggiation that includes the submediant
3. A pre-dominant that is expanded by voice exchange
4. A dominant that includes one suspension figure

EXERCISE 13.5 *Harmonizing Melodic Fragments Using the Submediant*

Harmonize the following soprano fragments by using at least one submediant harmony in each example; analyze. For Exercise C you must determine a suitable meter and rhythmic setting (you may change the given rhythms); add bar lines.

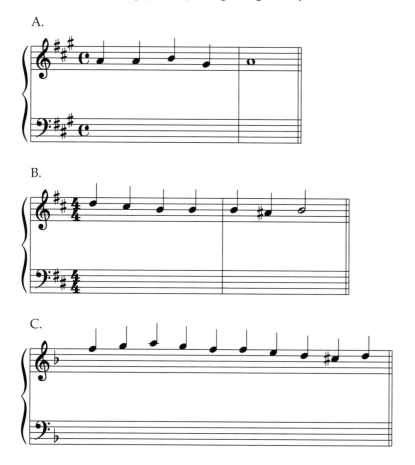

A.

B.

C.

ASSIGNMENT 13.3 EXERCISES FOR THE STEP-DESCENT BASS AND THE SUBMEDIANT HARMONY

WRITING

EXERCISE 13.6

In any major key (except C) write a progression that includes the following tasks. Begin by logically ordering the tasks so that your progression makes harmonic sense.

1. A deceptive harmonic progression
2. A bass suspension
3. A tonic expansion using a passing figure in the bass
4. A pre-dominant seventh chord
5. A descending fifth progression using vi

ANALYSIS

EXERCISE 13.7   *vi and the Step-Descent Bass*

 STREAMING AUDIO
www.oup.com/us/laitz

> Listen to each excerpt, determining first whether there is a direct, tetrachordal descent to V, or whether there is an indirect descent of a fifth. Finally, analyze using two levels.

A. Handel, "Thou Art Gone Up on High," *Messiah*, HWV 56

   Is there a textual motivation for the contour of the vocal line? What effect does this contour create with the bass?

B. Handel, Sarabande, Suite in G minor, HWV 432

   In this example the descent occurs on the downbeat chords. The intervening weak-beat chords elaborate it. The elaboration may be viewed as essential, given the voice-leading problems that would result if they were absent.

C. Corelli, Concerto Grosso no. 8 in G minor, op. 6, *Vivace*

ASSIGNMENT 13.4   COMPOSITION AND ANALYSIS OF THE STEP-DESCENT BASS AND THE SUBMEDIANT

WRITING

EXERCISE 13.8   *Writing the Step-Descent Bass*

Complete the soprano line, adding roman numerals as you go. Then, add inner voices and complete your analysis by adding a second-level analysis.

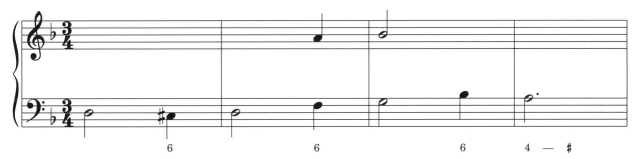

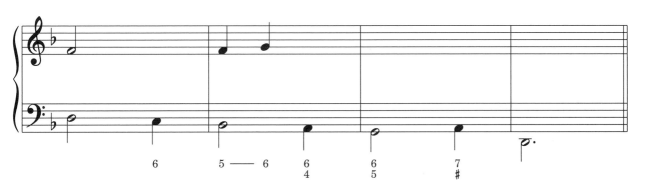

EXERCISE 13.9

Study the following broken-chord harmonic progression and the embellishment. Then write two additional four-measure phrases in a similar texture. Each phrase should use a different harmonic progression and should incorporate at least one example of the submediant harmony (e.g., an indirect step-descent bass or the submediant as a predominant).

After Schumann, "Hör' ich das Liedchen klingen," from *Dichterliebe*

ANALYSIS

EXERCISE 13.10

STREAMING AUDIO
www.oup.com/us/laitz

Analyze the following examples that include the submediant.

A. Schubert, Impromptu, op. posth. 142, no. 2, D. 935
   This excerpt features many accented embellishing tones.

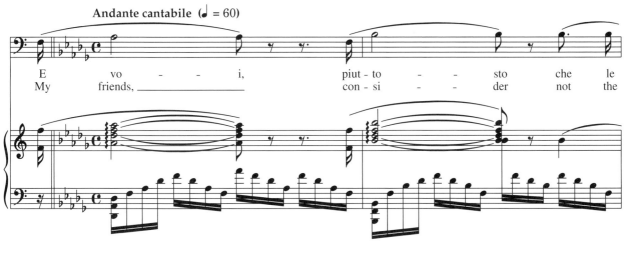

B. Leoncavallo, *I Pagliacci*, Prologue

E   vo -   i,   piut - to   —   —   sto   che   le
My   friends, _____   con - si   —   —   der   not   the

vo - stre   po   —   —   —   ve re gab - ba   —   ne   d'i-stri-o   —   —   —
gay   at - tire   we must a - dopt,   since   we are ac   —   —   —

The Mediant, the Back-Relating Dominant, and a Synthesis of Diatonic Harmonic Relationships

ASSIGNMENT 14.1
EXERCISES FOR THE MEDIANT

EXERCISE 14.1

STREAMING AUDIO
www.oup.com/us/laitz

Analyze the following excerpts that incorporate the mediant and subtonic harmony.

A. Schumann, *Davidsbundlertänze*, no. 11

B. Puccini, *La Bohème*, act 2

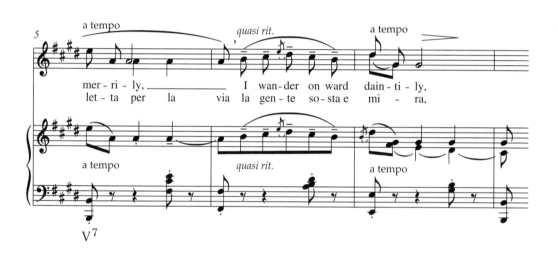

C. Corelli, Trio Sonata, op. 4, no. 5, Gavotta

D. Brahms, Clarinet Quintet, op. 115

WRITING

EXERCISE 14.2A   *Warm Up for Writing*

Exercise 1 provides roman numerals; add four voices. Exercises 2 and 3 require adding upper voices and roman numerals.

1.   2.   3.

EXERCISE 14.2B *Harmonization*

Harmonize the following soprano and bass fragments, incorporating iii (and in minor, V/III [VII]) when possible.

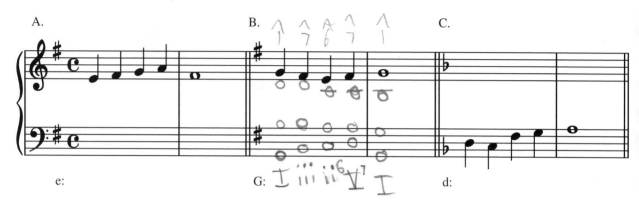

ASSIGNMENT 14.2
EXERCISES FOR THE MEDIANT

EXERCISE 14.3   *Analytical Synthesis*

STREAMING AUDIO
www.oup.com/us/laitz

These examples share certain musical characteristics, such as similar harmonic progressions. There are, of course, contrasting features as well. Listen to and analyze each excerpt. Then, in a paragraph, compare and contrast them.

A. Grieg, "Spring Dance," op. 38, no. 5, *Allegro giocoso*
   The A♯ that appears in mm. 7–10 is the temporary leading tone of the harmony that controls these measures.

B. Mahler, "Die zwei blauen Augen" ("The Two Blue Eyes"), *Lieder eines fahrenden Gesellen (Songs of a Wayfarer)*, no. 4

EXERCISE 14.4   *Figured Bass*

The following figured bass includes III and VI. Write a soprano voice, provide a first- and second-level analysis, and then add the inner voices.

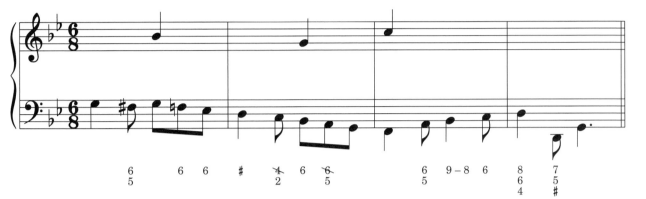

EXERCISE 14.5   *Analytical Synthesis*

The following two examples share certain musical characteristics, such as harmonic progression. There are, of course, contrasting features as well. Listen to and analyze each excerpt. Then, in a paragraph, compare and contrast them.

1. Mozart, Piano Sonata in A minor, K. 310

   Do you hear m. 1 as a motion from I to I⁶ or as I to iii? Measure 2 begins with a six-four chord. Is it consonant or dissonant? (*Hint*: We have encountered this six-four chord many times before but only in the context of V.)

2. Mozart, Piano Sonata in C major, K. 330, *Andante cantabile*

   Consider your analysis of six-four chords in light of what you did in the preceding example.

EXERCISE 14.6   *Multiple Harmonization of a Soprano Melody*

Harmonize the melody in two significantly different ways by adding a bass voice and roman numerals (you do *not* need to include inner voices). Use at least one example of the mediant and the submediant harmonies in each harmonization. Review the process of harmonizing a melody that was presented at the end of Chapter 12. Play each solution on the piano, singing either outer voice while playing the other voice.

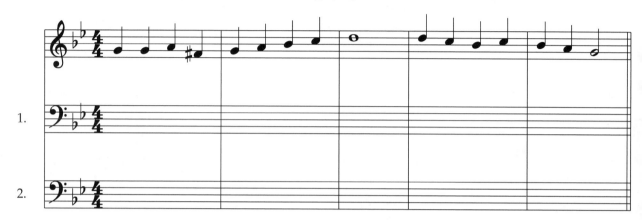

ASSIGNMENT 14.4   EXERCISES FOR THE BACK-RELATING DOMINANT

EXERCISE 14.7   *Functions of the Dominant*

STREAMING AUDIO
www.oup.com/us/laitz

Examples follow in which the dominant prominently appears. Determine whether the dominant is structural (i.e., it moves the harmonic progression forward) or whether it is a voice-leading chord (e.g., a passing chord in a bass descent to vi or a weak back-relating dominant).

A.

B.

C.

D. Beethoven, Piano Sonata no. 7 in D major, op. 10, no. 3, Menuetto, *Allegro*

WRITING

EXERCISE 14.8 *Unfigured Bass and Soprano*

Determine implied harmonies using roman numerals. Expect to encounter step descents, the mediant and submediant, and back-relating dominants. Add inner voices and a second-level analysis. Then add embellishing tones to create a more fluid sound, distributing them between voices in order to create a balanced texture.

CHAPTER 15

The Period

EXERCISE 15.1   *Analysis of Periods*

STREAMING AUDIO
www.oup.com/us/laitz

Make formal diagrams of the following examples and include a label and any comments that support your interpretation or illuminate motivic structures. Label each component of the phrase model (either T–PD–D [HC] or T–PD–D–T [AC], or T–PD–D [PHRY], or T–PD–D–T [DC]), except for continuous periods, whose tonal motion unfolds as a single progression. Don't forget that an EPM may occur within the tonic function. *Note:* Some examples may not be periods.

A. Mozart, String Quartet no. 19 in C major, "Dissonant," K. 465, *Allegro assai*

B. Chopin, Mazurka in D major, op. 33, no. 2, BI 115

C. Beethoven, Romance in F major for Violin and Orchestra, op. 50, *Adagio cantabile*

EXERCISE 15.2 *Melody Harmonization*

The following phrases function as either an antecedent or consequent phrase in a two-phrase period. Determine the type of period and then:

1. Write the corresponding phrase (e.g., if you are given a consequent phrase, you will create an antecedent, and vice versa). Your choices are PIP, CIP, and CCP.
2. Harmonize each period by using roman numerals (ca. one roman numeral per measure).

A. Schumann, "Volksliedchen," from *Children's Pieces*, op. 51, no. 2

Wenn ich früh in den Gar - ten geh', in mei - nem ___ grü - nen Hut,

B. Mozart, Symphony in G major, K. 110

C. Haydn, String Quartet in E♭ major, op. 64, no. 6, Trio

D. Mozart, Symphony in D major, K. 97, Trio

WRITING

EXERCISE 15.3 *Figured Bass*

The following figured bass is presented in an unmetered context. First determine roman numerals and possible cadences. Then fit the figured bass into a periodic structure by imposing a meter and providing each note with a duration. Make sure that there is no more than one chord per quarter note in $\frac{3}{4}$ or $\frac{4}{4}$ or one chord per eighth note in $\frac{6}{8}$.

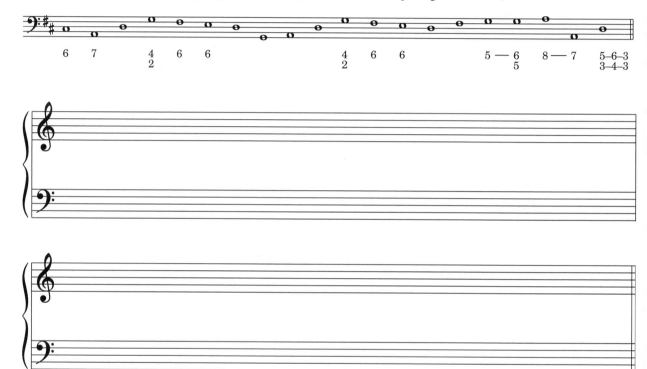

ASSIGNMENT 15.2
ANALYSIS AND COMPOSITION OF PERIODS

EXERCISE 15.4   *Analysis of Periods*

STREAMING AUDIO
www.oup.com/us/laitz

Make period diagrams of each example that follows. Include a label and any comments that support your interpretation or illuminate motivic structures. Label each component of the phrase model (either T–PD–D [HC] or T–PD–D–T [AC], or T–PD–D [PHRY], or T–PD–D–T [DC]). Don't forget that an EPM may occur within the tonic function. Do not analyze every chord.

A. Lehar, Waltz from *The Merry Widow*

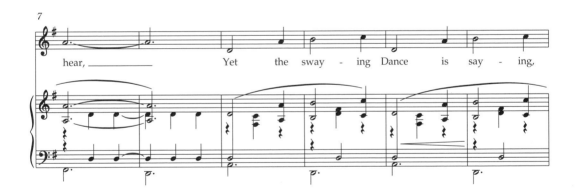

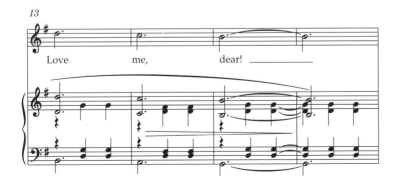

B. Beethoven, Piano Sonata no. 2 in A major, op. 2, no. 2, Scherzo, *Allegretto*

V^6_5 of V

C. Mozart, Piano Sonata in C major, K. 330, *Andante cantabile*

This example contains subphrases; consider them as you undertake your phrase analysis.

D. Chopin, *Grande Valse Brillante* in A minor, op. 34, no. 2, BI 64

WRITING

EXERCISE 15.5   *Completing Figurated Periods*

Maintaining the texture and the harmonic rhythm of the given antecedent phrase, write an appropriate consequent phrase. Provide a full label for the period.

A.

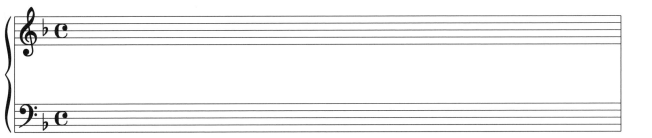

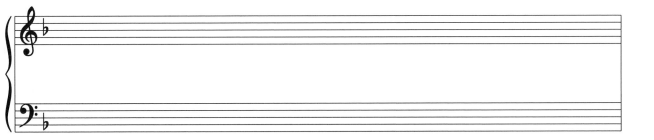

B.

ASSIGNMENT 15.3
ANALYSIS AND COMPOSITION OF PERIODS

ANALYSIS

EXERCISE 15.6   *Analysis of Periods*

STREAMING AUDIO
www.oup.com/us/laitz

Make period diagrams of each of the following examples.

A. Mozart, *Abduction from the Seraglio*, act 2, scene 1

B. Mozart, Violin Sonata in F major, K. 376

WRITING

EXERCISE 15.7   *Figured Bass*

The following figured bass is presented in an unmetered context. First, determine roman numerals and possible cadences. Then fit the figured bass into a periodic structure by imposing a meter and providing each note with a duration. Make sure that there is no more than one chord per quarter note in $\frac{3}{4}$ or $\frac{4}{4}$ or one chord per eighth note in $\frac{6}{8}$.

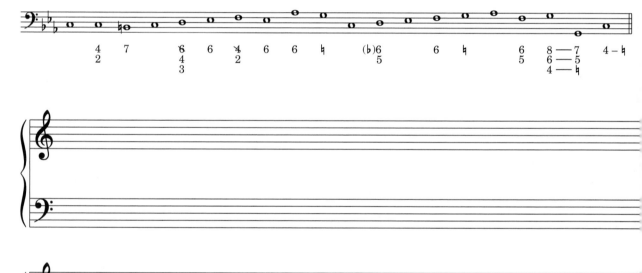

CHAPTER 16

Other Small Musical Structures: Sentences, Double Periods, and Modified Periods

ASSIGNMENT 16.1 COMPOSITION AND ANALYSIS OF SENTENCE STRUCTURES

EXERCISE 16.1 *Analysis of Sentence Structures*

STREAMING AUDIO
www.oup.com/us/laitz

Study the following various types of sentence structures, and provide diagrams of their structure.

A. Haydn, Symphony no. 101 in D major, "Clock," Menuet

B. Beethoven, Piano Sonata no. 3 in C major, op. 2, no. 3

Allegro con brio

C. Mozart, Piano Trio in E major, K. 542

D. Beethoven, Piano Concerto no. 3 in C minor, op. 37

ANALYSIS/WRITING

EXERCISE 16.2   *Melody Harmonization and Period/Sentence Structure*

For each example label the formal type (phrase or period) and whether it is cast in sentence structure. Then choose one example and determine the harmonic rhythm and harmonize the tune. Provide a harmonic analysis.

A. Mozart, Bassoon Concerto in B♭ major, K. 191, Rondeau: Tempo di Menuetto

B. Schubert, "Wiegenlied" ("Cradle Song"), op. 92, no. 2, D. 498

Schla - fe, schla - fe,   hol - der, sü - sser Kna - be,   lei - se   wiegt dich dei - ner Mut - ter Hand;

C. Mozart, Horn Concerto in D major, K. 412, *Allegro*

D. Schubert, "An mein Klavier" ("To My Piano"), D. 342

E. Mozart, Horn Concerto in D major, K. 412, *Allegro*

WRITING

EXERCISE 16.3   *Writing Sentence Structures*

A. Continue the given opening and compose a typical eight-measure sentence (2 + 2 + 4 measures). The opening tonic should be prolonged in mm. 3–4 with a contrapuntal harmony, and
the melodic material of the first two measures should be restated and, if necessary, altered to
suit the underlying harmony of these measures. Measures 5 and 6 should lead toward a cadence
and might use the material from one of the measures of the opening in sequence. Measures 7–8
should be cadential.

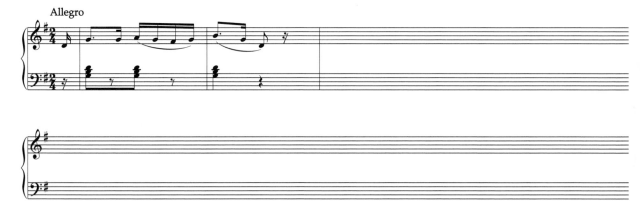

B. Write an eight-measure period that is cast in sentence structure (2 + 2 + 4 measures). Begin
either by improvising on your own instrument, singing, or just exploring ideas at the piano in
order to find a suitable melodic and rhythmic motive in a meter, key, and mode of your choice.

    The first part of your sentence will be a two-measure unit that will be repeated either literally,
or with small changes, to comprise four measures. The second part of your sentence will be a single four-measure idea that should borrow at least some elements from the opening two-measure

idea. As you write your melodies, consider the underlying harmonic structure and its harmonic rhythm; you may even wish to sketch in a few bass notes and roman numerals. The harmonic structure should approximate the following model:

A (2 mm.)	A' (2 mm.)	B (4 mm.)
I–I or V	I–I or V	I–PAC

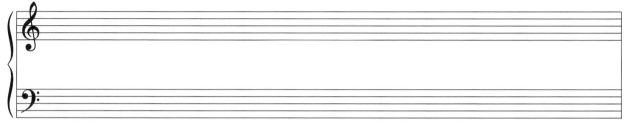

EXERCISE 16.4   *Composition*

Provided is the accompaniment for an antecedent phrase. Write a melody to the accompaniment, and then complete an interrupted period by writing a consequent phrase.

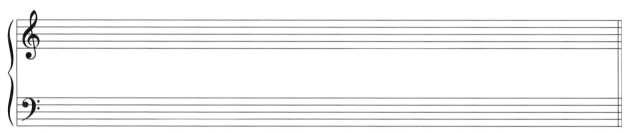

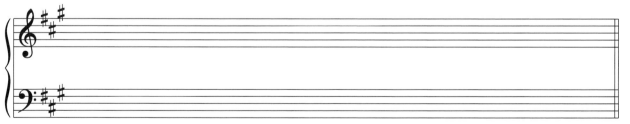

ASSIGNMENT 16.2
COMPOSITION OF SENTENCE STRUCTURES

EXERCISE 16.5   *Analysis of Sentence Structures*

STREAMING AUDIO
www.oup.com/us/laitz

Study the following various types of sentence structures, and provide diagrams of their structure.

A. Beethoven, Piano Sonata in C minor, op. 10, no. 1, *Allegro molto e con brio*

B. Beethoven, Piano Sonata in C minor, op. 10, no. 1, *Adagio*

C. Mozart, Symphony no. 40 in G minor, K. 550

WRITING

EXERCISE 16.6   *Melody Harmonization: The Sentence*

The following melodies are cast in sentence structure. They may take the form of single four-measure phrases or eight-measure periods comprising two four-measure phrases.

Determine cadential points and add appropriate bass notes. Then harmonize the rest of the tune. Remember, the two subphrases that together comprise half the sentence should be related, though they need not have identical harmonizations.

COMPOSITION

EXERCISE 16.7   *Harmonic Models and Periods and Sentences*

Choose two of the following harmonic models to write periods or double periods. Some examples work well as sentences. Decide on a key, meter, and harmonic rhythm, and add a bass voice. Finally, add a tune for voice or solo instrument and complete the texture by adding the missing chord tones to the implied harmonies above your bass, the result of which will be a homophonic accompaniment to your melody.

Phrase 1	Phrase 2
Model 1: I–prolongation of I–either to PD or V	V–deceptive progression–cadence: PAC
Model 2: i–step-descent bass leading to PD–HC	i–step-descent bass leading to expanded PD–PAC
Model 3: i–ascending ARP leading to Phrygian HC	i–descending ARP to expanded PD–PAC

CHAPTER 17

Harmonic Sequences

ASSIGNMENT 17.1
EXERCISES FOR TRIADIC SEQUENCES

EXERCISE 17.1 *Analysis of Sequences*

STREAMING AUDIO
www.oup.com/us/laitz

The following examples contain a mixture of the four sequence types. Also, all but the A2 (+5/−4) sequence may incorporate first-inversion variants. Bracket the model and copies for each sequence and provide a sequence label.

A.

B. Mozart Symphony no. 40 in G minor, K. 550, *Andante*

C. Corelli, Trio Sonata in D major, op. 4, no. 4

D. C. P. E. Bach, Sonata in A major, *Sechs Sonaten für Kenner und Liebhaber*

EXERCISE 17.2 *Composition: Continuing Sequences*

The following sequences begin on tonic. The model and the outer-voice counterpoint of the first chord of the copy are given.

1. Label the sequence type.
2. Continue and lead each sequence to a pre-dominant.

3. Close with an authentic cadence.
4. Write bass and soprano first, filling in the tenor and alto only after you are sure that the repetitions replicate the model exactly. Use no accidentals within the sequence; these are entirely diatonic sequences.

A.

B.

C.

D.

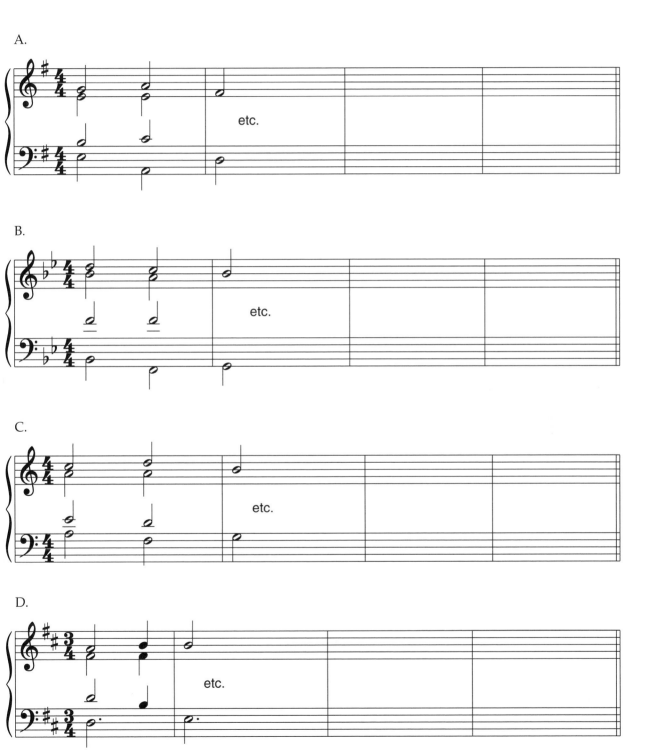

E.

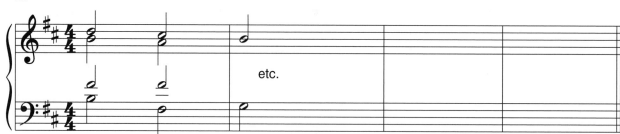

etc.

ASSIGNMENT 17.2
EXERCISES FOR TRIADIC SEQUENCES

EXERCISE 17.3 *Figured Bass and Sequences*

Bass, figures, and the soprano are given. The example includes two or more sequences. Bracket and identify the type of sequence. (Look for the intervallic pattern that repeats every two chords.) Add inner voices and provide a two-level roman numeral analysis. Do not analyze individual chords within a sequence.

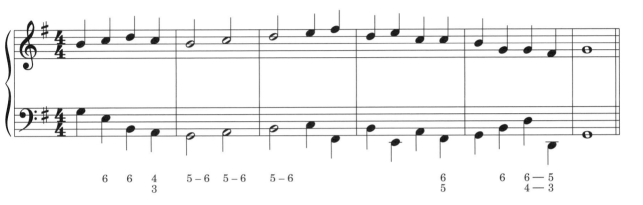

EXERCISE 17.4 *Composition*

Given is the accompaniment of an antecedent phrase. You will add a melody for a solo instrument or voice. Then realize the figured bass given, which will provide the consequent phrase; use the accompanimental figuration given in the antecedent and compose a suitable melody that is related to the one you wrote for the antecedent phrase. Analyze.

EXERCISE 17.5 *Analysis*

Analyze the following excerpts that contain sequences.

A. Mozart, Violin Concerto no. 2 in D major, K. 211, Rondeau

B.

ASSIGNMENT 17.3
EXERCISES FOR TRIADIC SEQUENCES

ANALYSIS

EXERCISE 17.6   *Comparison of Sequential Passages from the Literature*

STREAMING AUDIO
www.oup.com/us/laitz

The following three examples from Mozart's *Die Zauberflöte* (*The Magic Flute*), K. 620, contain a sequence. Listen to each and then, in a short paragraph, compare and contrast their content. Include in your discussion not only specific types of sequences but also their functions within the larger musical context.

A. "Drei Knäbchen" ("Three Little Boys"), act 1, scene 5

B. "Hölle Rache" ("Hell's Revenge"), act 2, scene 8

C. "Wie, wie, wie?" ("What, What, What?"), act 2, scene 5

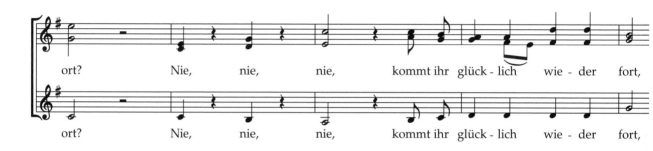

EXERCISE 17.7   *Continuing Sequences*

Based on the given models, continue the sequences for two repetitions. Close each example with a cadence. Label each sequence.

A. After J. S. Bach, Sonata for Flute in E♭ major, BWV 1031, *Allegro*

B. After Vivaldi, Sonata for Oboe in B♭ major, RV 34, *Allegro*

B1.

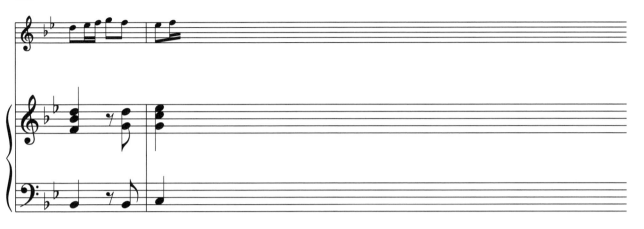

B2.

WRITING

EXERCISE 17.8 *Melody Harmonization*

1. Label the sequence implied by the given soprano melody.
2. Add a bass voice and inner voices; maintain the model's voicing in each repetition.
3. Add embellishments (passing tones, chordal leaps, suspensions, etc.) and maintain the sequential pattern.

A.

Bb:

B.

g:

C.

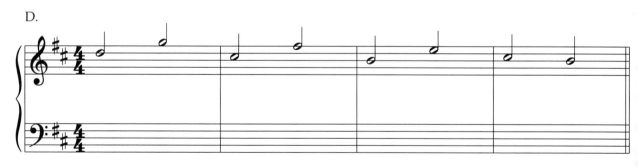

D:

D.

b:

ASSIGNMENT 17.4
EXERCISES FOR TRIADIC SEQUENCES

EXERCISE 17.9   *Analysis*

STREAMING AUDIO
www.oup.com/us/laitz

Analyze the following excerpts that contain sequences.

A. J. S. Bach, Chaconne, from Partita no. 2 in D minor for Solo Violin BWV 1004

B. Mozart, Flute Sonata no. 5 in C major, K. 14, *Allegro*

C. Mascagni, *Cavalleria rusticana*, Interlude

D. Brahms, Symphony no. 4 in E minor, op. 98, *Allegro non troppo*
  Note: The excerpt begins with a melodic sequence, not a harmonic sequence.

E. Quantz, Flute duet in A minor, op. 5, no. 5
  Compare the relationship between the instruments in mm. 9–16 and mm. 17–24.

F. Scarlatti, Sonata in D minor, K. 1 (transcribed for guitar)

WRITING

EXERCISE 17.10   *Elaborating Contrapuntal Models*

Six 1:1 (first-species) outer-voice models of various sequences follow. Choose a meter and a key different from the given key. Vary the mode (i.e., use both major and minor modes). Using a harmonic rhythm of half notes, or even whole notes, ornament each sequence by adding embellishing tones.

For example, given the three contrapuntal models shown, see how Corelli, Heinichen, and Bach embellished the basic model by adding recurring rhythmic patterns of neighbors, passing tones, and chordal leaps.

Sample solutions:

1. Corelli, Trio Sonata in B minor, op. 3, no. 4

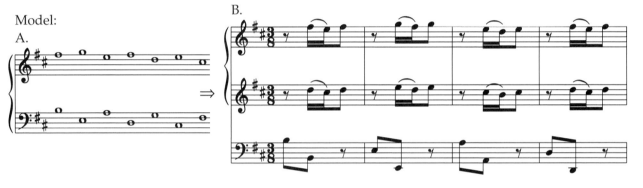

2. Heinichen, Sonata in C minor for Oboe and Bassoon

3. J. S. Bach, Flute Sonata in G minor, BWV 1020

Exercises:

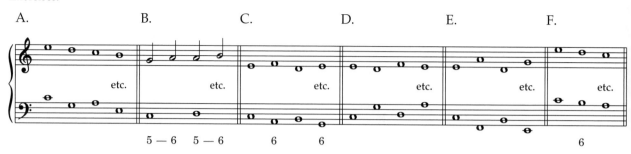

ASSIGNMENT 17.5
EXERCISES FOR SEQUENCES WITH SEVENTH CHORDS

EXERCISE 17.11   *Analysis*

STREAMING AUDIO
www.oup.com/us/laitz

For each of the following examples from the literature, identify the sequence with brackets and label. Include figures that show the alternating or interlocking seventh chords.

A. Brahms, "Wach auf, mein Hort," *Deutsche Volkslieder*, WoO 33, no. 13

What rhythmic device does Brahms use in this excerpt?

mich   der Treu   ge - nie -   ßen.
mir   freund - lich   zu   Wil -   len.
du   mir gönnst   von   Her -   zen

B. Brahms, Intermezzo in B♭ minor, op. 117, no. 2

This example begins on a neighboring harmony that leads to the tonic in six-three position (m. 1). Be aware that incomplete chromatic neighbors appear in each measure, beginning with the E♮ in m. 1.

C. Kreisler, Praeludium and Allegro

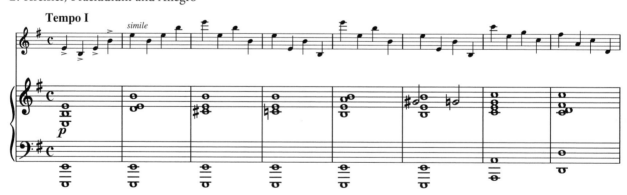

$$\text{V}^6_5/\text{iv}$$

$$\text{V}^7/\text{V}$$

WRITING

EXERCISE 17.12   *Completion of Sequence Patterns*

1. Write at least two repetitions of the sequence models given. Lead each sequence to an authentic cadence. Analyze.
2. Rewrite one of your solutions by adding at least two embellishing tones (e.g., suspension, passing tone, etc.) to the model and its copies.

1.
A.

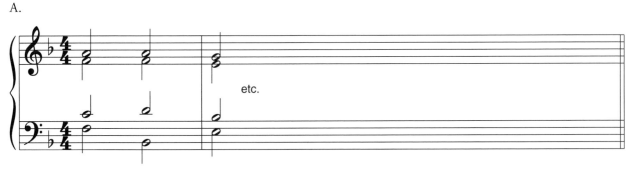

etc.

B.

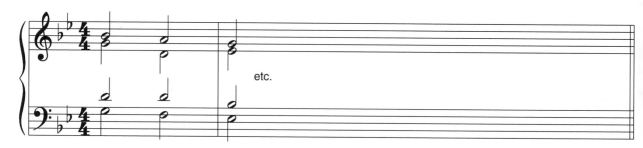

C.

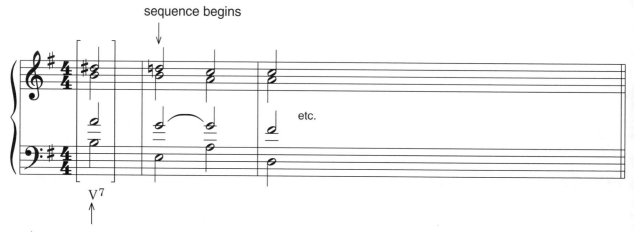

sequence begins

etc.

V^7

(prepares 7th in next chord)

2.

ASSIGNMENT 17.6   EXERCISES FOR SEQUENCES WITH SEVENTH CHORDS

EXERCISE 17.13   *Analysis*

STREAMING AUDIO
www.oup.com/us/laitz

Analyze the following examples that contain D2 (−5/+4) sequences with root-position and inverted seventh chords. Circle each chordal seventh and label its preparation and resolution. Are there any exceptions to the usual practice of preparing and resolving dissonances?

A. Telemann, Sonata in C minor for Flute, Oboe, and Basso Continuo, TV 41, no. 2, *Adagio*
  One might say that the sevenths of the sequence in the continuo do not resolve correctly. Is this really true?

B. Leclair, Sarabanda, Trio Sonata in D major, op. 2, no. 8

C. Marcello, Trio Sonata in B♭ major, op. 2, no. 2, *Largo* (continuo realization only)

WRITING

EXERCISE 17.14   *Figured Bass*

Realize the following figured bass in four voices and label all sequences. Analyze with two levels. Sequence choices are:

1. D2 (−5/+4): five-threes, six-threes, sevenths (alternating or interlocking)
2. A2 (+5/−4)
3. D3 (−4/+2): five-threes or six-threes (the descending 5–6)
4. A2 (−3/+4) (the ascending 5–6)

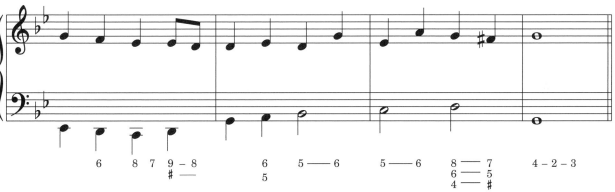

ASSIGNMENT 17.7
EXERCISES FOR ALL SEQUENCE TYPES

EXERCISE 17.15 *Melody Harmonization and Sequences*

Based on the contour of the following soprano fragments, determine an appropriate sequence type and then on a separate sheet of manuscript paper harmonize each in four voices (SATB). Examples A–D require one chord change for each melody note. Examples E–F contain embellishing tones and are incomplete. For these, determine the larger sequential pattern, add the sequential bass and complete the sequence, and lead to a cadence. Label each sequence type as shown in the sample solution.

Sample solution:

F: D2 (–5/+4) with $^6_3$s

A.

F *and* d:

B.

a *and* C:

C.

D.

E.

etc.

F.

etc.

EXERCISE 17.16   *Reduction of Sequences*

STREAMING AUDIO
www.oup.com/us/laitz

Determine the sequence type in the given examples, and reduce the texture to three or four voices. A sample solution is provided that contains three sequences.

Sample solution:

D2

A. Haydn, String Quartet in A major, op. 20, no. 6, *Allegro*

B. Corelli, Trio Sonata in A minor, op. 1, no. 4, *Allegro*

C. Corelli, Concerto Grosso no. 10 in C major, Corrente

Applied Chords

EXERCISE 18.1 *Recognizing Applied Chords*

STREAMING AUDIO
www.oup.com/us/laitz

Analyze the following short excerpts, each of which provides a "snapshot" of applied dominants in musical contexts.

A. Haydn, String Quartet in E♭ major, op. 20, no. 1

B. Haydn, String Quartet in C major, op. 20, no. 2, *Moderato*

C:

C. Haydn, String Quartet in F minor, op. 55, no. 2

f:

D. Schubert, Piano Sonata in D major, D. 850, Scherzo

D:

ANALYSIS

EXERCISE 18.2 *Recognizing Applied Chords*

STREAMING AUDIO
www.oup.com/us/laitz

The following examples contain up to four applied chords. The applied chords that we will focus on are V$^{(7)}$/ii, V$^{(7)}$/iii, V^7/IV, V$^{(7)}$/V, and V$^{(7)}$/vi. All are possible in both major and minor keys except for V/ii in minor (remember that dissonant triads such as ii° cannot be tonicized). For each excerpt, do the following:

1. Analyze all diatonic chords with roman numerals and give a second-level analysis.
2. Circle and label each applied chord with a roman numeral.

A sample analysis has been given. Remember to use your eye and ear to pinpoint new chromatic tones and harmonies foreign to the key.

Sample analysis:

Mozart, Trio, String Quartet in E♭ major, K. 171

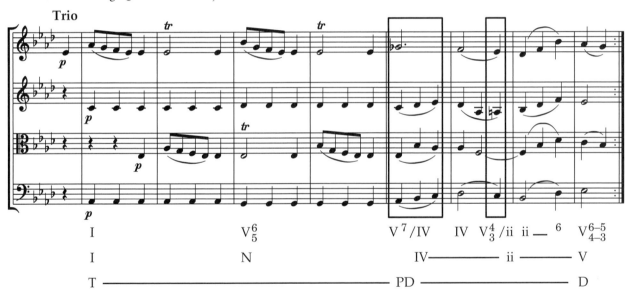

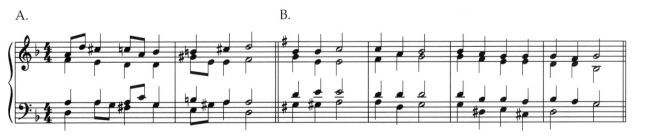

C. Beethoven, "Neues Liebe"

| | führ - ret | mich | im Au | - gen | - blick_ | | zu | ihr, |
| *Then,* | *as* | *by* | *a fai* | *- ry* | *chain,* | | *To* | *her,* |

WRITING

EXERCISE 18.3   *Error Detection of Applied Chords*

The following applied triads and seventh chords are either incorrectly notated or incorrectly analyzed.

- For Exercises A–C: *assume the roman numeral analysis and given key to be correct.* Renotate incorrect pitches in each chord to correctly represent the roman numerals.
- Exercises D–F: *assume the notated pitches and given key to be correct.* Change incorrect roman numerals to correctly represent the pitches and given key.
- Exercises G–I: *assume both roman numerals and given key to be correct.* Renotate pitches in each incorrectly spelled applied chord and resolution to correctly represent the analysis and the given key. Correct any voice-leading errors.

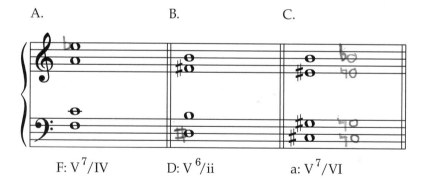

A.   B.   C.

F: V^7/IV   D: V^6/ii   a: V^7/VI

D.   E.   F.

C: V$^6_5$/iii I^6_3/IV   G: V$^4_3$/V V^4_3/vi   f: V$^6_5$/VI I^6_5/III

G.   H.   I.

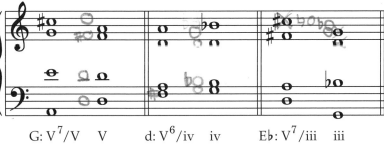

G: V^7/V   V   d: V^6/iv   iv   E♭: V^7/iii   iii

ASSIGNMENT 18.2
EXERCISES FOR APPLIED DOMINANTS

EXERCISE 18.4   *Recognizing Applied Chords*

STREAMING AUDIO
www.oup.com/us/laitz

The following examples contain up to four applied chords. The applied chords that we will focus on are V$^{(7)}$/ii, V$^{(7)}$/iii, V^7/IV, V$^{(7)}$/V, and V$^{(7)}$/vi. All are possible in both major and minor keys except for V/ii° in minor. For each excerpt do the following.

1. Analyze all diatonic chords with roman numerals and give a second-level analysis.
2. Circle and label each applied chord with a roman numeral.

A.

B. Schubert, Waltz in B♭ major, *German Dances and Ecossaises*, D. 783

WRITING

EXERCISE 18.5   *Resolving Applied Chords*

Analyze each applied chord according to the given key, then lead each to its respective
tonic, resolving all tendency tones correctly.

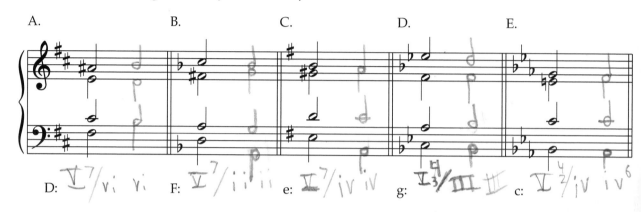

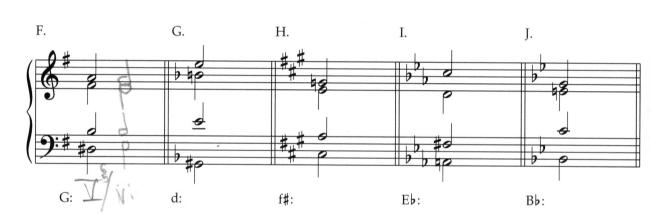

ASSIGNMENT 18.3
EXERCISES FOR APPLIED DOMINANTS

WRITING

EXERCISE 18.6   *Adding Four Voices*

Notate the chords as specified by the roman numerals, connecting each by using good voice leading.

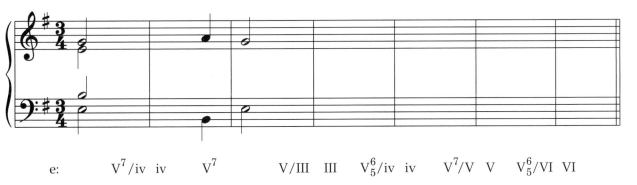

e: V^7/iv   iv V^7 V/III   III V^6_5/iv   iv V^7/V   V V^6_5/VI   VI

EXERCISE 18.7   *Harmonizing Melodic Fragments with Applied Chords*

In a logical meter and rhythmic setting of your choice, harmonize the melodic fragments using applied chords. Arrows indicate applied-chord placement. Your harmonic progression should make sense. Analyze.

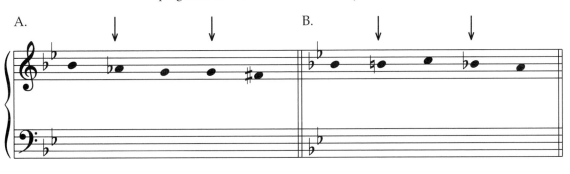

A.

B.

g: Bb:

C.

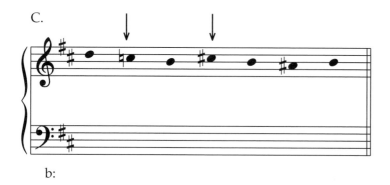

b:

EXERCISE 18.8 *Analysis*

Analyze the following examples using a first- and second-level analysis.

A. Mozart, String Quartet in F major, K. 158, *Allegro*

B. Elgar, "Salut d'Amour" ("Love's Greeting"), op. 12

Make a phrase–period diagram.

Andantino

ASSIGNMENT 18.4   EXERCISES FOR APPLIED LEADING-TONE TRIADS AND SEVENTHS

EXERCISE 18.9

In chorale style, complete the following applied leading-tone paradigms.

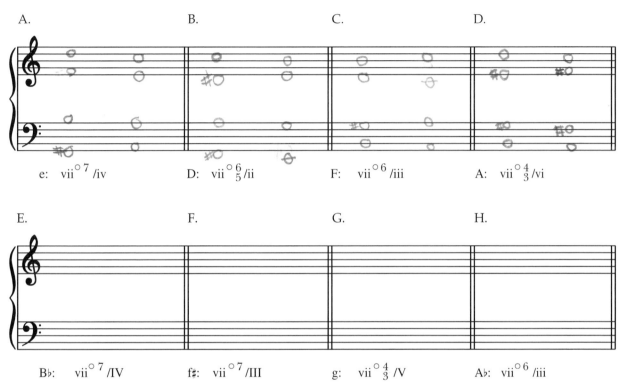

A.   B.   C.   D.

e: vii°7/iv   D: vii°6/5/ii   F: vii°6/iii   A: vii°4/3/vi

E.   F.   G.   H.

B♭:   vii°7/IV   f♯:   vii°7/III   g: vii°4/3/V   A♭:   vii°6/iii

EXERCISE 18.10

Realize the following figured bass, which includes applied vii°⁶ and vii°⁷ chords. The soprano is given. Provide a two-level analysis.

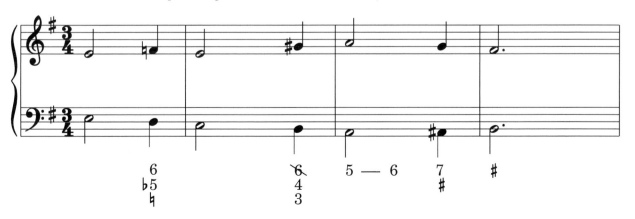

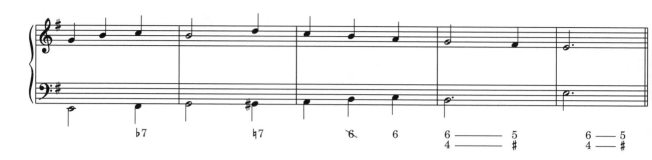

EXERCISE 18.11 *Analysis*

STREAMING AUDIO
www.oup.com/us/laitz

Provide a two-level harmonic analysis for the following examples from the literature.

A. Mozart, "Agnus Dei," *Requiem*, K. 626 ("Lamb of God, you take away the sins of the world")
Observe the metrical and harmonic qualities of this excerpt, and their relation to the text.
Looking at the first level of your analysis, what words are underlined by the music, and how is
this done? Looking at the second level, how is the meaning of the entire clause reflected in the
tonal motion?

B. Schubert, Piano Sonata in D major, D. 850, Scherzo
The *sforzandi* and ties contradict the written time signature. What might the time be in this
extract? Stem the heavily accented tones in the top and bottom voices. What resulting shapes
give this passage its underlying coherence?

ASSIGNMENT 18.5   EXERCISES FOR APPLIED DOMINANTS AND APPLIED LEADING-TONE CHORDS

WRITING

EXERCISE 18.12   *Applied vii°⁶ and vii°⁷*

Complete the following progressions that incorporate applied vii°⁶ and vii°⁷ chords.

1. Fill in the applied chords and resolve them, then compose an ending to the progression following the instructions in each example.
2. Provide a two-level analysis.

A. After resolving the applied chord, continue using an A2 (−3/+4) + ⁶₃ sequence that leads to the dominant. Include two additional applied chords in this progression.

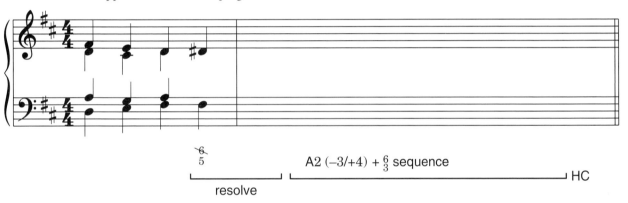

B. After resolving the applied chord, continue the progression for at least two measures, using harmonies of your choice. There must be at least two additional applied chords. Use ii°⁶₅ as the pre-dominant. Close with an authentic cadence that includes a suspension.

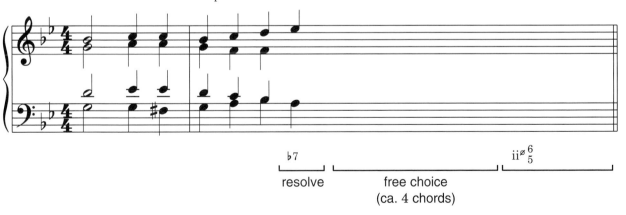

EXERCISE 18.13 *Harmonizing Melodic Fragments with Applied Chords*

In a logical meter and rhythmic setting of your choice, harmonize the melodic fragments by using applied chords. Arrows indicate applied-chord placement. Analyze.

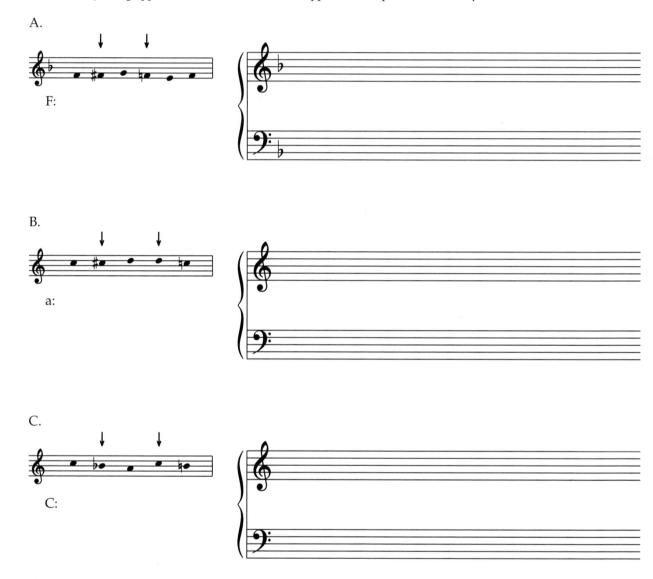

EXERCISE 18.14   *Analysis*

STREAMING AUDIO
www.oup.com/us/laitz

The following excerpts contain various applied chords. The goal is to work through these quickly, developing analytical fluency.

A. Haydn, String Quartet in G minor, op. 20, no. 3, Finale

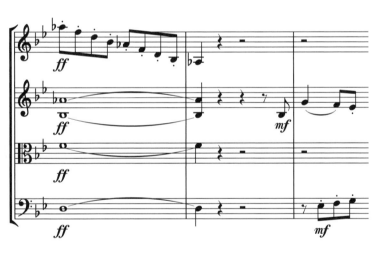

B. Haydn, String Quartet in C major, op. 64, no. 1, Minuet

C. Schubert, Piano Sonata in E♭ major, D. 568, *Allegro Moderato*

D. Schubert, piano sonata in E♭ major, D. 568, *Andante Molto*

E. Haydn, String Quartet in B♭ major, op. 71, no. 1, *Allegro*

ASSIGNMENT 18.6
EXERCISES FOR APPLIED-CHORD SEQUENCES

EXERCISE 18.15 *Analysis*

Listen to and analyze each excerpt, marking the beginning and ending points of each applied-chord sequence. Next, identify the sequence type by label. Finally, provide roman numerals for the remaining chords in each example.

A.

B.

C.

EXERCISE 18.16   *Completing Applied-Chord Sequences*

Determine the type of applied-chord sequence; continue the sequence and close with either an AC or a HC. Begin by writing the diatonic chords, and then insert the appropriate preceding applied chord.

E.

F.

ASSIGNMENT 18.7
EXERCISES FOR APPLIED-CHORD SEQUENCES

EXERCISE 18.17   *Figured Bass*

The following figured bass includes applied-chord sequences. Add roman numerals and inner voices. One sequence alters the soprano—why?

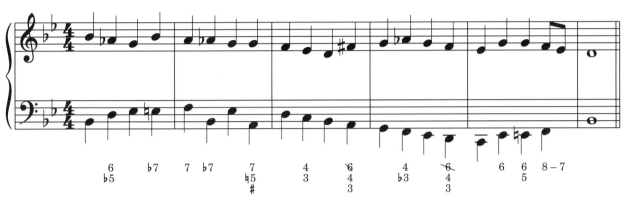

EXERCISE 18.18   *Harmonizing Bass Lines*

Harmonize each of the following bass lines. Each implies a diatonic or applied-chord sequence. Determine a suitable meter; you may change the note values. Analyze.

A.

F:

B.

A:

C.

b:

D.

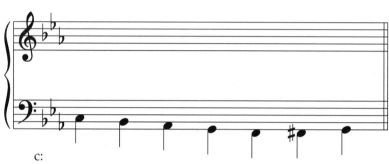

c:

EXERCISE 18.19 *Analysis*

Analyze the following examples, each of which contains an applied-chord sequence.

A. Vivaldi, Concerto Grosso in C minor, op. 9, no. 11, Ryom 198a, *Allegro*

F:

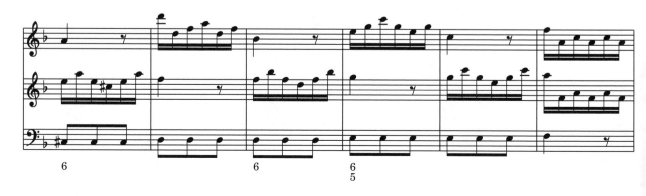

B. Schubert, Sonata in A major, D. 664, *Allegro*

CHAPTER 19

Tonicization and Modulation

ASSIGNMENT 19.1
EXERCISES FOR TONICIZED AREAS

EXERCISE 19.1 *Analysis*

STREAMING AUDIO
www.oup.com/us/laitz

The following excerpts are from the literature in which a nontonic harmony is expanded through tonicization. You are to:

1. listen to each phrase and bracket the expanded harmony,
2. provide a chord-by-chord analysis of the harmonies within the expansion,
3. analyze the remaining chords,
4. provide a second-level analysis that places the tonicized area within the overall harmonic progression of the entire passage.

A. Mendelssohn, Cello Sonata no. 1 in B♭ major, op. 45

B. Corelli, Concerto Grosso, op. 6, nos. 9 and 11, *Adagio*

Two *Adagio* sections from two Corelli concertos are provided. Analyze and, in a short paragraph, compare and contrast their harmonic content.

1. Excerpt B1 begins with what looks like a pedal six-four chord, but considering the chord that follows, is this the best label?
2. Consider B2 to be in G minor.

B1.

B2.

C. Schumann, "Du bist wie eine Blume" ("You Are So Like a Flower"), *Myrten*, op. 25, no. 24

WRITING

EXERCISE 19.2   *Figured Bass and Tonicized Areas*

1. Study the bass for cadential patterns and the figures for chromaticism, both of which will provide a general idea of which nontonic harmonies are being tonicized.
2. Lightly bracket each tonicized area and use a roman numeral to label it in relation to the main tonic.
3. Realize the figured bass by looking for short harmonic paradigms; add a soprano, and then inner voices. Refine your initial analysis, making sure that your first-level roman numerals are consistent with the deeper-level tonicized areas.

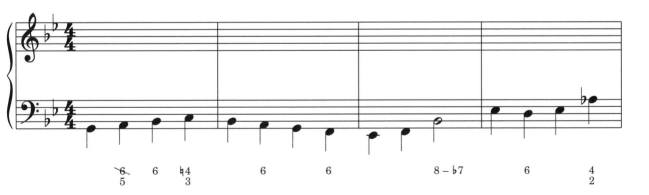

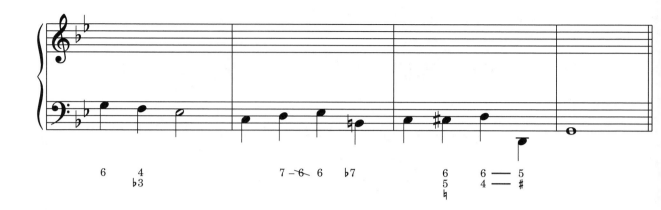

ASSIGNMENT 19.2   EXERCISES FOR TONICIZED AREAS AND MODULATION

EXERCISE 19.3   *Analysis*

STREAMING AUDIO
www.oup.com/us/laitz

Study the following excerpts, each of which features one or more expanded nontonic harmonies.

A. Bellini, *Cavatina*, "Casta Diva," from *Norma*, act 1, scene 4

B. Beethoven, Piano Sonata no. 27 in E minor, op. 90

Mit Lebhaftigkeit und durchaus mit Empfindung und Ausdruck

C. Brahms, *Hungarian Dance* no. 1, WoO1

WRITING

EXERCISE 19.4 *Key Choices*

List the closely related keys to each of the given keys. Review the various ways you can determine closely related keys.

A. D major __ __ __ __ __   B. A♭ major __ __ __ __ __   C. E minor __ __ __ __ __

D. B♭ major __ __ __ __ __   E. F minor __ __ __ __ __   F. C♯ minor __ __ __ __ __

EXERCISE 19.5   *Modulating Figured Basses*

Realize the following figured basses in four voices. Analyze and label the pivot chords.

A.

B.

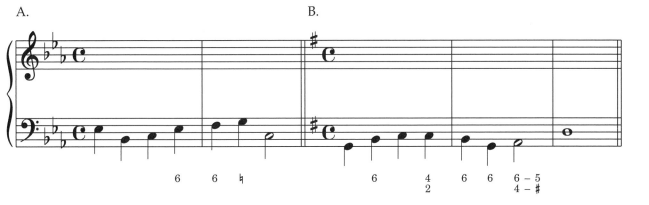

EXERCISE 19.6   *Analysis*

STREAMING AUDIO
www.oup.com/us/laitz

Each example that follows modulates. Analyze and label the pivot chord.

A. Schubert, *Eighteen Viennese Ladies' Ländler and Écossaises*, D. 734, no. 13

B. Haydn, Symphony no. 97 in C major, Hob I.97, *Allegretto*

C. Haydn, String Quartert in E♭ major, op. 71, no. 3, *Andante con moto*

D. Mozart, Symphony no. 40 in G minor, K. 550, *Allegro*

ASSIGNMENT 19.3
EXERCISES FOR MODULATIONS

WRITING

EXERCISE 19.7

Each of the following examples begins in G major and includes a vi (submediant) chord placed roughly halfway through what will become a complete progression. Each example's instructions specify a tonal destination (only one closes in the original tonic of G).

In chorale style, establish tonic, and, using the given submediant chord as a pivot, lead each progression to its destination. Make sure you use a strong authentic cadence in each case.

A. Head to V

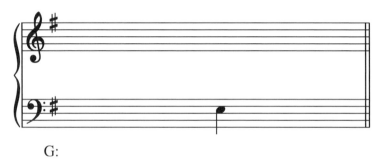

G:

B. Remain in G major

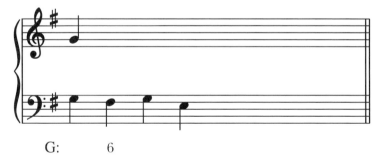

G: 6

C. Head to iii

G:

D. Head to vi

G:

ANALYSIS

EXERCISE 19.8   *Two-Voice Modulations*

STREAMING AUDIO
www.oup.com/us/laitz

Analyze the following examples. Include a formal and a harmonic analysis.

A.

B.

C.

ASSIGNMENT 19.4   EXERCISES FOR MODULATIONS EMPLOYING SEQUENCES AND COMPOSITION PROJECT

EXERCISE 19.9

STREAMING AUDIO
www.oup.com/us/laitz

Analyze the following excerpts, each of which modulates through the use of sequence. Bracket and label each sequence, then using pivot notation determine how the last chord of the sequence functions in the new key.

A. Dvořák, Cavatina, *Romantické kusy* (*Romantic Pieces*), op. 75, no. 1, *Allegro moderato*

B. Leclair, Violin Sonata in G major, op. 1, no. 5, *Allegro*

EXERCISE 19.10   *Modulating Figured Basses*

Realize the following figured basses in four voices. Analyze and label the pivot chords fully.

A.

B.

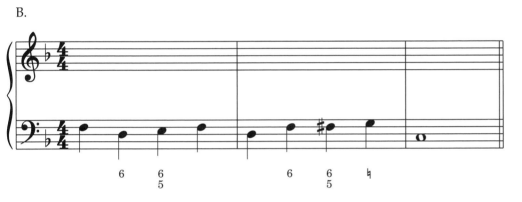

EXERCISE 19.11   *Composition*

A. Analyze the following antecedent phrase using roman numerals and figured bass; label embellishing tones. On a separate sheet of manuscript paper write three different consequent phrases to the antecedent, creating the following three period types: PIP, CIP, and PPP (you may close in either v or III).

B. 1. Analyze the following chord progression.
    2. Realize the figured bass (in four voices) that concludes the first phrase.
    3. Write a second phrase that modulates to and closes in a new key of your choice.
    4. Finally, write a suitable melody for both phrases.

ASSIGNMENT 19.5
MORE EXERCISES FOR MODULATIONS

WRITING

EXERCISE 19.12   *Modulating Figured Basses and Composition*

Realize the following figured bass in four voices. Analyze and label the pivot chord fully.

A.

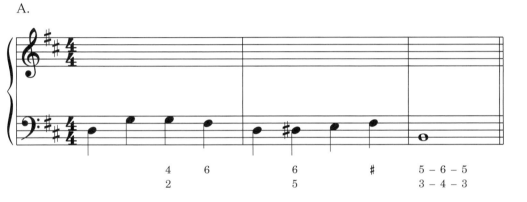

Continue the given opening and compose a sentence which modulates to the dominant. The opening five measures will be an expansion of the initial tonic, and the final two will be a cadence in the new key. Use the harmony in mm. 5 or 6 as a pivot chord.

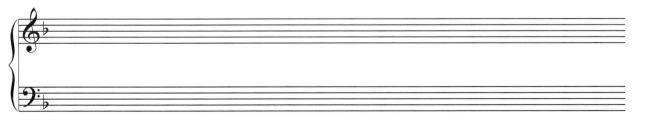

EXERCISE 19.13   *Soprano Harmonization*

Harmonize each soprano tune that follows in two different ways. Incorporate applied chords, diatonic and applied-chord sequences, and tonicized areas. Begin by breaking up the melodies into harmonic paradigms.

A.

B.

EXERCISE 19.14   *Analysis of Modulating Sequences*

Bracket and label the following modulating sequence. Then using pivot notation, determine how the last chord of the sequence functions in the new key.

Mozart, Divertimento in B♭ major, K. 254, *Allegro assai*

CHAPTER 20

Binary Form and Variations

ASSIGNMENT 20.1
ANALYSIS OF BINARY FORM

EXERCISE 20.1

STREAMING AUDIO
www.oup.com/us/laitz

Study each score, provide a formal diagram and label, and answer the accompanying questions.

A. Haydn, String Quartet in B minor, op. 33, no. 1, *Scherzando*

1. Provide a first- and second-level analysis for mm. 1–7.
2. Most of the melodic material in the movement is generated from violin 1's initial melody. Study mm. 1–7, marking motivic patterns between the instruments. Is there a single interval that is particularly important?

B. Türk, "Evening Song"

1. Diagram the first period in the piece.
2. What key is tonicized in mm. 9–10? (Use a roman numeral in relation to the main tonic.) Provide roman numerals to represent the work's overall tonal motion.

WRITING

EXERCISE 20.2   *Composition Project*

Analyze the following antecedent phrase. Then write two consequent phrases, one that modulates to V and one that modulates to iii. Add a melody for any solo instrument or voice.

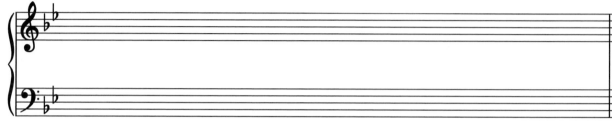

ASSIGNMENT 20.2   ANALYSIS AND COMPOSITION OF BINARY FORM

EXERCISE 20.3   *Analysis*

Make a form diagram for each of the following pieces.

A. Mozart, Duet for Two Violins in G major, K. 487

B. Haydn, Duo in F minor from Six Duos Concertante for Two Flutes, op. 101, no. 1, Hob
III.25, Trio

Label each suspension in mm. 1–5 and 11–22. Do you find any unprepared dissonance in
mm. 1–10?

EXERCISE 20.4 *Binary Composition*

- Analyze the following antecedent phrase.
- Write a consequent that modulates to III. Include repeat signs at the beginning
  of the antecedent and the end of the consequent.
- Write a melody for both phrases that contains a recurring rhythmic or pitch
  motive.

- Write another passage of approximately six to eight measures that is sequential and leads to the dominant.
- Finally, restate the opening eight-measure period, but rewrite the last phrase so that it closes in the tonic.
- You should end up with a rounded continuous binary form.

ASSIGNMENT 20.3
ANALYSIS OF BINARY FORM

EXERCISE 20.5

STREAMING AUDIO
www.oup.com/us/laitz

Make a form diagram for each of the following pieces.

A. Couperin, Concert Royal no. 1 in G major for Flute, Oboe, and Basso Continuo, Menuet

The basso continuo, which is written in the lower two staves, includes two instruments: harpsichord and cello (originally viola da gamba). Therefore, even though this is referred to as a trio, there are four players.

1. What is the form?
2. There are many melodic relationships between the instruments.
    a. What is the relationship between the opening winds and the continuo in mm. 1–2? Be specific.
    b. The continuo repeats the winds' material once literally and once in augmentation in the A section. Label these spots.
    c. Starting in m. 9, Couperin develops and intensifies the relationships between the instruments. For example, the descending melody is an inversion of the menuet's opening melody and imitation and pairing of voices occur between all instruments. Find two or three instances of such repetitions.
3. What single key controls mm. 9–16?
4. What is the large-scale tonal progression in mm. 1–20?

A.

B. Schumann, Romance in B♭ minor, *Three Romances*, op. 28, no. 1

1. Analyze mm. 1–8 and determine the overall tonal progression.
2. Label any sequences you find.
3. The C-major tonality is extended from m. 13 to the downbeat of m. 16. What is its harmonic function?

ASSIGNMENT 20.4   ANALYSIS AND COMPOSITION OF BINARY FORM

EXERCISE 20.6   *Analysis*

STREAMING AUDIO
www.oup.com/us/laitz

Given are complete themes and opening passages of two or three of their following variations. For Example A (Handel), only the first section of the theme is given.

Study each theme and its variations to determine:

1. whether the variation set is continuous or sectional;
2. what musical elements (e.g., harmony, embellishment) remain fixed (or only minimally changed) and which are varied. If the theme is sectional, label its overall form (except for Exercise A, which is incomplete).

Begin by providing roman numerals for the theme and studying the melody. Work through each variation beginning with a harmonic analysis and then focusing on the varied element.

Circle the original components of the melody to see exactly how the composer has altered it in the variations.

A. Handel, Gavotte from Keyboard Suite XIV in G major, HWV 222, *Allegro*

Variation 2

B. Mozart, Variations in C major on "Ah, vous dirai-je, Maman," K. 265

THEMA

VAR. I

VAR. II

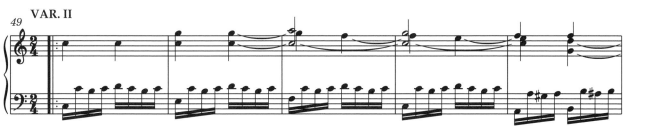

C. Tommaso Vitali, Variations in G minor

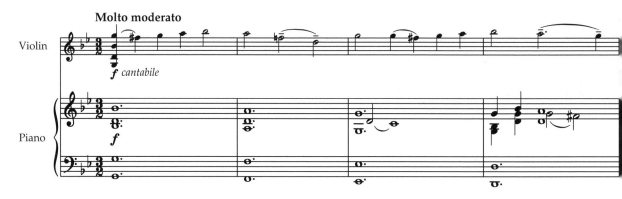

ASSIGNMENT 20.5   ANALYSIS AND COMPOSITION OF VARIATION FORM

ANALYSIS

EXERCISE 20.7

STREAMING AUDIO
www.oup.com/us/laitz

Given are complete themes and opening passages of two or three of their following variations.

Study each theme and their variations to determine:

1. whether the variation set is continuous or sectional;
2. what musical elements (e.g., harmony, embellishment) remain fixed (or only minimally changed) and which are varied. If the theme is sectional, label its overall form.

Begin by providing roman numerals for the theme and studying the melody. Work through each variation, focusing on the varied element.

Circle the original components of the melody to see exactly how the composer has altered it in the variations.

A. Schubert, Impromptu in B♭ Major, *Four Impromptus for Piano*, op. posth. 142, no. 3, D. 935

WRITING

EXERCISE 20.8

The first half of the theme and the incipits of five variations from one of Handel's keyboard works are shown. Analyze the theme and choose two variations whose first half you will complete.

Handel, Air from Keyboard Suite no. 3 in D minor, HWV 428

Air

1. Variation

2. Variation

3. Variation

4. Variation

5. Variation

CHAPTER 21

Modal Mixture

EXERCISE 21.1

STREAMING AUDIO
www.oup.com/us/laitz

Analyze the following excerpts from the literature, each of which contains one or more mixture harmonies.

Be aware that not all chromatically altered chords indicate mixture; some are applied chords. (Recall that mixture harmonies are independent chords that participate in the harmonic progression and usually carry a pre-dominant function. Applied harmonies, on the other hand, function exclusively as dominants, and they lead to their temporary tonics, to which they are subordinate.) Circle chromatic pitches and label scale degrees for mixture harmonies.

A. Bach, Chorale, "Vater unser im Himmelreich," BWV 90

B. Mozart, Clarinet Quintet in A major, K. 581, *Allegro*

What melodic/contrapuntal function does the harmony in mm. 4 and 6 serve?

C. Mahler, "Die zwei blauen Augen von meinem Schatz" ("The Two Blues Eyes of My Darling"), *Lieder eines fahrenden Gesellen* (*Songs of a Wayfarer*), no. 4

What is the mode of this excerpt? In spite of the pedal that runs through the entire excerpt, one can trace an implied progression of tonic–pre-dominant–dominant–tonic in the excerpt. Mark these functions.

Ich bin aus - ge - gan - gen in stil - ler Nacht, In __ stil - ler Nacht wohl __ ü - - ber die dunk - le __ Hal - - de;

D. Schubert, Piano Sonata in D major, D. 850, *Allegro vivace*

WRITING

EXERCISE 21.2

Complete each of the following tasks in chorale style. Expect to encounter multiple examples of modal mixture.

A. Unfigured bass

B. Figured bass

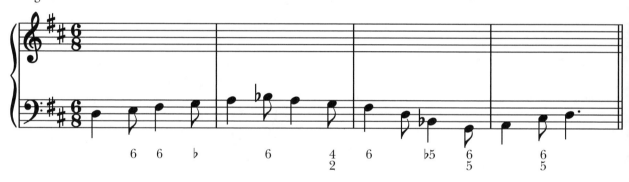

C.

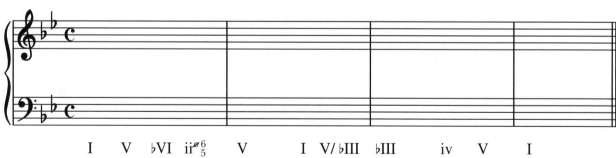

ASSIGNMENT 21.2
EXERCISES FOR MODAL MIXTURE

WRITING

EXERCISE 21.3   *Figured Bass*

Realize the following figured bass in four voices and analyze.

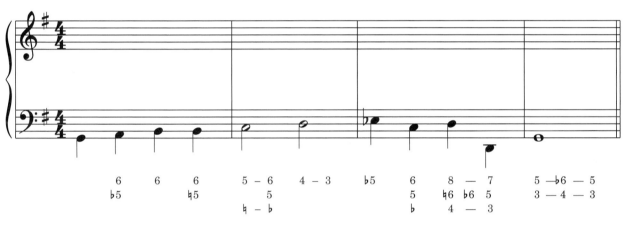

EXERCISE 21.4   *Analysis*

STREAMING AUDIO
www.oup.com/us/laitz

The following examples contain occurrences of modal mixture. Analyze each harmony with roman numerals and figured bass. Mixture choices include: minor tonic (i), diminished supertonic (ii°), half-diminished supertonic (ii°$^6_5$, ii°$^4_3$) lowered mediant ($\flat$III), minor subdominant (iv^7), minor dominant (v), lowered submediant ($\flat$VI).

A.

B.

C. Schubert, "Jägers Liebeslied," op. 96, no. 2

Mässig geschwind (Allegro moderato)

schieß den Hirsch im grü - nen Forst, im stil - len Tal das Reh,_____

den Ad - ler auf dem Klip - pen-horst, die En - te auf dem See.

D. Schubert, "Das Zügenglöcklein"

Ist's der Fro - hen Ei - ner, der die Freu-den rei - ner

Lieb' und Freund schaft theilt, gönn' ihm noch die Won - nen un - ter die-ser Son - nen,

gönn' ihm noch die Won - nen un - ter die-ser Son - nen, wo er ger - ne

ASSIGNMENT 21.3 EXERCISES FOR MODAL MIXTURE AND PLAGAL RELATIONS, CHROMATIC BASS DESCENTS, AND OTHER TYPES OF CHROMATICISM

EXERCISE 21.5 *Unfigured Bass*

Based on the harmonic implications of the bass, determine a logical chord progression, add inner voices, and analyze. Include as many mixture harmonies as possible.

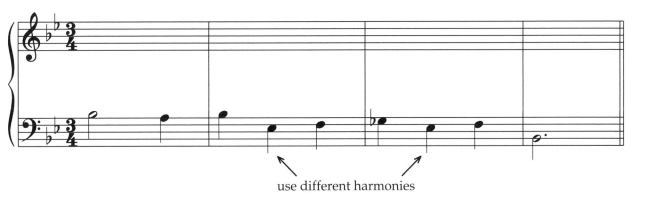

use different harmonies

EXERCISE 21.6 *Plagal Relations, III, and VI*

Write the following progressions:
  A. In E♭ major: I–III–IV–V⁷– ♭VI
  B. In B♭ major: I–VI–IV–V–I
  C. In F major: I– ♭VI–ii°⁶₅–V⁴₂–I⁶–III–IV–iv ♭ –I
  D. In C major: V–V/ ♭VI– ♭VI–iv ♭ –V/ ♭III– ♭III–ii°⁶₅–I

A.   B.

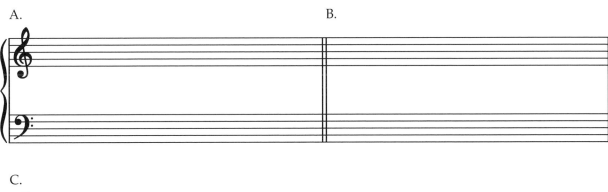

C.

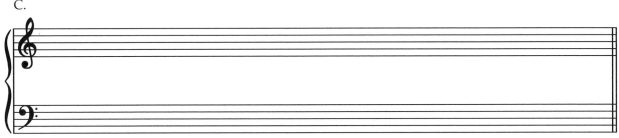

D.

EXERCISE 21.7 *Analysis*

STREAMING AUDIO
www.oup.com/us/laitz

Analyze the following chromatic bass descents using roman numerals.

A.

B. Beethoven, Piano Sonata no. 28 in A major, op. 101, *Lebhaft. Marchmässig*

C. Beethoven, Violin Sonata no. 5 in F major, "Spring," op. 24, Scherzo

What is unusual about the mixture harmony's function in the large-scale tonal framework?

ASSIGNMENT 21.4   ANALYSIS AND COMPOSITION INCORPORATING MODAL MIXTURE

EXERCISE 21.8   *Analysis*

STREAMING AUDIO
www.oup.com/us/laitz

A. Beethoven, Violin Sonata no. 9 in A major, "Kreutzer," op. 47, *Adagio sostenuto*

Explore the possibility that Beethoven is introducing modal mixture in stages, first melodically with the support of subordinate harmonies and then harmonically (with structural chords). Consider whether the F major harmony in m. 7 is best interpreted as ♭VI in A or IV in C major.

B. Brahms, "Sind es Schmerzen," *Die schöne Magelone*, op. 33, no. 3

Ach, und fällt die Trä - ne nie - der, ist es dun - kel um mich her;

den noch kömmt kein Wunsch__ mir wie - der,

WRITING

EXERCISE 21.9 *Figured Bass*

Realize the following figured bass that incorporates plagal relations and III and VI.

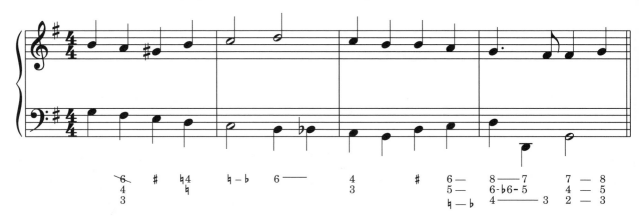

EXERCISE 21.10   *Composition*

Write a 16-measure double period that is based on the following model. Choose a meter and melodic structure (parallel or contrasting). Begin in G major and move to its V. Details of each phrase follow.

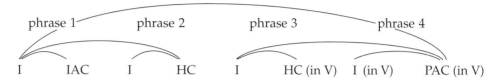

Phrase 1: Include a sequence of your choice that uses suspensions.
Phrase 2: Include one applied chord and one example of mixture.
Phrase 3: Use a mixture harmony to lead to the HC in V.
Phrase 4: Include a step-descent bass.

CHAPTER 22

Expansion of Modal Mixture Harmonies: Chromatic Modulation and the German Lied

ASSIGNMENT 22.1
EXERCISES FOR CHROMATIC MODULATIONS

EXERCISE 22.1 *Analysis*

STREAMING AUDIO
www.oup.com/us/laitz

Listen to the following examples of prepared (i.e., pivot-chord) chromatic tonicizations. Then do the following:

1. Locate and label the chromatic tonicization.
2. Locate and interpret the pivot chord or pivot area.
3. Use roman numerals to write out the overall harmonic progression.

Note: You do *not* need to analyze every harmony. Two sample solutions are provided.

Sample solution 1:

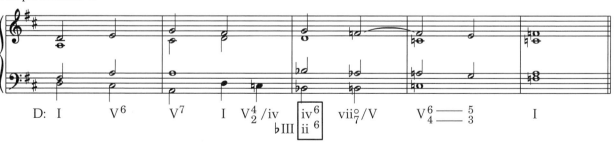

Sample solution 2: Beethoven, Violin Sonata, op. 24, "Spring," *Adagio molto espressivo*

A.

B.

C. Beethoven, Piano Sonata in A major, op. 2, no. 2, *Largo appassionato*

WRITING

EXERCISE 22.2 *Figured Bass*

Realize the following figured bass in four voices and analyze.

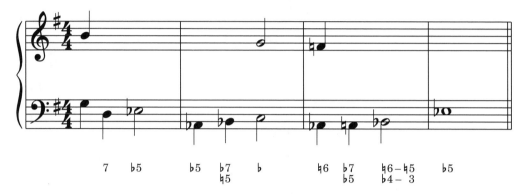

ASSIGNMENT 22.2 EXERCISES FOR CHROMATIC MODULATIONS

EXERCISE 22.3 *Analysis*

 STREAMING AUDIO
www.oup.com/us/laitz

Listen to the following examples of prepared (i.e., pivot-chord) chromatic tonicizations. Then do the following:

1. Locate and label the chromatic tonicization.
2. Locate and interpret the pivot chord or pivot area.
3. Use roman numerals to write out the overall harmonic progression.

Note: You do *not* need to analyze every harmony.

A.

B. Schubert, Suleika II (Ach um deine feuchten Schwingen), D. 717

C. Mozart, String Quartet in A major, K. 464, *Allegro*
  What type of formal construction occurs in mm. 1–16?

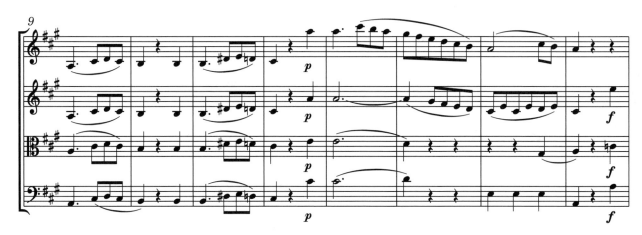

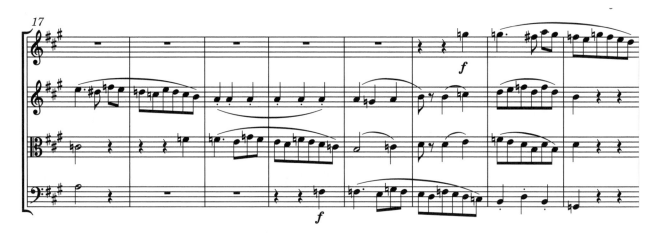

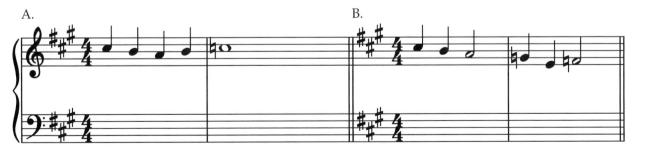

EXERCISE 22.4   *Melody Harmonization*

Harmonize the following soprano melodic fragments in four voices, each of which implies a chromatic tonicization. Analyze with roman numerals and mark the pivot carefully.

ASSIGNMENT 22.3   EXERCISES FOR COMMON-TONE CHROMATIC MODULATIONS

EXERCISE 22.5   *Multiple Harmonizations of a Soprano Melody*

Given are two modulating soprano melodies that may be harmonized in a variety of ways. Analyze and add a bass line. You need not add inner voices.

A.

B.

EXERCISE 22.6   *Prepared and Common-Tone Chromatic Modulations*

STREAMING AUDIO
www.oup.com/us/laitz

Following are two types of chromatic third modulations: pivot-chord and common-tone.

1. Use roman numerals to label the chromatic destination.
2. Determine whether the composer has used a pivot-chord modulation (in which a mixture chord in the first key becomes a diatonic chord in the new key) or a common-tone modulation (a single pitch is reinterpreted in the new key). If you encounter a pivot-chord modulation, mark the pivot. If you encounter a common-tone modulation, circle and beam the common pitch class(es).

A. Chopin, Etude in A♭ major, op. 10, no. 10

B. Brahms, "Die Mainacht" ("May Night"), *Vier ernste Gesänge* (*Four Serious Songs*), op. 43, no. 2
   Consider B major to be an enharmonic respelling of C♭ major.

ASSIGNMENT 22.4 ANALYSIS OF TEXT–MUSIC RELATIONS AND WRITING CHROMATIC MODULATIONS

EXERCISE 22.7 *Interactive Analysis*

STREAMING AUDIO
www.oup.com/us/laitz

Schubert, "An Emma" ("To Emma"), D. 113c

This song presents chromatic third relations prepared by modal mixture. Study the text and listen to the song. Then analyze to the best of your ability using roman numerals. Star any passages whose resolutions or progressions you find puzzling or interesting. Then attempt a second analysis with the following leading discussion guiding you.

Was da-hin ist und ver-gan-gen, Em-ma, kann's die Lie-be sein? Ih - rer

Flam - me Him - mels-glut, stirbt sie wie ein ir - disch Gut?

Weit in nebelgrauer Ferne	Far in the great misty distance
Liegt mir das vergangne Glück,	lies my past happiness.
Nur an einem schönen Sterne	My gaze still lingers fondly
Weilt mit Liebe noch der Blick.	on one lovely star alone;
Aber, wie des Sternes Pracht,	but the splendor of the star,
Ist es nur ein Schein der Nacht.	it is only an illusion of the night.
Deckte dir der lange Schlummer,	If the long sleep of night
Dir der Tod die Augen zu,	had closed your eyes
Dich besässe doch mein Kummer,	my grief might still possess you;
Meinem Herzen lebtest du.	you would live on in my heart.
Aber ach! du lebst im Licht,	But oh, you live in the light,
Meiner Liebe lebst du nicht.	but you do not live for my love.
Kann der Liebe süss Verlangen,	Emma, can love's sweetness
Emma, kann's vergänglich sein?	fade and die?
Was dahin ist und vergangen,	That which is past and gone,
Emma, kann's die Liebe sein?	Emma—can that be love?
Ihrer Flamme Himmelsglut,	Can the heavenly glow of its ardor die,
Stirbt sie wie ein irdisch Gut?	like some earthly possession?

(trans. John Reed, *The Schubert Song Companion*)

The goal of *Lied* analysis is to discern how the musical material may be aligned with the underlying poetic drama. The subject of this poem is timeless. A jilted lover reflecting on happier times is repeatedly jarred back to the reality of his loss. The rhyme scheme of the text is ababcc. The last two lines of each strophe are segregated both by rhyme scheme and meaning, acting as a refrain. In the first two strophes, this refrain and the preceding verse are set in opposition to each other. The verse expresses the protagonist's longing for love, while the refrain redirects this thought toward the painful truth. The first verse emphasizes past happiness, and the distance between the speaker and the object of his gaze—the star—is symbolic of the time that separates him from the object of his affection, Emma.

1. Are particular words highlighted in the musical setting? By what means? Consider the use of accidentals, chromatic harmony, and dramatic pause.
2. Locate all the A-major triads. Are certain words associated with this chord and with D minor (its resolution chord)?
3. Are there harmonic progressions left incomplete? How might these interact with the text?
4. In the second verse (mm. 20ff), consider the analogy of death with night and slumber. Is the beloved dead, or only dead to the love of the speaker?
5. Is there a change in the speaker's perspective? Where is the climax in this section? In the closing verse the speaker poses a question to his beloved: If true love can never die, and that which we shared has died, then how could it have been love? Why is there the curious sojourn into A♭ major?

WRITING

EXERCISE 22.8 *Common-Tone and Other Types of Modulation*

Complete the following tasks using five to seven chords and in four voices; analyze.

A. Modulate from C major to A♭ major by means of a common-tone modulation.
B. Modulate from E major to ♭III by means of a common-tone modulation.
C. Modulate from B♭ major to D major by means of a mixture-chord pivot.
D. Modulate from A major to F major, using any sequence as a pivot.
E. Given an F-minor triad as a pivot, modulate from:
   1. C major to A♭ major
   2. E♭ major to C minor
   3. A♭ major to F minor

A.   B.

C.   D.

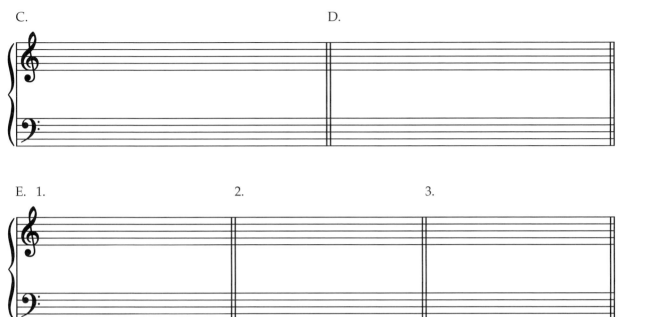

E. 1.   2.   3.

ASSIGNMENT 22.5   COMPARATIVE ANALYSIS AND WRITING CHROMATIC MODULATIONS

EXERCISE 22.9   *Comparative Analysis*

Analyze the following excerpts from Beethoven's and Schubert's settings of Goethe's poem "Kennst du das Land?" Focus on chromaticism that results from tonicization and modal mixture. Study the two text settings, and compare and contrast the way Beethoven and Schubert have merged text and music.

A. Beethoven, "Mignon," op. 75, no. 1

B. Schubert, "Kennst du das Land?" ("Mignons Gesang") ("Do You Know the Land?"), D. 321

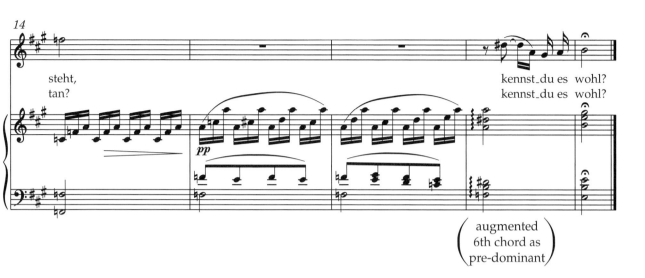

(augmented 6th chord as pre-dominant)

Kennst du das Land, wo die Zitronen blühn,	Do you know where the lemon grows,
Im dunkeln Laub die Gold-Orangen glühn,	In dark foliage the golden-orange glows,
Ein sanfter Wind vom blauen Himmel weht,	A gentle breeze blows from the blue sky,
Die Myrte still und hoch der Lorbeer steht?	Do the myrtle and the laurel, stand high?
Kennst du es wohl? . . .	Do you know it well? . . .
Kennst du das Haus? Auf Säulen ruht sein Dach,	Do you know the house, its roof on columns fine?
Es glänzt der Saal, es schimmert das Gemach,	Its hall glows brightly and its chambers shine,
Und Marmorbilder stehn und sehn mich an:	And marble figures stand and gaze at me;
Was hat man dir, du armes Kind, getan?	What have they done, oh poor child, to you?
Kennst du es wohl? . . .	Do you know it well? . . .

WRITING

EXERCISE 22.10 *Composition*

Study the given measures and perform the followig tasks.

1. Add inner voices to the first two measures according to the implications of the melody and bass, following the accompaniment pattern laid out in the first measure.
2. Add a bass to the second two measures that modulates to ♭III. Write the bass tones for the cadence before considering where you will place the chromatic pivot chord (which you should be mindful of as you write your bass).
3. Add inner voices.
4. Analyze, using two levels.
5. Write a parallel consequent phrase, setting the next two lines of Wordworth's poem, ending in V.

When all at once I saw a crowd,
A host, of golden daffodils;

CHAPTER 23

The Neapolitan Chord (♭II)

ASSIGNMENT 23.1 EXERCISES FOR THE NEAPOLITAN SIXTH CHORD

EXERCISE 23.1 *Analysis*

STREAMING AUDIO
www.oup.com/us/laitz

Analyze the following examples, each of which contains the Neapolitan chord.

A. Meyerbeer, "Scirocco"

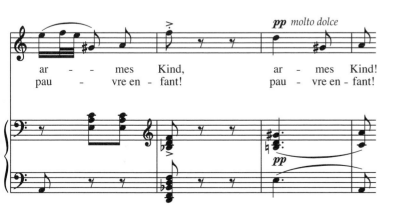

B. Beethoven, "Sehnsucht," WoO 134

Nur   wer   die Sehn - sucht kennt weiss, was   ich lei -   de!
Ach!   der   mich liebt und kennt   ist   in   der Wei -   te.

C.

D. Brahms, Clarinet Sonata in F minor, op. 120, no. 1

WRITING

EXERCISE 23.2 *Spelling, Identifying, and Writing ♭II⁶*

Given the following triads, determine the minor key in which each triad functions as ♭II⁶ and provide a key signature. Then resolve each as required.

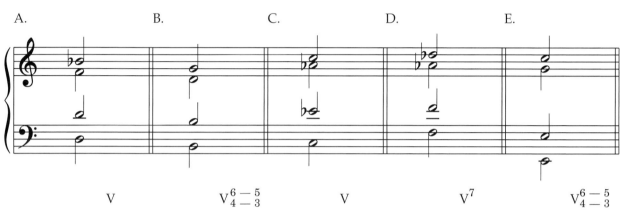

EXERCISE 23.3 *Figured Bass and the Neapolitan*

Realize the following figured basses in four voices. Analyze.

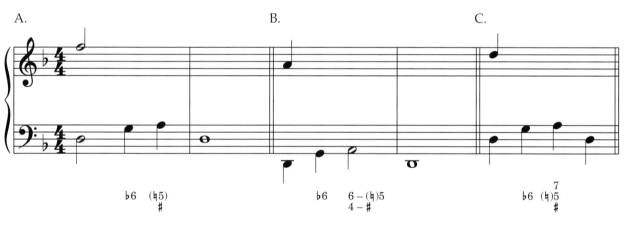

ASSIGNMENT 23.2   EXERCISES FOR THE NEAPOLITAN SIXTH CHORD

WRITING

EXERCISE 23.4   *More Spelling, Identifying, and Writing ♭II⁶*

Given is the bass of ♭II⁶ chords in various keys. Determine the key for each example and provide a key signature. Then complete the ♭II⁶ chord in four voices (double the bass in each case) and precede and follow it as required.

A.   B.

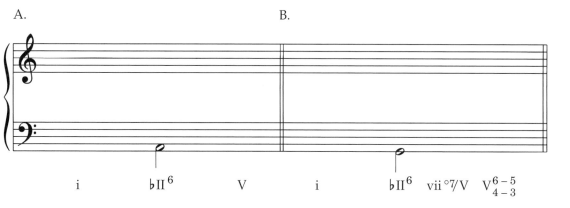

i   ♭II⁶   V   i   ♭II⁶   vii°7/V   V⁶⁻⁵₄₋₃

C.

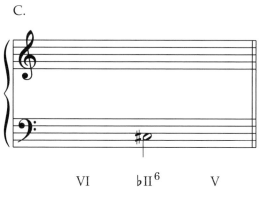

VI   ♭II⁶   V

EXERCISE 23.5 *Figured Bass*

Realize the following figured bass. Analyze.

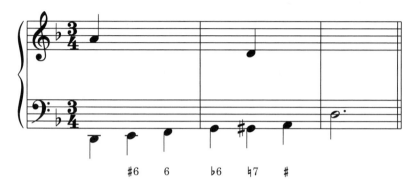

EXERCISE 23.6 *Analysis*

Analyze the following examples.

STREAMING AUDIO
www.oup.com/us/laitz

A. Wagner, "Leb Wohl," *Die Walküre*, act 3, scene 3

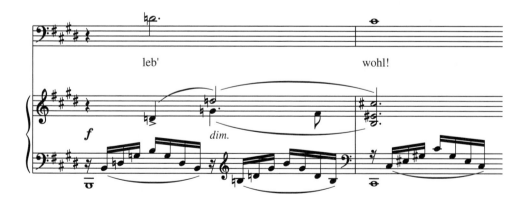

B. Locatelli, Sonata no. 3 in G minor, Twelve Sonatas for Flute and Continuo, *Largo*

1. What is the form of this piece?
2. The interval of the third, especially encompassing 1̂–3̂, is very important throughout the piece. Mark various statements of the third. Explore how thirds in multiple voices may occur simultaneously, creating voice exchanges and other interesting contrapuntal motions.
3. A progressive period occurs in the A section. Analyze the pivot area. Compare this pivot with that which leads back to the tonic at the end of the digression.
4. Label all sequences.
5. Perform a roman numeral analysis of mm. 1–4.

ASSIGNMENT 23.3   EXERCISES FOR EXPANDED NEAPOLITAN PROGRESSIONS

WRITING

EXERCISE 23.7   *Harmonic Progressions*

Choose a suitable meter and rhythmic setting and write the following progressions in four voices. Analyze. *Optional:* Play your progressions on the piano in keyboard style. Be able to sing either upper voice while playing the remaining three voices.

   A. B minor: i–vii°⁶–i⁶– ♭II⁶–vii°⁷/V–V–I
   B. C minor: i–V⁶/III–III– ♭II⁶–cad. $^{6-5}_{4-3}$–i

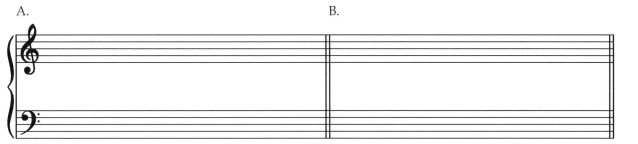

EXERCISE 23.8   *Melodic Fragments*

Write a logical bass line, analyze, and add inner voices. The Neapolitan must appear at least once in each exercise.

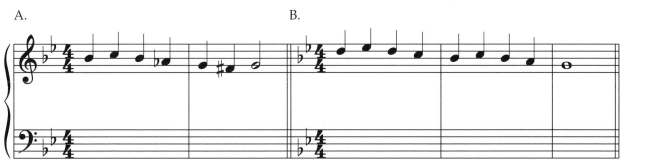

STREAMING AUDIO
www.oup.com/us/laitz

EXERCISE 23.9 *Analysis*

Analyze the following example. Use a two-level analysis.

Beethoven, Rondo in C major, op. 51, no. 1

ASSIGNMENT 23.4   EXERCISES FOR EXPANDED NEAPOLITAN PROGRESSIONS

WRITING

EXERCISE 23.10   *Figured Bass*

Realize the following figured bass and given melody by adding inner voices. Analyze. What type of progression opens the exercise?

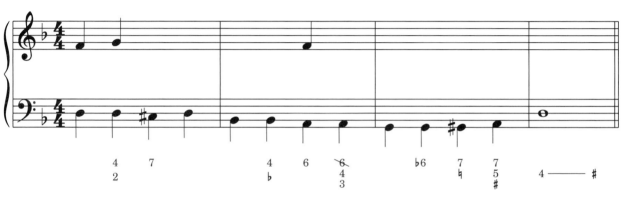

EXERCISE 23.11   *Unfigured Bass and Melody*

Based on the harmonic implications of the bass and soprano, add inner voices and analyze.

EXERCISE 23.12   *Analysis*

Analyze the following examples. Employ a first- and second-level analysis when appropriate. Determine the form.

A. Vivaldi, Manchester Violin Sonata no. 12, RV 754, Sarabanda

B. Mozart, Violin Sonata in G major K. 379, Tema con variazioni

The Augmented Sixth Chord

ASSIGNMENT 24.1   EXERCISES FOR THE AUGMENTED SIXTH CHORD

EXERCISE 24.1

STREAMING AUDIO
www.oup.com/us/laitz

Listen to and analyze the following analytical snapshots, each of which contains an augmented sixth chord. Label the augmented sixth as follows: It⁶₃, Ger⁶₅, or Fr⁴₃.

A. Bach, "Ich hab' mein' Sach' Gott heimgestellt," BWV 351
The pitch that creates the characteristic interval of the augmented sixth appears just after the other chord tones of the sonority. How does Bach postpone this pitch?

B. Mozart, Piano Trio no. 7 in E♭ major, K. 498, *Allegretto*

C. Beethoven, Violin Sonata no. 7 in C minor, op. 30, no. 2, Finale, *Allegro*

One could argue that all three forms (a world tour) of the augmented sixth appear in this example. Label each form.

D. Mozart, Piano Concerto in E♭ major, K. 449, *Allegro*

EXERCISE 24.2   *Writing and Resolving Augmented Sixth Chords*

We now generate the three forms of the augmented sixth chord from the Phrygian cadence. Follow this procedure:

1. Determine the minor key implied by the key signature.
2. Write a Phrygian cadence (i.e., iv⁶–V).
3. Transform the Phrygian cadence into an It⁶ (raise $\hat{4}$).
4. Transform the It⁶ into a Ger$^6_5$ (add a fifth above the bass: $\hat{3}$) and resolve the chord to a cadential six-four chord.
5. Transform the Ger$^6_5$ into a Fr$^4_3$ (substitute an augmented fourth above the bass by lowering the fifth of the Ger$^6_5$ a semitone: $\hat{2}$).

Sample solution:

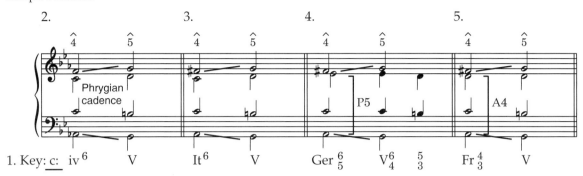

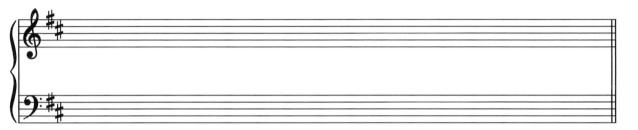

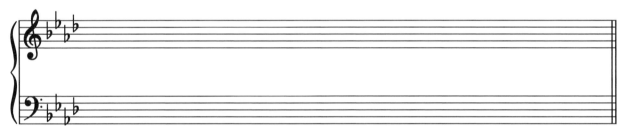

EXERCISE 24.3   *Spelling Augmented Sixth Chords*

Notate the following augmented sixth chords and resolve them to the dominant. Add necessary chromaticism; do not use key signatures.

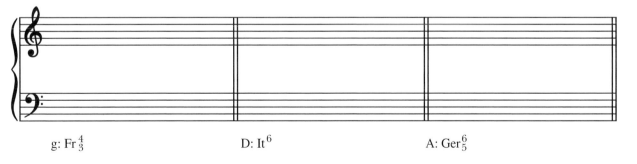

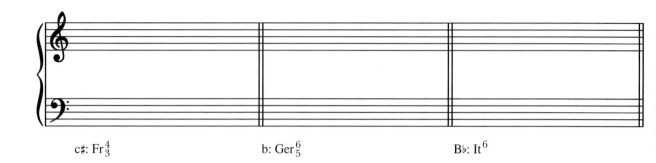

c#: Fr$^4_3$ b: Ger$^6_5$ B♭: It^6

ASSIGNMENT 24.2 EXERCISES FOR THE AUGMENTED SIXTH CHORD

EXERCISE 24.4

STREAMING AUDIO
www.oup.com/us/laitz

Listen to and analyze the following two examples. Label augmented sixth chords fully (It$^6_3$, Ger$^6_5$, or Fr$^4_3$).

A. Schubert, Waltz in F major, *36 Originaltänze*, no. 34, D. 365

1. One can view the B♭/D as an anticipation to the V^7 in m. 5. Does this ninth resolve?
2. What is the form of this piece? *Hint:* Is this a binary form or merely a period?

B. Mozart, String Quartet no. 15 in D minor, K. 421, *Allegro*

1. What type of bass line occurs twice in this example? What is the basic difference between the two appearances?
2. How would you explain the dissonant B♭ in violin 1 of m. 3?
3. How does Mozart prepare in the first phrase for the augmented sixth chord that appears in the second phrase?

WRITING

EXERCISE 24.5   *Motion to and from Augmented Sixth Chords*

Determine and label the key in which each of the augmented sixth chords occurs. Then do the following:

1. Precede each augmented sixth with a root-position tonic chord.
2. Resolve each augmented sixth chord to the dominant.

Sample solution:

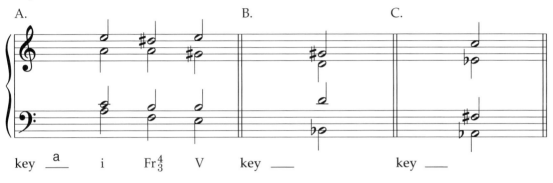

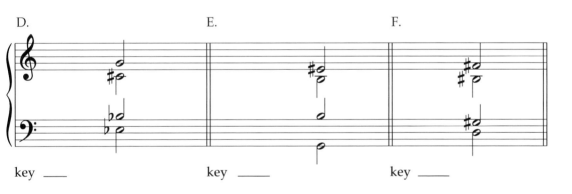

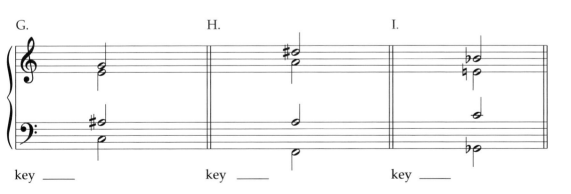

EXERCISE 24.6 *Figured Bass*

Realize the following figured basses in four voices and analyze.

A.   B.

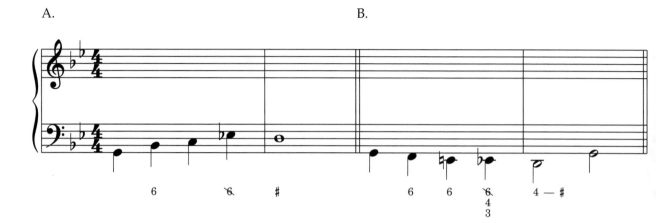

ASSIGNMENT 24.3   EXTENDED EXERCISES FOR THE AUGMENTED SIXTH CHORD

EXERCISE 24.7   *Melody Harmonization*

Study the following melodic fragments and harmonize each in four voices according to the instructions. Analyze.

A. Include an It⁶ and step-descent bass.

B. Include a Ger$^6_5$ and an applied chord.

C. Include a Fr$^4_3$ and deceptive cadence.

D. Include an applied chord and an augmented sixth chord.

EXERCISE 24.8   *Figured Bass*

Realize the following figured bass in four voices and analyze.

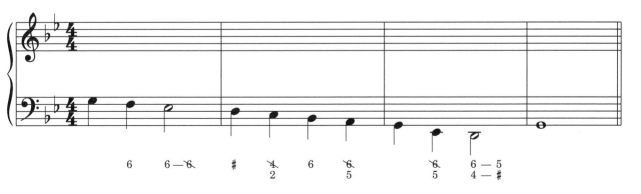

EXERCISE 24.9

Each of the following three operatic excerpts contains tonicizations of two or more keys, and each tonicization is signaled by an augmented sixth chord. Label each key, then analyze the pre-dominant to dominant motion.

A. Verdi, "Qual voce come tu donna?" from *Il Trovatore*, part 4, no. 18

B. Ponchielli, "Ombre di mia prosopia," from *La Gioconda*

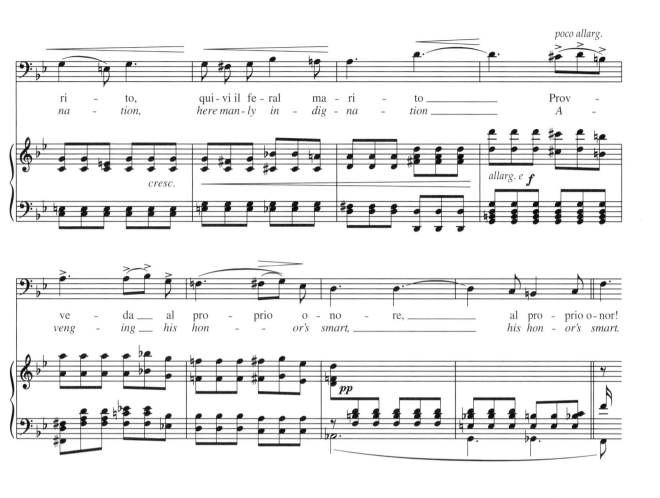

C. Wagner, "Mein Herr und Gott," from *Lohengrin*

ASSIGNMENT 24.4   EXTENDED EXERCISES FOR THE AUGMENTED SIXTH CHORD

EXERCISE 24.10   *Figured Bass*

Realize the following figured bass in four voices. Analyze.

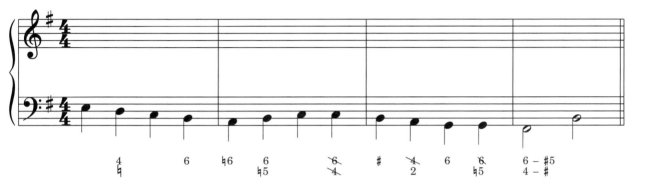

EXERCISE 24.11   *Analysis*

STREAMING AUDIO
www.oup.com/us/laitz

Listen to the following examples, and analyze. Answer any accompanying questions.

A. Haydn, String Quartet in C major, op. 74, no. 1, Hob III.72, Menuett
Identify the type of binary form. (You will be listening to the A section, the digression, and the three measures that immediately follow the digression.) What type of sequence is used in the digression, and what harmony does it extend?

B. Schubert, Waltz in A major, *Wiener-Damen Ländler*, no. 6, D. 734
   What is the form of this piece?

C. Kozeluch, String Quartet in A major, op. 33, no. 2

EXERCISE 24.12   *Writing the Diminished Third Chord*

Write the following chords and resolve them to the dominant:

- A. Ger^7 in C minor
- B. Ger$^6_5$ in D minor
- C. Ger^7 in C♯ minor
- D. Ger$^6_5$–P$^6_4$–Ger^7 in A minor
- E. Ger$^6_5$–Ger$^{○7}$ with voice exchange in G minor

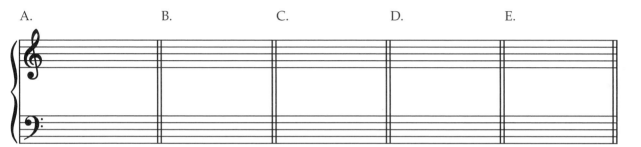

EXERCISE 24.13   *Figured Bass*

Realize the following figured bass. Include a harmonic analysis.

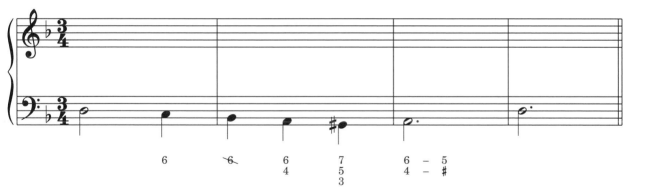

EXERCISE 24.14 *Expanded Pre-Dominants and Augmented Sixth/Diminished Third Chords*

Analyze the excerpts that combine extended pre-dominants and augmented sixth chords. Circle the pre-dominant area; then analyze each sonority.

A. Haydn, Piano Sonata in E major, Hob XVI.31, *Allegretto*

B. Beethoven, String Quartet no. 11 in F minor, "Serioso," op. 95, *Larghetto espressivo*

C. Gluck, Ritornello from *Orpheus and Eurydice*, act 1, no. 6

D. Mussorgsky, *Songs and Dances of Death*, no. 4

ASSIGNMENT 24.6   EXERCISES FOR ENHARMONIC MODULATIONS USING THE AUGMENTED SIXTH CHORD

EXERCISE 24.15   *Analysis of Enharmonic Modulations Using the Dominant Seventh Chord*

STREAMING AUDIO
www.oup.com/us/laitz

Identify the point at which the dominant seventh is transformed enharmonically into an augmented sixth chord in the following musical excerpts. No roman numeral analysis is necessary. Even though you will encounter tonicizations, rather than "modulations," use the pivot-chord labeling technique.

Sample solution:

$$
\begin{array}{ll}
\text{I:} & \boxed{V^7} \\
\text{♭II:} & \boxed{\text{Ger}^6_5}
\end{array}
$$

A.

B.

C. Beethoven, Piano Sonata no. 27 in E major, op. 90, *Nicht zu geschwind und sehr singbar vorzutragen*

D. Schubert, Piano Sonata in A minor, op. 42, D. 845, *Moderato*

E. Schubert, *Originaltänze*, op. 9, no. 14, D. 365

WRITING

EXERCISE 24.16   *Brain Teaser*

Consider the following two harmonies: C–E–G–B♭ and C–E–G–A♯. Determine the key in which these function as a dominant seventh and a German sixth, respectively. Then write a progression that demonstrates each chord's behavior.

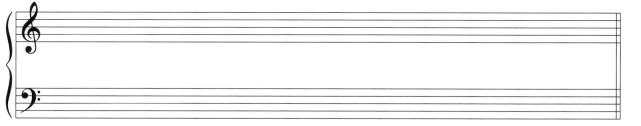

WRITING

EXERCISE 24.17   *Composition*

Write a consequent phrase to the given antecedent to create a parallel progressive period. Incorporate one example of ♭II and an augmented sixth chord. Analyze.

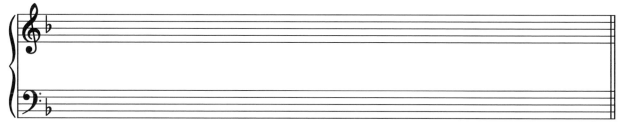

ASSIGNMENT 24.7   EXERCISES FOR THE AUGMENTED SIXTH CHORD AND DIMINISHED THIRD CHORD

EXERCISE 24.18

Complete the following passage in four-voice chorale style. You are given the following:

mm. 1–2: unfigured bass   mm. 3–4: melody harmonization
mm. 5–6: figured bass   mm. 7–8: figured bass + melody

Add the remaining voices and analyze. Include one of each type of augmented sixth chord.

EXERCISE 24.19

STREAMING AUDIO
www.oup.com/us/laitz

Analyze the following examples using roman numerals.

A. Mozart, Piano Trio in G major, K. 564, *Allegretto*

B. Chopin, Mazurka in C♯ minor, op. 63, no. 3

C. Leopold Mozart, from Trio Sonata in E♭ major, op. 1, no. 2, *Andante*

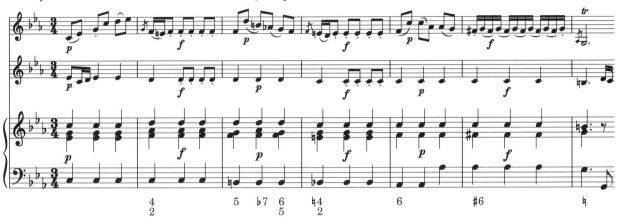

D. Schubert, Symphony no. 8 in B minor, "Unfinished," D. 759, *Andante*

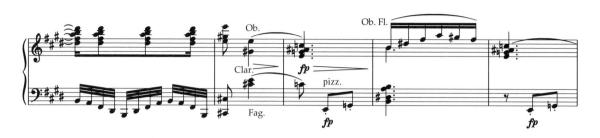

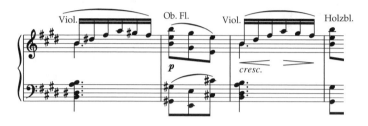

Ternary Form

EXERCISE 25.1   *Ternary and Binary Forms*

There may be some ambiguity between a work cast in ternary form with transitions and retransitions and one that is written in rounded binary form. To compare and contrast these forms, study the following examples. Could these examples be viewed as being either binary or ternary? Listen to and study the pieces to develop an interpretation. Then, make formal diagrams that include the major sections, transitions, and retransitions. Finally, summarize your interpretation in a paragraph.

A. Haydn, Trio, Piano Sonata in D major, Hob XVI.14

Label any sequences and discuss in a sentence or two their function within the passage.

B. Chopin, Mazurka in E minor, op. 17, no. 2, BI 77

1. Discuss examples of the important role that unprepared dissonance plays in this piece.
2. Discuss the phrase–period structure in mm. 1–12 and in mm. 1–24.
3. What is the underlying harmonic motion in mm. 1–12?
4. The material in mm. 25ff contrasts with the material in the first section. One could argue, however, that many of the melodic gestures could be traced back to the first section. Support this assertion with examples; in particular, focus on the opening melody of the *Dolce* section and the chromatic material over the G pedal that follows.

ASSIGNMENT 25.2   ANALYSIS: COMPARISON OF TERNARY AND BINARY FORMS

EXERCISE 25.2   *Ternary and Binary Forms*

STREAMING AUDIO
www.oup.com/us/laitz

Study the piece to be able to develop an interpretation. Next, make a formal diagram that includes the major sections, transitions, and retransitions. Answer the leading questions that accompany the example. Finally, summarize your interpretation in a paragraph.

A. Beethoven, Bagatelle no. 8 in G minor, op. 119, no. 1

1. How many phrases occur in mm. 1–16? Do they combine to form one or more periods?
2. There is an interesting relationship between mm. 1–4 and mm. 5–8. Discuss. *Hint:* Study the relationship between the hands.
3. Given the prominence of the upper-neighbor figure, $\hat{5}$–$\hat{6}$–$\hat{5}$, might this be viewed as a motive? Trace other statements of this figure—both on the surface and below the surface (i.e., migration to the bass and harmonic structure)—and/or any other motivic ideas that you may find interesting.

B. Heinichen, Sonata in C minor for Oboe and Bassoon

Label cadences and sequences.

Larghetto e cantabile

ASSIGNMENT 25.3
ANALYSIS

EXERCISE 25.3 *Ternary and Binary Forms*

STREAMING AUDIO
www.oup.com/us/laitz

Listen to and study the piece carefully, to be able to develop an interpretation. Next, make a formal diagram that includes the major sections, transitions, and retransitions. Answer the leading questions that accompany the example. Finally, summarize your interpretation in a paragraph.

Haydn, String Quartet in F major, op. 74, no. 2, Hob III.73, Menuetto, *Allegro*

1. Provide a two-level harmonic analysis that details (a) the deepest-level tonal relations of the movement and (b) tonicizations within formal sections.
2. What type of period opens the movement? How many phrases are there? How are they linked harmonically?
3. The chromaticism that appears in m. 4 is striking, almost shocking. Haydn often injects chromaticism into the opening of a piece, and, as we have seen in the work of other composers, the chromaticism appears throughout the movement and may be often developed in ways that help explain unusual tonal relations as simply harmonizations, and thus stabilizations, of chromatic pitches. Explore the reappearance of such chromaticism.
4. What is the function of the material in mm. 28–41? What would be a good label for this section?
5. Label and discuss the tonal functions of sequential passages.

CHAPTER 26

Rondo

ASSIGNMENT 26.1
ANALYSIS OF RONDO FORM

EXERCISE 26.1 *Analysis*

STREAMING AUDIO
www.oup.com/us/laitz

Listen to and study the score, make a form diagram, and answer the following questions.

Haydn, Finale, Piano Sonata no. 50 in D major, Hob XVI.37, *Presto ma non troppo*

1. The sectional character of this rondo is enhanced by nested forms that are either ternary or binary types. Label the specific type of these nested forms.
2. Discuss any changes that occur in the restatements of the refrain.
3. One could view the material that begins in m. 29 as derived from earlier material. Explore this possibility.

FINALE

ASSIGNMENT 26.2
ANALYSIS OF RONDO FORM

EXERCISE 26.2 *Analysis*

STREAMING AUDIO
www.oup.com/us/laitz

Rondos appear in a variety of genres, including opera. The following piece is an aria cast in rondo form.

1. Make a formal diagram that includes section labels and key structure. Make sure that you show transitions and retransitions and include measure numbers.
2. Discuss how the highly contrasting sections are demarcated.
3. What is the recurring harmonic pattern called that appears throughout one of the episodes?
4. The material that occurs in m. 108 is interrupted by a section marked *tutti*. What musical role does this interruption play?

Handel, "Vaghe pupille" ("O Lovely Eyes"), from *Orlando*, HWV 31, act 2, scene 9

Vaghe pupille, non piangete, nò,	O lovely eyes, weep no more!
che del pianto ancor nel regno	Because in this realm of woe,
può in ogn' un destar pietà.	It will awaken pity in everyone.
Vaghe pupille, non piangete, nò!	O lovely eyes, flow no more!
Ma sì, pupille, che sordo al	But yes, eyes, endure your
vostro incanto	enchantment
ho un core d'adamanto,	I have an adamant heart
nè calma il mio furor, nò.	And my fury will not be calmed.
Ma sì, pupille, piangete, sì.	But yes, eyes, weep forever.

A tempo di Gavotta

EXERCISE 26.3

A. Here is the opening of a finale from an early Mozart piano sonata, but with a repeat mark inserted in m. 8 where none appears in the original score. Although the movement is set in sonata form, its opening theme is decidedly rondoesque, and becomes unambiguously so with the added repeat mark (compare it with the Handel work in Exercise 26.2). Over the course of the assignments of this chapter, we will construct a rondo from Mozart's theme.

Analyze these measures, using two levels. On a separate sheet of manuscript paper, copy this selection. Write a simple four- or eight-measure digression and a′ section ending in the tonic, to make it into a small binary form; you might use the opening of the Handel as a model. This will be your refrain. Notate some ornamental variants or truncations you might use when the refrain returns.

Mozart, Piano Sonata in E♭ major, K. 282, *Allegro*

B. Here are three openings that could begin the first episode of your rondo based on the finale of Mozart's K. 282. Choose one of these openings (or, alternatively, invent one of your own) and compose a binary structure to act as the B section. Observe that in 1 and 2 the voice leading of the melody follows that of the tenor in the accompaniment, but in 3 the melody is independent. The continuation marks shown at the end of each fragment provide suggestions for the opening pitches of the following material.

In order to give the impression of an episode, you should consider employing some chromatic harmonies to contrast this section with the stability and simplicity of the refrain. You might use the first episode of the Beethoven's String Quartet in C minor, op. 18, no. 4, *Allegro* (see the *Anthology*), as a model. You can choose to write a closed binary form, rounded or otherwise, or to transition from the first episode into the refrain. You might write out the refrain that follows this episode, perhaps with some alterations.

C. Here are three openings that could begin the second episode of your rondo based on the finale of Mozart's K. 282. As in the Handel (Exercise 26.2), our C section will be larger than either the previous episode or the refrain, and will lead to the final statement of the A section.

Choose one of these openings (or, alternatively, invent one of your own) and compose a binary form. When choosing or writing the beginning of your second episode, keep in mind the material used for your first episode, as well as your refrain: Is there enough of a contrast of mood, key, texture, register, etc.?

Add a transitional phrase that leads toward the dominant of the home key using a harmonic sequence or other large directed progression. Ensure that this dominant links well to the beginning of the refrain.

Finally, properly order your refrains and episodes to create a rondo movement.

Sonata Form

ANALYSIS

EXERCISE 27.1   *Beethoven, Piano Sonata no. 1 in F minor, op. 2, no. 1,* **Allegro**

STREAMING AUDIO
www.oup.com/us/laitz

Following is a movement cast in sonata form. Listen to the piece, then make a formal diagram that includes the location, name, and key of each section. Finally, answer the questions concerning the piece.

1. Although this is Beethoven's first piano sonata with an opus (he wrote several earlier sonatas while in Bonn), it has many unusual characteristics. For example, the first tonal area can be viewed as being exceptionally short, while the beginning of the second tonal area might be considered to balance the short FTA by its considerable length. Discuss these and other unusual features of this sonata.
2. Beethoven builds remarkable energy in mm. 1–8. Discuss how he accomplishes this by focusing on harmonic rhythm.
3. The E♮ is left conspicuously hanging in m. 8. Some composers, including Beethoven, created connections between phrases and even sections of a work by endowing specific pitches with associative power. Explore this possibility in this movement, beginning with the E♮^{5} in m. 8.
4. What type of sequence appears in the transition? Where is the first authentic cadence in the STA? Is this unusual?
5. There are several sequences in the development. Label each.
6. One might view most of the development to lie in the key of A♭ (III). Given this, list any keys that Beethoven tonicizes in relation to A♭. Does A♭ lead directly to the retransition, or is there another key that links A♭ and the retransition's dominant?
7. This sonata illustrates how an initial surface motive can control almost all of the movement's subsequent melodic and harmonic material. Shown is a reduction of mm. 1–8.

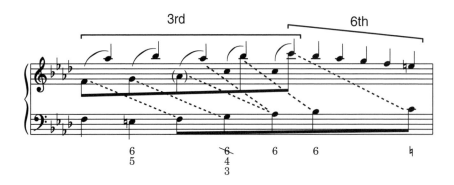

The opening ascending arpeggiation in the right hand moves to A♭⁵, followed by a turn figure around F. It is repeated a step higher and moves to B♭, followed by a turn around G. Both A♭⁵ (m. 5) and the B♭⁵ (m. 6) are marked *sforzando* and ascend to the C (m. 7), which is marked *fortissimo*. This ascent to C is balanced by a descent of a sixth from C⁶ to the hanging E♭⁵.

The bass voice also exhibits a melodic pattern in mm. 1–8. The F³ is prolonged by its lower neighbor, E♮³, before it rises to C⁴ by stepwise motion. In fact, this same fifth ascent is manifested in the upper voice, by the F⁴ (m. 1) moving to G⁴ (m. 3), to A♭⁴ (m. 5), to B♭⁴ (m. 6), and finally to C⁵ (m. 7). We can now understand that by delaying the ascent in the bass for one measure, the neighboring V⁶₃, (m. 3) transforms what would have been parallel octaves, resulting from the fifth ascent between the two voices, into a canon between the two voices.

Might this motivic sixth in the FTA also occur in other formal sections of the sonata? You may wish to look not only at the surface of thematic events, but also at any lines that occur below the surface, such as between the beginning and ending points of sequences. You could even explore the development for the opening motive's deep-level repetition, a feature that we also saw in Mozart's B♭-major sonata K. 333, which was discussed in the text. Do not ignore rhythmic correspondences.

ASSIGNMENT 27.2
ANALYSIS OF SONATA FORM

ANALYSIS

EXERCISE 27.2 *Haydn, String Quartet in G minor, "Horseman," op. 74, no. 3, Hob III.74,* **Allegro**

STREAMING AUDIO
www.oup.com/us/laitz

Make a formal diagram that represents the entire piece as well as the sections. Include keys and measure numbers.

1. What in the music might have provided the impetus for the subtitle "Horseman"?
2. Discuss any motives that you feel are important. Consider the possibility that such motives might take the form of something as simple as a specific interval.

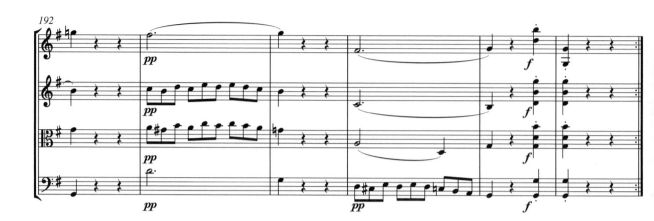

CHAPTER 28

New Harmonic Tendencies

ASSIGNMENT 28.1   EXERCISES FOR TONAL AMBIGUITY (INCLUDING MIXTURE, SEMITONAL VOICE LEADING, RECIPROCAL PROCESS, AND ENHARMONIC PUNS)

EXERCISE 28.1   *Analysis*

STREAMING AUDIO
www.oup.com/us/laitz

The following excerpts contain ambiguities resulting from modal mixture, semitonal voice leading, the reciprocal process, and enharmonic puns. Bracket the area or areas in which tonal ambiguity occurs. Label the type of ambiguity, and answer any accompanying questions.

A. Wagner, *Das Rheingold*, act 1, scene 3 (Alberich demonstrates the magical powers of the Tarnhelm)
In what key is this example? Is there a functional harmonic progression? Begin by looking at the close of the excerpt.

Helm: ob sich der   Zau - ber auch zeigt?   Nacht   und Ne - bel
head: now will   the   spell   al - so speed?   Night   and dark - ness

B. Beethoven, Symphony no. 7 in A major, op. 92, *Vivace* and *Presto*
   The first excerpt begins on V/A. What key succeeds A major, and how is it secured? The second
   excerpt also illustrates a tonal motion. Compare and contrast the two methods of tonicization.

1. *Vivace*

2. *Presto*

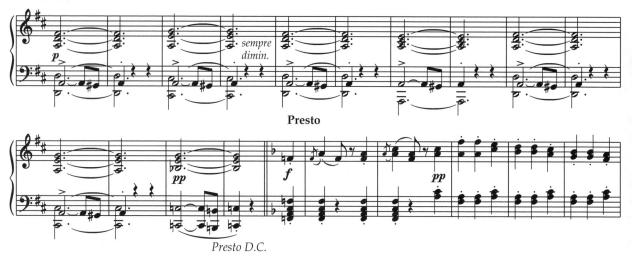

C. Brahms, "Mein Herz ist schwer" ("My Heart Is Heavy"), op. 94, no. 3
  This song is in G minor; discuss the tonic's strength and function at the close.

Herz ____ ist schwer, ____ mein Au - ge wacht, mein
heart ____ is heavy, ____ my eyes are awake, my

Herz ist schwer, mein Au - ge wacht. _
heart is heavy, my eyes are awake. _

WRITING

EXERCISE 28.2 *Figured Bass*

Fill in inner voices and include a second-level analysis.

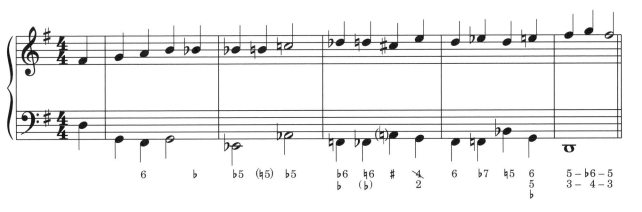

ASSIGNMENT 28.2   EXERCISES FOR ENHARMONIC USAGE OF DIMINISHED SEVENTH CHORDS AND OFF-TONIC BEGINNINGS/DOUBLE TONALITY

ANALYSIS

EXERCISE 28.3   *Enharmonically Reinterpreted Diminished Seventh Chords*

STREAMING AUDIO
www.oup.com/us/laitz

Mark the pivot in the following examples, which modulate by means of an enharmonically reinterpreted diminished seventh chord.

A.

B.

C. Wolf, "Verschling' der Abgrund meines liebsten Hütte" ("May the Abyss Swallow Up My Beloved's Cottage"), *Italienisches Liederbuch*, no. 45

Hüt-te,

p _____ *cresc.*

WRITING

EXERCISE 28.4   *Figured Bass*

Realize the following figured bass, which contains an enharmonic modulation that uses the diminished seventh chord. Analyze, including the pivot chord.

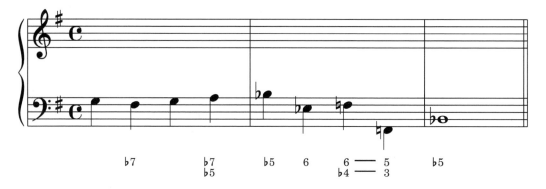

ASSIGNMENT 28.3   MORE ENHARMONICALLY REINTERPRETED DIMINISHED SEVENTH CHORDS

EXERCISE 28.5   *Analysis of Enharmonically Reinterpreted Diminished Seventh Chords*

Mark the pivot in the following examples, which modulate by means of an enharmonically reinterpreted diminished seventh chord. Analyze the remaining chords with roman numerals.

A.

B.

EXERCISE 28.6   *Figured Bass*

Realize the following figured bass, which contains an enharmonic modulation that uses the diminished seventh chord. Analyze, including the pivot chord.

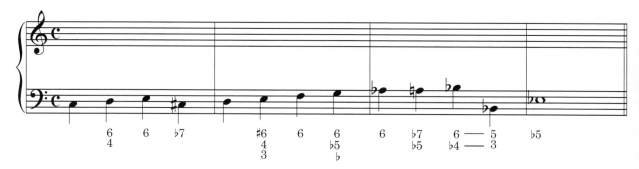

EXERCISE 28.7   *Composition*

Using an enharmonically reinterpreted diminished seventh chord, write a modulating consequent phrase to the given antecedent phrase. Note that the diminished seventh chord is prepared in the antecedent phrase. Analyze, and play your solution.

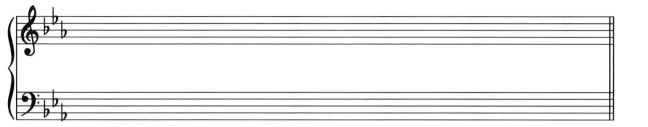

ASSIGNMENT 28.4   ENHARMONICALLY REINTERPRETED DIMINISHED SEVENTH CHORDS

ANALYSIS

EXERCISE 28.8   *Enharmonically Reinterpreted Diminished Seventh Chords*

STREAMING AUDIO
www.oup.com/us/laitz

Mark the pivot in the following examples, which modulate by means of an enharmonically reinterpreted diminished seventh chord.

A. Wagner, Overture, *Der fliegende Holländer* (*The Flying Dutchman*)

B. Beethoven, Symphony no. 2 in D major, op. 36, *Larghetto*

Begin by finding cadences, then determine how the reinterpreted diminished seventh secures the key.

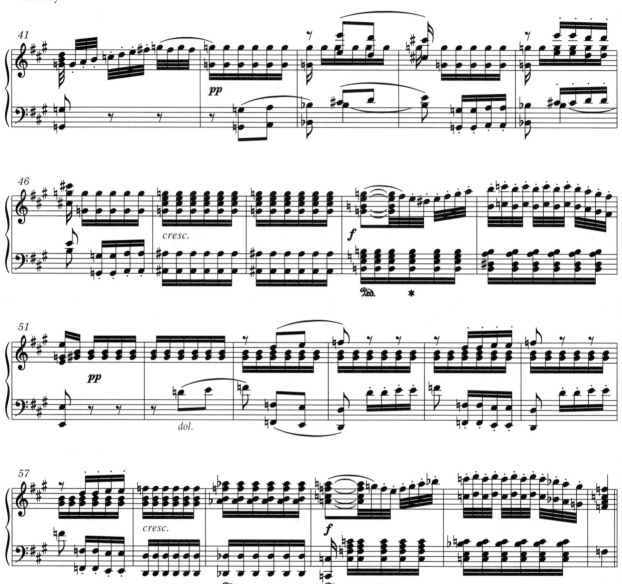

WRITING

EXERCISE 28.9   *Figured Bass*

Realize the following figured bass, which contains an enharmonic modulation that uses the diminished seventh chord. Analyze, including the pivot chord.

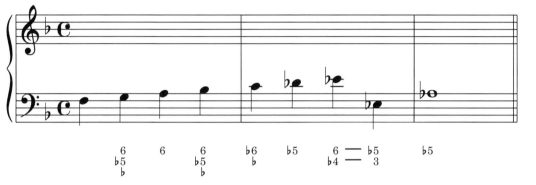

ASSIGNMENT 28.5   OFF-TONIC BEGINNINGS; MODEL COMPOSITION

EXERCISE 28.10   *Analysis*

STREAMING AUDIO
www.oup.com/us/laitz

Analyze the following examples, which do not begin on the tonic. Determine how best to interpret their off-tonic structure within the overall key scheme.

A. Lamm, "Saturday in the Park"

B. Schubert, Waltz, 12 *Ländler*, op. 171, no. 4, D. 790

C. Schubert, Waltz, *18 German Dances and Ecossaises*, op. 33, no. 5, D. 783

D. Mendelssohn, "Wedding March," *Midsummer's Night Dream*, op. 61

EXERCISE 28.11   *Composition*

Sing or play the following tune to determine the harmonic rhythm, implied harmonies, cadences, and form. Harmonize it and create an accompanimental pattern.

ASSIGNMENT 28.6   EXERCISES FOR AUGMENTED TRIADS AND ALTERED V⁷ CHORDS

ANALYSIS

EXERCISE 28.12 *Analysis of Augmented Triads and Altered V⁷ Chords*

STREAMING AUDIO
www.oup.com/us/laitz

Analyze the following examples, which contain augmented triads and altered dominant seventh chords. Determine whether the dissonant pitches are embellishing tones (usually passing tones) or chordal members. Use figured bass notation. Passing tones are represented by a horizontal line (e.g., "5— #5"). Chromatic alterations of chord members are shown by placing the alterations before the arabic numbers.

For example:

$$V^{\sharp 7}_{5} \quad \text{or} \quad V^{\flat 7}_{5}$$

A.

B.

C.

WRITING

EXERCISE 28.13 *Altered Triads and Seventh Chords*

Based on the roman numerals and figured bass, write a progression in chorale style.

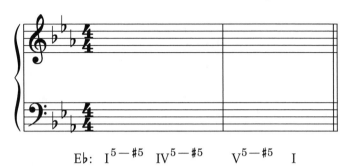

E♭: $I^{5-\sharp 5}$ $IV^{5-\sharp 5}$ $V^{5-\sharp 5}$ I

ASSIGNMENT 28.7
EXERCISES FOR ALTERED V⁷ CHORDS

ANALYSIS

EXERCISE 28.14   *Analysis of Augmented Triads and Altered V⁷ Chords*

STREAMING AUDIO
www.oup.com/us/laitz

Analyze the following examples, which contain augmented triads and altered dominant seventh chords. Determine whether the dissonant pitches are embellishing tones (usually passing tones) or chordal members. Use figured bass notation. Passing tones are represented by a horizontal line (e.g., "5— #5"). Chromatic alterations of chord members are shown by placing the alterations before the arabic numbers.

For example:

$$V^{\sharp 7}_{\sharp 5} \qquad \text{or} \qquad V^{\flat 7}_{3}$$

A. Schumann, "Fabel" ("Fable"), *Phantasiestücke*, op. 12, no. 6
   Be aware that this excerpt does not begin in the tonic.

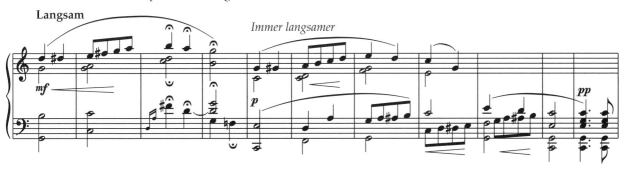

B. Beethoven, Variation XIV, *Diabelli Variations*, op. 120
   Suspensions create the dissonant harmony that appears on the downbeat of m. 3.

C. Puccini, *Madama Butterfly*, act 1
What sequence does Puccini use?

EXERCISE 28.15   *Writing*

Based on the roman numerals and figured bass, write a progression in chorale style.

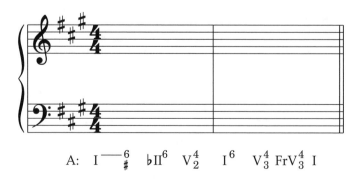

ASSIGNMENT 28.8   EXERCISES FOR COMMON-TONE DIMINISHED SEVENTH AND AUGMENTED SIXTH CHORDS

ANALYSIS

EXERCISE 28.16   *Chromatic Common-Tone Harmonies*

Diminished sevenths and augmented sixths may be used either as common-tone chords (in which they contrapuntally prolong an underlying harmony) or as functional chords (in which they participate in the harmonic progression (i.e., augmented sixths function as pre-dominants and diminished sevenths function as dominants). Employ a two-level analysis, making sure that you distinguish between contrapuntal and harmonic functions.

A.

B.

C.

EXERCISE 28.17   *Writing Common-Tone Harmonies*

Use common-tone diminished sevenths to embellish the tonic and dominant.

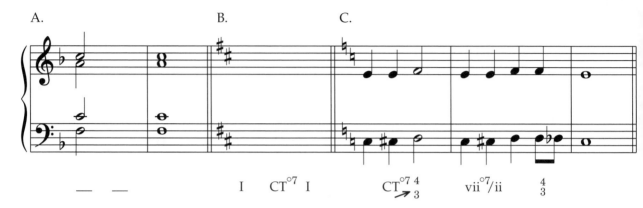

EXERCISE 28.18   *Composition Project*

Realize and analyze the unfigured bass, turning it into a florid eight-measure period by adding a bass accompaniment figure and decorated melody based on the given soprano pitches.

ASSIGNMENT 28.9   EXERCISES FOR COMMON-TONE DIMINISHED SEVENTH AND AUGMENTED SIXTH CHORDS

ANALYSIS

EXERCISE 28.19   *Chromatic Common-Tone Harmonies*

STREAMING AUDIO
www.oup.com/us/laitz

Employ a two-level analysis, making sure that you distinguish between contrapuntal and harmonic functions.

A. Chopin, Nocturne in A♭ major, op. 32, no. 2, BI 106

B. Brahms, "Salamander," op. 107, no. 2

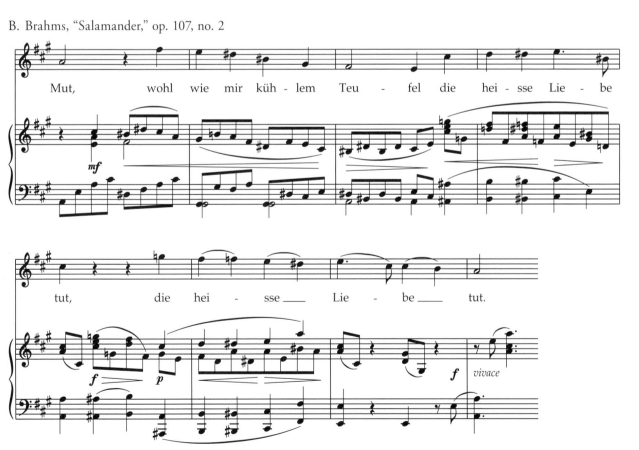

C. Brahms, Symphony no. 3 in F major, op. 90, *Allegro con brio*

WRITING

EXERCISE 28.20   *Writing Common-Tone Harmonies*

Use common-tone diminished sevenths to embellish tonic and dominant in chorale style.

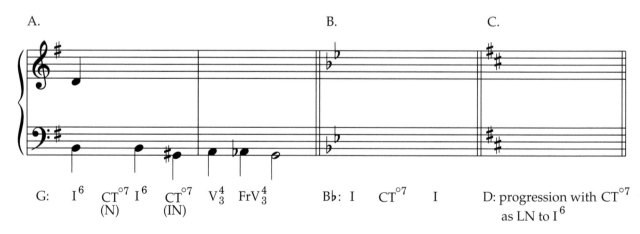

EXERCISE 28.21   *Melody Harmonization*

Set each soprano fragment in four voices, and include at least three chromatic chords in each example. You may use modal mixture, applied chords, common-tone harmonies, altered dominant and dominant seventh chords, ♭II chords, and augmented sixth chords. Analyze.

A.

b:

B.

d:

ASSIGNMENT 28.10 COMMON-TONE HARMONIES AND COMPOSITION PROJECT

WRITING

EXERCISE 28.22 *Unfigured Bass*

Add inner voices to create a four-voice texture. Use common-tone diminished seventh chords where possible. Analyze.

tonic expansion

EXERCISE 28.23 *Melody Harmonization*

Set the soprano line in four voices. Include at least four chromatic chords. You may use modal mixture, applied chords, common-tone harmonies, altered dominant and dominant seventh chords, ♭II chords, and augmented sixth chords. Analyze.

d:

WRITING

EXERCISE 28.24   *Composition Project*

This assignment focuses first on generating a harmonic progression and then on transforming the progression into a piece for a melody instrument or voice with piano accompaniment. The passage must be at least one period in length and consist of at least two four-measure phrases. It must:

1. Modulate to a chromatic key of your choice and back to the original key. Each of the keys must incorporate a pivot chord that moves either to the new key or back to the original key. Use either a mixture chord or an enharmonically respelled augmented sixth as one of the pivots.
2. Include at least two examples of each of the following chords or procedures: plagal relations, altered triads and dominants, and common-tone harmonies.

Begin your work by determining a good progression, then animate it by working out an accompanimental pattern (for keyboard). Finally, add a melody above (refer to the following excerpts from Schubert songs and Beethoven violin sonatas) that provide compositional models.

A. Beethoven, Violin Sonata in A major, op. 30, no. 1, *Adagio molto espressivo*

B. Beethoven, Violin Sonata in F major, "Spring," op. 24, *Allegro*

C. Schubert, "Des Müllers Blumen" ("The Miller's Flowers"), *Die schöne Müllerin*, op. 25, no. 9, D. 795

Am Bach viel klei - ne Blu - men stehn, aus hel - len, blau - en Au - gen sehn
Dicht un - ter ih - rem Fen - ster - lein, da will ich pflanzen die Blu - men ein
Und wenn sie tät die Äug - lein zu und schlaft in sü - ßer, sü - ßer Ruh

pp

D. Schubert, "Auf dem Flusse" ("By the Stream"), *Winterreise*, D. 911

Langsam (Lento)

staccato

p

Der du so lu - stig

6

rausch - test, du hel - ler, wil - der Fluß, wie still bist du ge - wor - den, gibst

(sehr leise) **(pp)**

ppp

CHAPTER 29

Melodic and Harmonic Symmetry Combine: Chromatic Sequences

ASSIGNMENT 29.1
EXERCISES FOR CHROMATIC SEQUENCES

EXERCISE 29.1 *Analysis of Chromatic Sequences*

STREAMING AUDIO
www.oup.com/us/laitz

Bracket and label each sequence in the following exercises. Circle each bass note involved in the sequence. Do not analyze each harmony within the sequence—only the harmonies that begin and end the sequence. Then determine the underlying tonal progression.

A. Carissimi, "Et ululantes filii Ammon" ("And Weeping, the Children of Ammon"), from *Jephthah*

B. Wagner, *Rienzi*, Overture

C. Schubert, Symphony no. 4 in C minor, "Tragic," D. 417, *Allegro*

D. Schumann, Symphony no. 1 in B♭ major, "Spring," op. 38, *Andante un poco maestoso—Allegro molto vivace*

WRITING

EXERCISE 29.2   *Pattern Completion*

1. Study the following sequential models, then write three copies for each sequence.
2. End with a strong cadence. Label each sequence type.

A.

B. Three voices only

C. The model begins on beat 3.

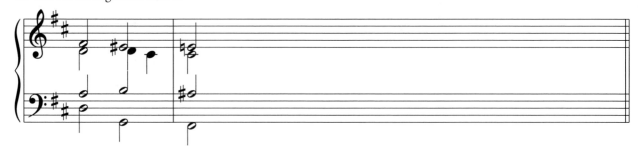

D.

ASSIGNMENT 29.2
EXERCISES FOR CHROMATIC SEQUENCES

EXERCISE 29.3   *Analysis*

STREAMING AUDIO
www.oup.com/us/laitz

Bracket and label each sequence in the following exercises. Circle each bass note involved in the sequence. Analyze only the harmonies that begin and end the sequence and then determine the underlying tonal progression.

A. Mendelssohn, Prelude in B minor, op. 104, no. 2

B. Beethoven, Symphony no. 1 in C major, op. 21, Menuetto

C. Donizetti, "Esci fuggi," from *Lucia di Lammermoor*, act 2, scene 5

229

tà,	sì,	-quan	- te	vol	-tead	un	so	- lo	tor	-men	to
thral,	*ah,*	*heav'n*	*- ly*	*love*	*hath*	*a*	*balm*	*for*	*thy*	*sor*	*- row,*

| dra, | sì, | sì, | la | mac | - chia d'ol | - trag | - gio sì | ne | - ro |
| *call,* | *the* | *maid* | *- en's* | *heart* | *hath* | *by* | *thee* | *- been per-* | *vert - ed* |

| drà, | sì, | sì, | la | mac | - chia d'ol | - trag | - gio sì | ne | - ro, __ | col | tuo |
| *call,* | *the* | *maid* | *- en's* | *heart* | *hath* | *by* | *thee* | *been per- vert* | *- ed, __* | *We* | *have* |

Più allegro

WRITING

EXERCISE 29.4   *Unfigured and Figured Basses*

Complete the unfigured bass exercise (A) in *three* voices and include 7–6 suspensions. Complete the two figured bass exercises (B and C) in *four* voices. Label any sequences. Be aware of modulations.

A.

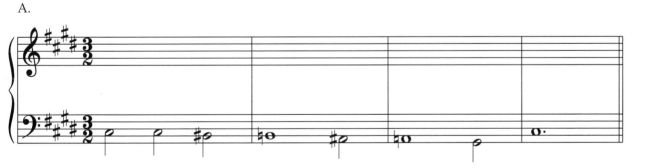

B.

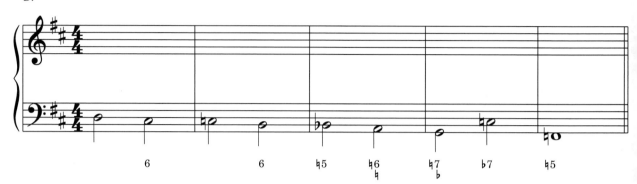

C.

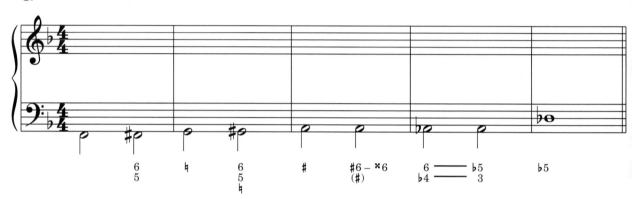

ASSIGNMENT 29.3
EXERCISES FOR CHROMATIC SEQUENCES

EXERCISE 29.5 *Analysis*

STREAMING AUDIO
www.oup.com/us/laitz

These excerpts from Chopin and Beethoven contain multiple sequences. Circle and label each.

A. Chopin, Piano Sonata in C minor, op. 4, BI 23, *Allegro maestoso*

B. Beethoven, Piano Concerto no. 1 in C major, op. 15, *Allegro*

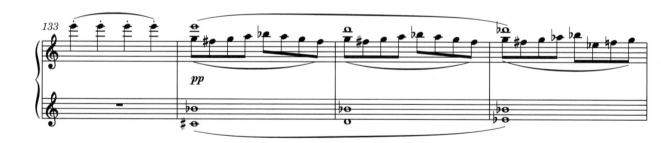

WRITING

EXERCISE 29.6 *Extended Illustrations*

Complete any two of the following tasks.

A. Write a three-voice progression in F♯ minor that begins on tonic, moves through a sequence of descending six-three chords with 7–6 suspensions and chromatic bass, and leads to a cadential six-four chord. The dominant will move deceptively to a mixture chord, followed by a cadence in a chromatic third–related key.

B. Write a three-voice progression in E♭ major that begins with an A2 (−3/+4) sequence using applied V⁶ chords that resolve to major triads. This sequence will move from I to III. Once you have arrived on III, treat it as a temporary tonic. Expand and cadence on III.

C. Write a three-voice progression in E♭ major that begins with a chromatic A2 (−3/+4) sequence, this time employing augmented triads that will serve as applied chords to the next chromatic chords. Move from I to III (e.g., I . . . ♭II . . . ♮II . . .). Don't modulate to III, but find a convenient way to get back to tonic and cadence there.

D. Write a four-voice progression in G major that initially moves from I to iv via a chromatic D2 (−4/+3) sequence. Expand this pre-dominant with a voice exchange that includes an augmented sixth chord. Close with a PAC.

ASSIGNMENT 29.4   EXERCISES FOR CONTRARY-MOTION CHROMATICISM

EXERCISE 29.7   *Analysis of Chromatic Sequences and Contrary-Motion Chromaticism*

STREAMING AUDIO
www.oup.com/us/laitz

Label and bracket sequences in the following examples, and analyze any harmonies outside of the sequence.

A. Brahms, "Salome," op. 69, no. 8
   Develop the idea that the chromaticism in this example might have been motivated by the text.

B. Schubert, Violin Sonata in D major, D. 384, *Allegro*

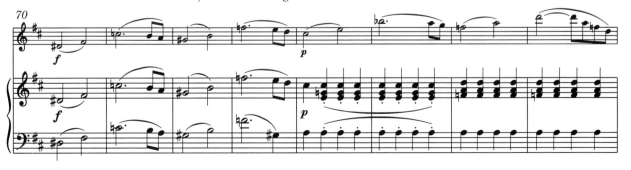

EXERCISE 29.8   *Figured Bass*

Realize the following figured basses. The first example includes a complete soprano, but the second example presents an incomplete soprano line. Analyze.

A.

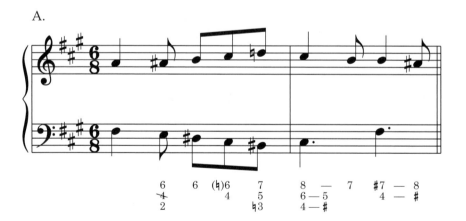

B.

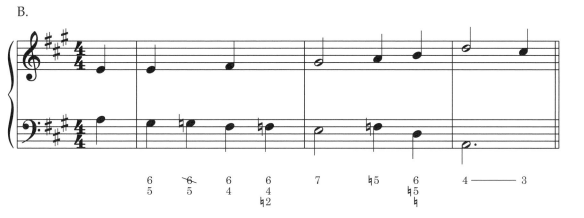

ASSIGNMENT 29.5   EXERCISES FOR CONTRARY-MOTION CHROMATICISM

EXERCISE 29.9   *Analysis of Chromatic Sequences and Contrary-Motion Chromaticism*

STREAMING AUDIO
www.oup.com/us/laitz

Label and bracket sequences in the following examples and analyze harmonies outside the sequence.

A. Schubert, String Quartet in G major, D. 887, *Allegro molto moderato*

B. Schubert, "Sanctus," Mass no. 6 in E♭ major, D. 950

EXERCISE 29.10   *Figured Bass*

Realize the following figured bass. Analyze.

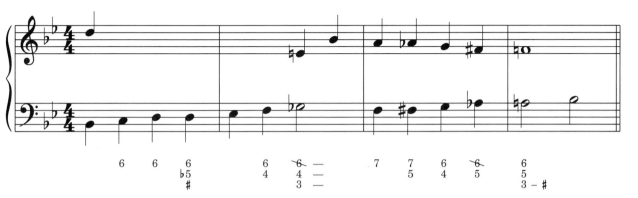

WRITING

EXERCISE 29.11   *Soprano Harmonization*

Harmonize in four voices the following soprano melodies; include each of the required elements. Analyze.

A.

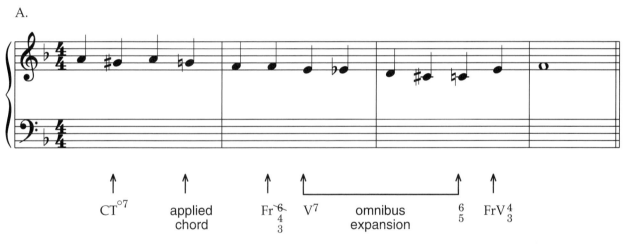

B.

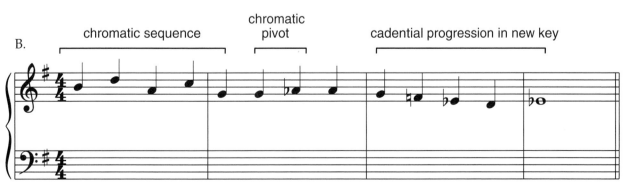

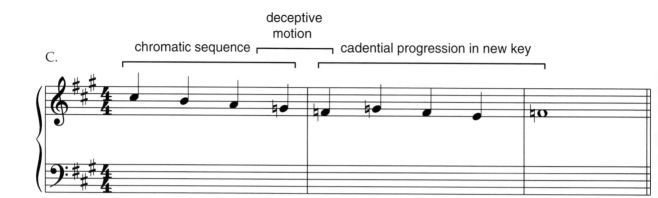

ASSIGNMENT 29.6 EXERCISES FOR NONSEQUENTIAL PROGRESSIONS THAT DIVIDE THE OCTAVE EVENLY

EXERCISE 29.12 *Analysis of Progressions that Divide the Octave Evenly*

STREAMING AUDIO
www.oup.com/us/laitz

Use second-level analytical brackets and specify whether each of the following excerpts illustrates an example of a sequential or nonsequential progression that divides the octave equally (into either major or minor thirds, each step of which is tonicized).

A. Wolf, "Und steht Ihr früh am Morgen auf" ("And When You Rise Early"), *Italienisches Liederbuch*, no. 34

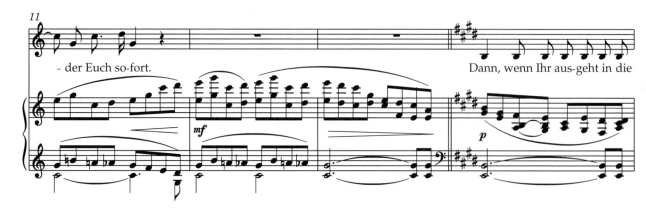

B. Wagner, *Lohengrin* act 1, scene 2

Allmählich noch etwas langsamer

C. Puccini, Tosca, act 2 (end)

EXERCISE 29.13 *Figured Bass*

Realize the following figured bass in four voices. Include a roman numeral analysis.
Mark all sequences and tonicizations.

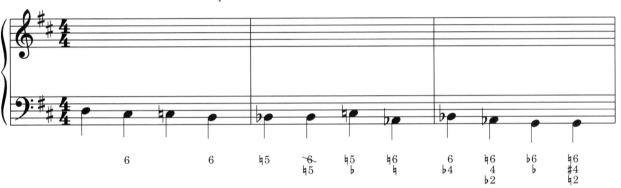

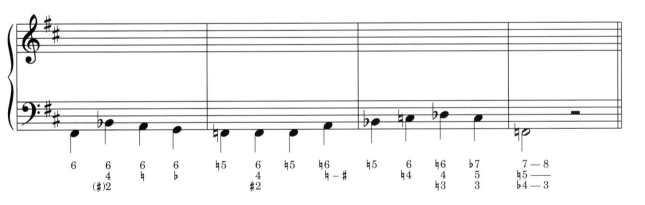

ASSIGNMENT 29.7   EXERCISES FOR LARGE-SCALE TONAL MOTIONS THAT DIVIDE THE OCTAVE EVENLY

ANALYSIS

EXERCISE 29.14   *Tchaikovsky, Symphony no. 4 in F minor, op. 36, Scherzo, Pizzicato ostinato*

STREAMING AUDIO
www.oup.com/us/laitz

Following are several thematic and tonal areas as well as transitions that link formal sections of this famous movement. Determine the means by which each new tonal area is secured. Then, interpret the large-scale tonal structure of the movement based on the unfolding keys. Summarize the results of your analysis in a few sentences.

A.

EXERCISE 29.15 *Unfigured Bass*

Consider the harmonic implications of the following two-voice counterpoint. Analyze and add the inner voices to create an SATB texture.

ASSIGNMENT 29.8
EXERCISES FOR INTERVALLIC CELLS

EXERCISE 29.16   *Figured Bass*

Realize the following figured bass in four voices. Analyze and summarize in a sentence or two any large-scale tonal patterns.

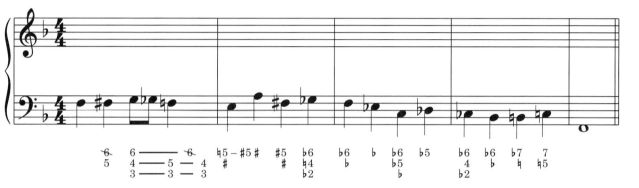

EXERCISE 29.17   *Intervallic Cells: Brahms, Intermezzo in F♯ minor, op. 76, no.1*

STREAMING AUDIO
www.oup.com/us/laitz

Trace repetitions of the circled intervallic cell labeling the transformation of each as follows: T (transposition), I (inversion), R (retrograde), RI (retrograde inversion), A (augmentation), and D (diminution). Repetitions may not be strict; for example, intervallic size between each pair of members of the cell may not be exact.

ASSIGNMENT 29.9   EXERCISES FOR INTERVALLIC CELLS AND HARMONIC DIVISIONS OF THE OCTAVE

EXERCISE 29.18   *Intervallic Cells in Symmetrical and Asymmetrical Tonal Contexts*

STREAMING AUDIO
www.oup.com/us/laitz

Berg, "Nacht" ("Night"), from *Sieben frühe Lieder* (*Seven Early Songs*), no. 1

This is the first in a collection of songs written just as Berg's compositional voice was beginning to emerge. While composed in the shadow of the nineteenth century, these songs also look to the future. We will focus only on the song's opening measures, in which an ambiguous structure gradually gives way to a more traditional harmonic progression—a vivid juxtaposition of old and new styles. Consider the following issues in your analysis.

1. Recall that structure—and with it, clarity—is often postponed until the end of musical units.
2. Is the key signature unnecessary, or is Berg using it traditionally? If Berg incorporates it traditionally, you may be able to make some harmonic sense out of the opening of the song.
3. Recall from our earlier studies that the whole-tone scale comprises intervals whose number of half steps is evenly divided by 2: for example, a major second (2 half steps), major third (4), tritone (6), minor sixth (8), and minor seventh (10).
4. Notice how the song begins with a single pitch, E, to which is added an F♯. Is there some additive process that generates subsequent sonorities?
5. Study the translation of the text. Is Berg sensitive to its sentiments? If so, how?

Dämmern Wolken über Nacht und Tal,	Over night and valley the clouds grow dark,
Nebel schweben, Wasser rauschen sacht.	Mists are hovering, water rushes by.
Nun entschleiert sich's mit einemmal:	Now the covering veil is lifted:
O gib acht! Gib acht!	Come look! Look!
Weites . . .	Distant . . .

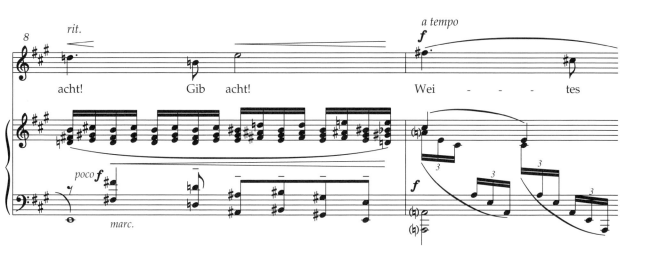

B. Chopin, Mazurka in B major, op. 56, no. 1, BI 153

You are given the opening passages for each of the large sections in Chopin's Mazurka. What is the probable form? Focus on tricky harmonic areas, such as the sequential passage that opens the piece and the transitional and re-transitional passages that link larger sections. In a few sentences, discuss what appears to be the large-scale tonal structure of the entire piece.

B1.

ASSIGNMENT 29.10   EXERCISES FOR DIVISION OF THE OCTAVE AND INTERVALLIC CELL

ANALYSIS

EXERCISE 29.19   *Analysis of Excerpts from Wagner's Operas*

STREAMING AUDIO
www.oup.com/us/laitz

Examples from four of Wagner's operas, *Der fliegende Holländer* (*The Flying Dutchman*), *Parsifal*, *Tristan und Isolde*, and *Die Walküre*, are given. Analyze each excerpt, then compare and contrast the final three.

A. Prelude to *Der fliegende Holländer* (*The Flying Dutchman*)

B. "Zum letzten Liebesmahle" ("At the Last Meal of Love"), from *Parsifal*, act 1

C. "Mild und leise" ("Mildly and Gently") (opening of "Liebestod"), from *Tristan und Isolde*, act 3, scene 3

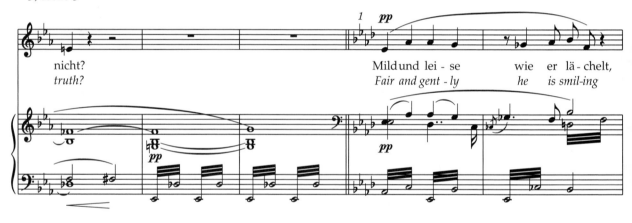

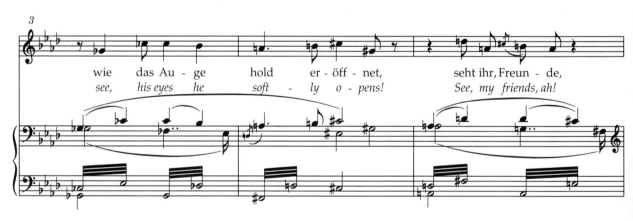

säh't ihr's nicht?   Im - mer lich - ter   wie_____ er leuch - tet,
see ye not?   *how he, bright and*   *bright - - er burn - ing,*

stern   um - strah - let hoch sich hebt?
stream - - ing star - light, heaves him high?

D. "Leb' wohl" ("Farewell"), "Wotan's Farewell," from *Die Walküre*, act 3, scene 3

schlies - sen   Denn so kehrt der Gott sich dir
e - ver.   *For so turns the god now from*

ab,   so   küsst er die   Gott - heit von   dir!
thee,   so   kis - ses thy   god - hood a - way!

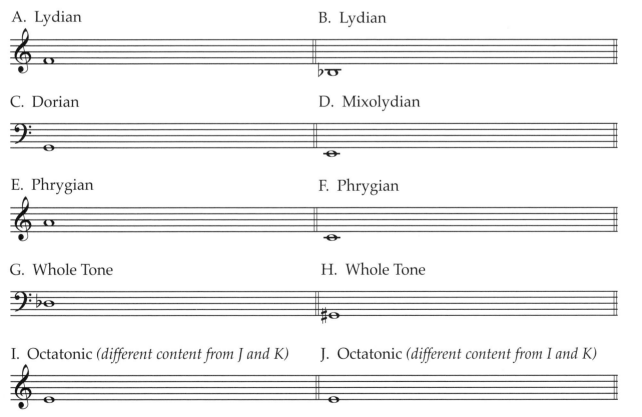

CHAPTER 30

Vestiges of Common Practice and the Rise of a New Sound World

EXERCISE 30.1 *Scale Notation*

Notate the specified scales/modes starting on the given notes.

A. Lydian

B. Lydian

C. Dorian

D. Mixolydian

E. Phrygian

F. Phrygian

G. Whole Tone

H. Whole Tone

I. Octatonic *(different content from J and K)*

J. Octatonic *(different content from I and K)*

K. Octatonic *(different content from I and J)*   L. Octatonic *(same content as J)*

ASSIGNMENT 30.2
EXERCISE FOR ARRANGING

EXERCISE 30.2   *Theme and Variations*

Sing and study this melody by Beethoven:

Imagine an arrangement of this melody for piano in classical style:

Now make your own arrangements of the melody using post-tonal resources as specified:

A. Use triadic extensions (as suggested for measure 1). When forming your harmonies, feel free to use notes from outside the key of F major.

B. Harmonize the melody with quartal and/or quintal sonorities. Avoid the monotony of simply repeating the same chord structure underneath every melody note.

C. Harmonize the melody with whole-tone harmony. Feel free to move back and forth between the two whole-tone collections, but don't feel obligated to make every melody note a member of the same whole-tone collection as the sonority underneath.

D. Rewrite the melody so that it remains within a single octatonic collection (while retaining its rhythm and contour). Then harmonize it with subsets of that same octatonic collection.

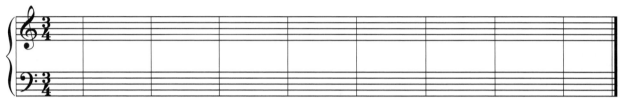

ASSIGNMENT 30.3
EXERCISE FOR COLLECTIONS

EXERCISE 30.3   *Collection Identification and Manipulation*

Identify the given collection. Use stems and beams to extract the specified subsets. The first one is done for you.

A. Collection: _____WHOLE-TONE_____. Extract two different augmented triads.

B. Collection: _____. Extract two different fully diminished 7th chords.

C. Collection: _____. Extract four different major triads.

D. Collection: _____. Extract two different minor triads.

E. Collection: _____. Extract three different major triads (stems up)
and three different minor triads (stems down).

F. Collection: _____. Extract three additional instances of the 2–3 trichord.

G. Collection: _____. How many different 2–4 trichords can you extract?

ASSIGNMENT 30.4
EXERCISES FOR ANALYSIS

EXERCISE 30.4   *Analysis I*

STREAMING AUDIO
www.oup.com/us/laitz

In one or two sentences, discuss pitch centricity at the end of Charles Ives's *Concord Sonata* (1919). Circle and describe five different examples of chordal extensions.

Concord Sonata

C. Ives
(1919)

EXERCISE 30.5 *Analysis II*

For each excerpt, notate and identify the underlying pitch collection(s) on the staff provided and answer any additional questions.

A.

U. S. Folk Song

B.

von Reuenthal

C. Ravel, Trio for Violin, Cello, and Piano, III, mm. 1–8 (piano)

Ravel

D. Ives, "Mists"

Discuss the relationship of the voice and piano with respect to pitch collections and tonal centers.

_____

_____

_____

_____

_____

_____

E. Casella, Preludio from _11 pezzi infantile_

Discuss the relationship of the right hand and left hand with respect to pitch collections and tonal centers.

_____

_____

_____

_____

_____

_____

_____

F. Bartók, *For Children*, Book 1, no. 10

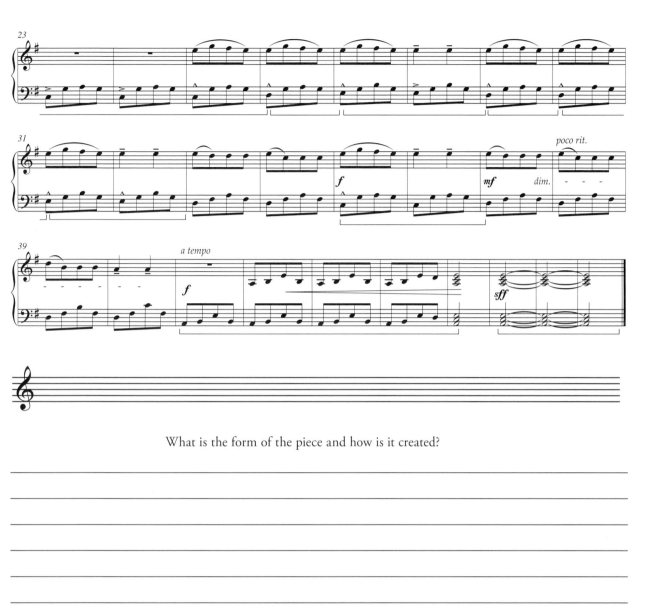

What is the form of the piece and how is it created?

_____

_____

_____

_____

_____

_____

G. Debussy, "Feuilles mortes" (Preludes for Piano, Book 1, no. 2)

H. Bartók, Violin Duos, no. 33

STREAMING AUDIO
www.oup.com/us/laitz

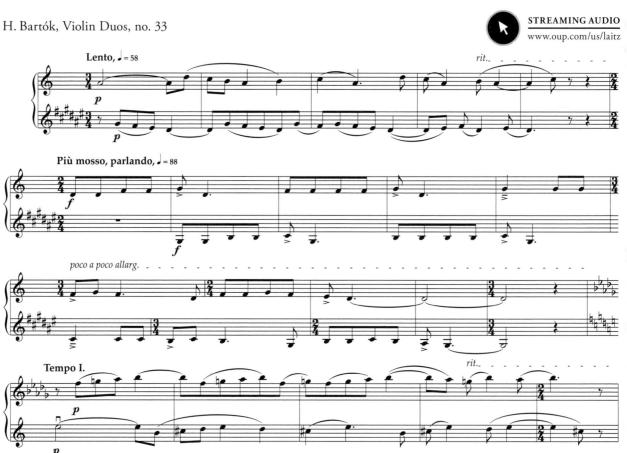

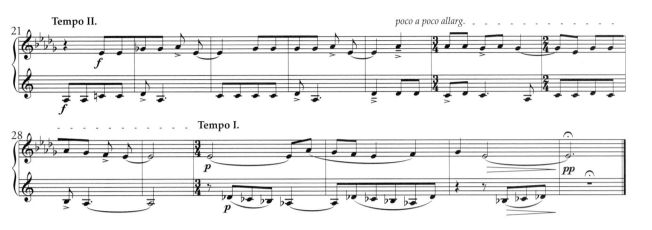

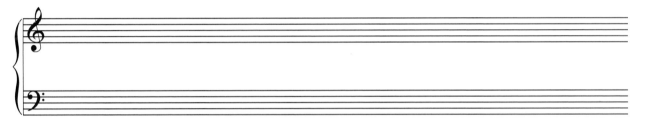

Make a chart of the overall form showing changes in pitch collections and tonal centers:

ASSIGNMENT 30.5
EXERCISE FOR COMPOSITION

EXERCISE 30.6   *Composition Projects*

A. Determine the modality of the melodic fragments, then compose a completion of the melodies retaining the same mode and tonal center.

B. Complete the composition using the fragmentary opening as inspiration.

Whole-Tone Invention

C. Continue the ostinato and compose a lyrical melody in the treble staff to go with it, employing the same octatonic collection. Create form in the piece from changes to different octatonic collections, or to different tonal centers while keeping the same octatonic collection.

Octatonic Ostinato

CHAPTER 31

Noncentric Music: Atonal Concepts and Analytical Methodology

ASSIGNMENT 31.1
EXERCISES FOR IDENTIFICATION

EXERCISE 31.1   *Pitches and Pitch Classes*

Label the notes in each excerpt as pitches and pitch classes. Then transpose as indicated and give the new labels for the transposed version. The first exercise is completed for you.

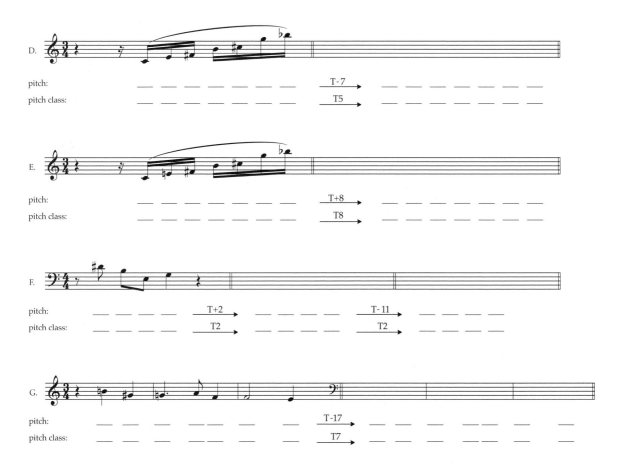

pitch:

pitch class:

EXERCISE 31.2   *Interval Types*

Give the four possible interval labels for each dyad.

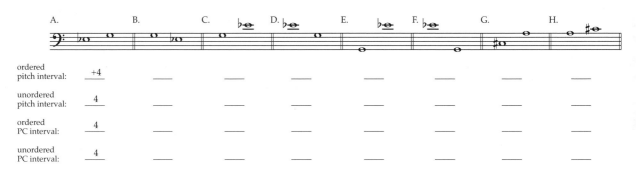

	A.	B.	C.	D.	E.	F.	G.	H.
ordered pitch interval:	+4	___	___	___	___	___	___	___
unordered pitch interval:	4	___	___	___	___	___	___	___
ordered PC interval:	4	___	___	___	___	___	___	___
unordered PC interval:	4	___	___	___	___	___	___	___

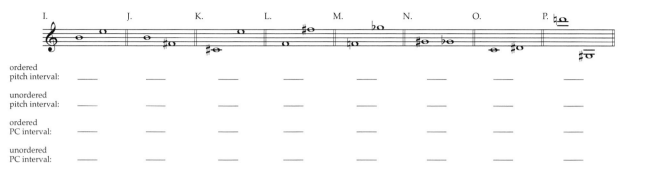

	I.	J.	K.	L.	M.	N.	O.	P.
ordered pitch interval:	___	___	___	___	___	___	___	___
unordered pitch interval:	___	___	___	___	___	___	___	___
ordered PC interval:	___	___	___	___	___	___	___	___
unordered PC interval:	___	___	___	___	___	___	___	___

EXERCISE 31.3 *Inversional Equivalence*

On the lower staff, notate the pitch-space inversion of the given set, using the given note as the starting point. Above or below all notes (on both staffs), indicate the PC label (integer). Finally, calculate the index number for the inversion you've notated. The first one is done for you.

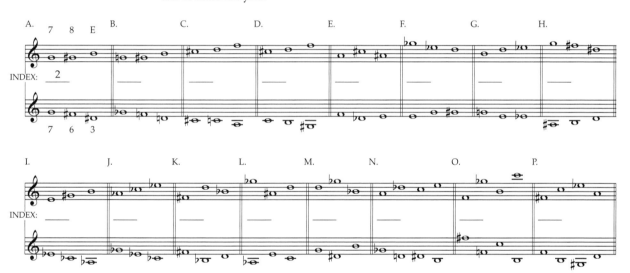

EXERCISE 31.4 *Sets and Set Classes*

Give the {normal order} and [prime form] for the PC set comprising all the notes in each excerpt.

	A.	B.	C.
normal order:	{347}	_____	_____
prime form:	[014]	_____	_____

ASSIGNMENT 31.2
EXERCISES FOR ANALYSIS

EXERCISE 31.5   *Post-Tonal Analysis: Webern, Movement for String Quartet, op. 5/2*

A. Identify the trichord type circled and labeled "a" in the viola:

    a. normal order: _____   prime form: _____

B. Circle and give letter labels "b" through "e" for four other formations of this same trichord type in the excerpt. In other words, locate four other trichords that are tranpositionally or inversionally equivalent to trichord "a." Only group together notes that are closely associated in some meaningful musical way. Indicate the normal order and prime form of these four trichords below:

    b. normal order: _____   prime form: _____

    c. normal order: _____   prime form: _____

    d. normal order: _____   prime form: _____

    e. normal order: _____   prime form: _____

C. Discuss the transpositional or inversional relationships among these trichords:

_____

_____

_____

_____

_____

D. What is the tetrachord type sounding among all three instruments at the end of the excerpt?

normal order: _____   prime form: _____

Give the normal order and location of one other instance of this tetrachord type formed by a logical musical grouping of notes in the excerpt:

normal order: _____   location: _____

E. Identify the following pentachords found in the excerpt:

All the notes in all three instruments held by the fermata in measure 1:

normal order: _____   prime form: _____

The next five notes in the viola after the "a" trichord:

normal order: _____   prime form: _____

Discuss similarities and differences between these two pentachords:

_____

_____

_____

_____

_____

_____

F. Find instances of the following sets among meaningful musical groupings in the excerpt:

[012]:   normal order: _____   location: _____

[014]:   normal order: _____   location: _____

[0246]: normal order: _____   location: _____

G. Identify the tetrachord type of the chord formed by 2nd violin and cello in the beginning of the excerpt:

normal order: _____   prime form: _____

Now examine the end of the piece:

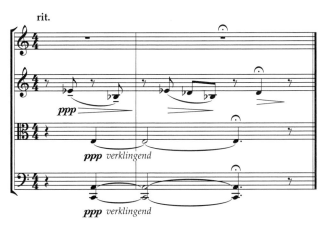

How does the end relate to the beginning?

_____

_____

_____

_____

_____

EXERCISE 31.6   *Post-Tonal Analysis: Schoenberg,*
Das Buch der hängende Gärten,
op. 15/11, piano introduction

STREAMING AUDIO
www.oup.com/us/laitz

A. Identify the tetrachords formed by the first four notes in each hand:

right hand: normal order: _____   prime form: _____

left hand: normal order: _____   prime form: _____

B. How many other formations of these tetrachord types can you find in musically meaningful groupings in the excerpt? What are their transpositional or inversional relationships?

_____

_____

_____

_____

_____

_____

C. What is the relationship between the structure of the right hand tetrachord and its subsequent transformations?

_____

_____

_____

_____

_____

_____

D. What are some other musically important note groupings in the excerpt? (Identify in normal order and prime form.) Mention any relationships you notice between these sets and the tetrachords identified in question A.

_____

_____

_____

_____

_____

_____

EXERCISE 31.7   *Post-Tonal Analysis: Berg, Piece for Clarinet and Piano, op. 5/1*

Note: The clarinet sounds a whole step lower than notated.

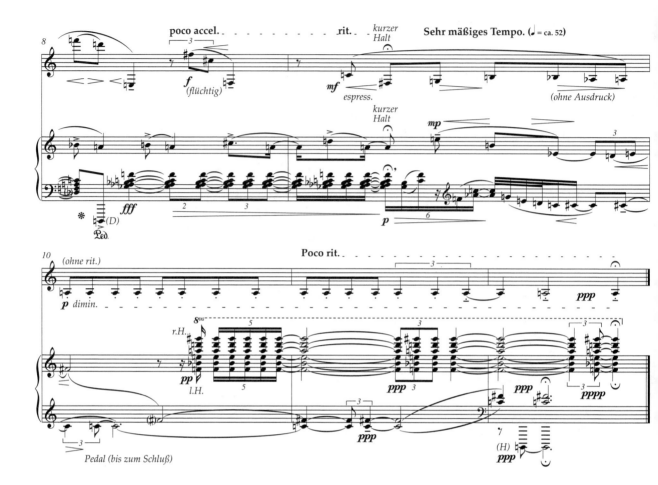

A. Listen to the piece several times. As you're listening, locate musically meaningful note groupings (pitch-class sets). Then identify these sets by normal order and prime form.

B. Which sets recur most frequently?

C. Which sets occur at structurally important moments?

D. How do the set types you have identified unify the work's pitch language and contribute to the creation of form?

E. How does the G^3 repeated in the clarinet in the last three measures relate to the pitch-space arrangement of the clarinet's notes in measure 9?

ASSIGNMENT 31.3
EXERCISE FOR COMPOSITION

EXERCISE 31.8   *Composing with Pitch-Class Sets*

A. Eight-Bar Etude for Piano.

Study the left-hand part provided. Determine the septachord type formed in first measure, then look for recurrences of this same chord type in other measures. Also identify set types in measures where the entire septachord isn't formed: How do the pitch groupings in these measures relate to the septachord? Compose a melody for the right hand based on the same septachord type and/or its subsets.

B. Dialogue.

Imagine a duet for treble and bass instruments in which the two musical lines seem to exchange thoughts or ideas as if in dialogue. A treble part is provided below. Compose a bass part that is in dialogue with it. Form PC sets in the bass part, and in the parts in combination, that interrelate in interesting ways.

CHAPTER 32

New Rhythmic and Metric Possibilities, Ordered PC Relations, and Twelve-Tone Techniques

ASSIGNMENT 32.1
EXERCISES FOR RHYTHM IDENTIFICATION

EXERCISE 32.1 *Rhythm in Post-Tonal Music*

Match each excerpt to the technical term that best describes it.

A. Boulez

B. Scriabin

C. Carter

D. Messiaen

E. Bartók

A. Boulez	asymmetrical meter
B. Scriabin	polyrhythm
C. Carter	changing meter
D. Messiaen	metric modulation
E. Bartók	non-retrogradable rhythm

EXERCISE 32.2 *Analysis of Rhythmic Techniques*

Write a short paragraph explaining the metric structure and rhythmic techniques found in each excerpt. Employ technical terminology from the chapter whenever possible.

A. Stravinsky, *L'histoire du soldat*, "Marche du soldat," mm. 1–21, piano arrangement

B. Carter, String Quartet no. 2, first movement, mm. 97–100, first violin

C. Ligeti, "Fém," No. 8 from Etudes for Piano, Book II, mm. 1–12

D. Cowell, "Exultation" for Piano, first section

Note: The notation in the left hand indicates black-key tone clusters between the upper and lower notes.

ASSIGNMENT 32.3
EXERCISE FOR COMPOSITION

EXERCISE 32.3   *Composition Exercises*

A. Compose a melody in ⅝ that changes beat groupings in the middle and then changes back. (Start and end at 2+3 and switch to 3+2 in the middle, or start and end at 3+2 and switch to 2+3 in the middle.) Use only notes of a certain pitch collection for one grouping and a different collection for the other. For example, you might employ the odd whole-tone collection at the beginning and end, and the even whole-tone collection when the grouping changes in the middle. Or perhaps switch from one octatonic collection to another, or from a certain hexachord to another.

B. Compose a melody in changing meter. Take this opportunity to explore a certain pitch collection or favorite hexachord. Experiment with the notion of "nonharmonic tones" within a post-tonal context. Or use a twelve-tone row—that you've created, or that you've borrowed from one of the examples in this chapter—to determine the PC content of the melody.

C. Compose a melody that becomes gradually faster though a process of *metric modulation*. Use pitch material as suggested above.

ASSIGNMENT 32.3
EXERCISES FOR ANALYSIS

EXERCISE 32.4 *Analysis of Twelve-Tone Rows*

For each row:

- Convert the twelve different notes to pitch-class integer notation.
- Give the ordered PC intervals between consecutive pitch classes.
- Give the {normal order} and [prime form] of the non-overlapping hexachords, tetrachords, and trichords.
- Describe any row features that seem interesting and/or compositionally exploitable (including aspects not revealed in the work you've already done).

A. Schoenberg, Variations for Orchestra, op. 31

PC: _____ _____ _____ _____ _____ _____ _____ _____ _____ _____ _____ _____

ordered PC
intervals: _____ _____ _____ _____ _____ _____ _____ _____ _____ _____ _____

hexachords: {_____} {_____}

[_____] [_____]

tetrachords: {_____} {_____} {_____}

[_____] [_____] [_____]

trichords: {_____} {_____} {_____} {_____}

[_____] [_____] [_____] [_____]

Discuss:

_____

_____

_____

_____

_____

_____

B. Webern, String Quartet, op. 28

PC: _____ _____ _____ _____ _____ _____ _____ _____ _____ _____ _____ _____

ordered PC
intervals: _____ _____ _____ _____ _____ _____ _____ _____ _____ _____ _____

hexachords: {_____}   {_____}

[_____]   [_____]

tetrachords: {_____}   {_____}   {_____}

[_____]   [_____]   [_____]

trichords: {_____} {_____} {_____} {_____}

[_____] [_____] [_____] [_____]

Discuss:

_____

_____

_____

_____

_____

_____

_____

C. Berg, *Der Wein*

PC: ___ ___ ___ ___ ___ ___ ___ ___ ___ ___ ___ ___

ordered PC
intervals: ___ ___ ___ ___ ___ ___ ___ ___ ___ ___ ___

hexachords: {_____}   {_____}

              [_____]   [_____]

tetrachords: {_____}   {_____}   {_____}

              [_____]   [_____]   [_____]

trichords: {_____}   {_____}   {_____}   {_____}

              [_____]   [_____]   [_____]   [_____]

Discuss:

_____

_____

_____

_____

_____

_____

D. Nono, *Il canto sospeso*

PC: ___ ___ ___ ___ ___ ___ ___ ___ ___ ___ ___ ___

ordered PC
intervals: ___ ___ ___ ___ ___ ___ ___ ___ ___ ___ ___

hexachords: {_____}   {_____}

               [_____]   [_____]

tetrachords: {_____}   {_____}   {_____}

               [_____]   [_____]   [_____]

trichords: {_____} {_____} {_____} {_____}

               [_____] [_____] [_____] [_____]

Discuss:

_____

_____

_____

_____

_____

_____

_____

EXERCISE 32.5 *Calculating and Labeling Row Forms*

Write the specified forms of the rows in Exercise 32.4 in pitch-class integer notation. Assume that the Exercise 32.4 rows are all P-forms (for example, Schoenberg's row in question 32.4A is P10).

A. Schoenberg, Variations for Orchestra

P1: ___ ___ ___ ___ ___ ___ ___ ___ ___ ___ ___ ___

I7: ___ ___ ___ ___ ___ ___ ___ ___ ___ ___ ___ ___

R10: ___ ___ ___ ___ ___ ___ ___ ___ ___ ___ ___ ___

RI7: ___ ___ ___ ___ ___ ___ ___ ___ ___ ___ ___ ___

B. Webern, String Quartet

P1: ___ ___ ___ ___ ___ ___ ___ ___ ___ ___ ___ ___

I1: ___ ___ ___ ___ ___ ___ ___ ___ ___ ___ ___ ___

R4: ___ ___ ___ ___ ___ ___ ___ ___ ___ ___ ___ ___

RI7: ___ ___ ___ ___ ___ ___ ___ ___ ___ ___ ___ ___

C. Berg, *Der Wein*

P1: ___ ___ ___ ___ ___ ___ ___ ___ ___ ___ ___ ___

I7: ___ ___ ___ ___ ___ ___ ___ ___ ___ ___ ___ ___

R3: ___ ___ ___ ___ ___ ___ ___ ___ ___ ___ ___ ___

RI11: ___ ___ ___ ___ ___ ___ ___ ___ ___ ___ ___ ___

D. Nono, *Il canto sospeso*

P9: ___ ___ ___ ___ ___ ___ ___ ___ ___ ___ ___ ___

I6: ___ ___ ___ ___ ___ ___ ___ ___ ___ ___ ___ ___

R7: ___ ___ ___ ___ ___ ___ ___ ___ ___ ___ ___ ___

RI3: ___ ___ ___ ___ ___ ___ ___ ___ ___ ___ ___ ___

EXERCISE 32.6   *Recognizing Row Forms*

Each of the following rows is a form of one of the rows in Exercise 32.4. For each, identify the source (Schoenberg, Webern, Berg, or Nono) and give the form label. The first one is done for you.

		source	label
A.	1 7 9 6 8 0 5 4 T E 2 3	Schoenberg	P1
B.	E 5 7 4 6 T 3 2 8 9 0 1		
C.	5 6 3 4 0 E 2 1 9 T 7 8		
D.	T 4 2 5 3 E 6 7 1 0 9 8		
E.	T E 9 0 8 1 7 2 6 3 5 4		
F.	9 5 6 2 0 7 4 3 1 E T 8		
G.	0 T 9 7 5 4 1 8 6 2 3 E		
H.	9 8 E T 2 3 0 1 5 4 7 6		
I.	T 9 E 8 0 7 1 6 2 5 3 4		
J.	8 7 4 3 9 T 5 1 E 2 0 6		

EXERCISE 32.7   *Twelve-Tone Analysis: Schoenberg,*
                    Piece for Piano, op. 33a

Here is a clear presentation of a P-form of Schoenberg's row:

A. Make a twelve-tone matrix for this row:

I0
↓

P0 →

B. Determine the {normal order} and [prime form] of this row's non-overlapping
    hexachords, tetrachords, and trichords:

hexachords: {_____}   {_____}

[_____]   [_____]

tetrachords: {_____} {_____} {_____}

[_____] [_____] [_____]

trichords: {_____} {_____} {_____} {_____}

[_____] [_____] [_____] [_____]

C. Let's look first at a passage near the beginning where Schoenberg introduces a new theme in contrasting style, reminiscent of the second theme in a sonata form. Directly on the score of this passage, indicate the row forms used and place an order position number (1–12) next to each note.

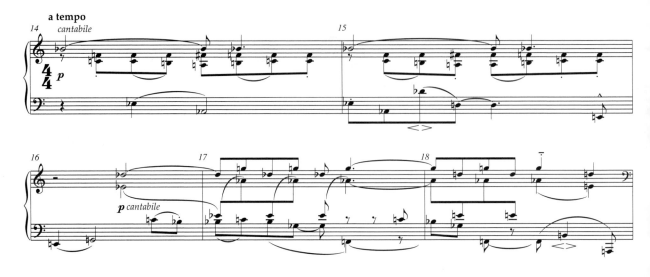

D. Explain Schoenberg's rationale for choosing these row forms in this passage for giving them musical expression as he does. Mention properties that are built into the row and exploited here with particular clarity.

_____

_____

_____

_____

_____

_____

E. Now look at the piece's opening section (below). Indicate the row form and order position numbers on the score.

EXERCISE 32.8   *Twelve-Tone Analysis: Webern, Symphony, op. 21*

Here is the P-form of the row presented at the beginning of Webern's Symphony:

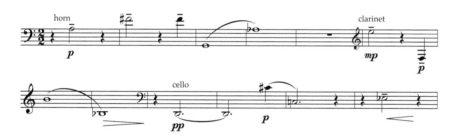

A. Make a 12-tone matrix for this row:

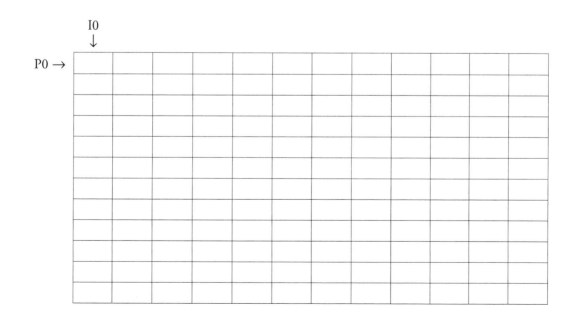

B. Determine the {normal order} and [prime form] of this row's non-overlapping hexachords, tetrachords, and trichords:

hexachords: {_____} {_____}

[_____] [_____]

tetrachords: {_____} {_____} {_____}

[_____] [_____] [_____]

trichords: {_____} {_____} {_____} {_____}

[_____] [_____] [_____] [_____]

C. Discuss the structure and properties of this row:

_____

_____

_____

_____

_____

_____

D. The second movement of Webern's symphony is a theme and variation. On the score for the first variation (next page), indicate the row forms Webern uses and number the order positions (1–12) in each form.

E. Discuss the row usage in this excerpt. Explain how the row usage groups the four instrumental lines into two pairs.

_____

_____

_____

_____

_____

_____

Webern, Symphony, op. 21, second movement, variation 1 (mm. 11–23).

F. Now look at variation 7 from the same movement (next two pages). This variation presents the same row forms as variation 1. Mark the distribution of these forms on the score.

G. Compare the row presentation in variations 1 and 7: How is it similar, and how is it different?

H. How does Webern create harmonic consistency in variation 7 when he associates notes from different row forms (e.g., mm. 78–79, cello and viola)? Cite evidence from throughout the variation in support of your answer.

_____

_____

_____

_____

_____

_____

Webern, Symphony, op. 21, second movement, Variation 7 (mm. 77–89).

EXERCISE 32.9   *Twelve-Tone Analysis: Dallapiccola, "Fregi" from* **Quaderno musicale di Annalibera**

A. A P-form of the row is presented in the right hand in mm. 1–4 (ending on the E4). Make a twelve-tone matrix for this row:

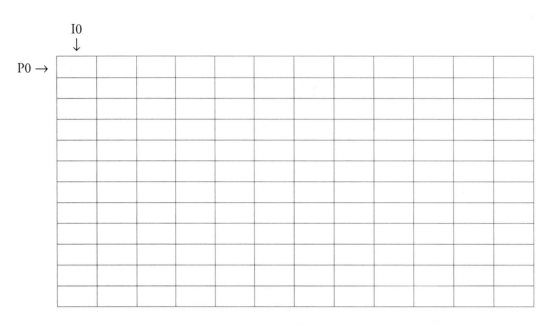

I0

P0 →

B. Determine the {normal order} and [prime form] of this row's non-overlapping hexachords, tetrachords, and trichords:

hexachords: {_____}   {_____}

[_____]   [_____]

tetrachords: {_____} {_____} {_____}

[_____] [_____] [_____]

trichords: {_____} {_____} {_____} {_____}

[_____] [_____] [_____] [_____]

C. On the score below, indicate which row forms are used in this movement. Place an order position number next to each note.

D. Discuss the intervallic structure of the initial P-form in the right hand of mm. 1–4.

_____

_____

_____

_____

_____

E. Now look at the first two row forms in the right hand. How does Dallapiccola
    draw attention to the specific transformational relationship between these two
    forms?

F. Where is there a varied return of the opening melody? What is different about
    it, and what is the same? How does Dallapiccola draw attention to the specific
    transformational relationship between the original melody and its variation?

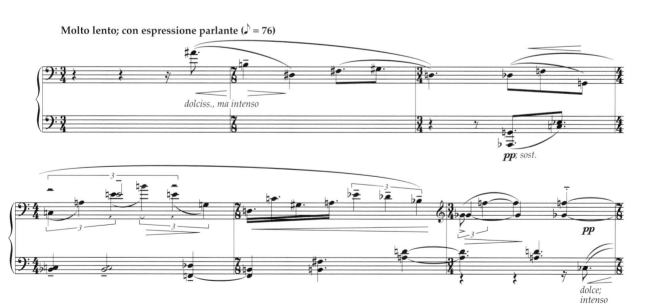

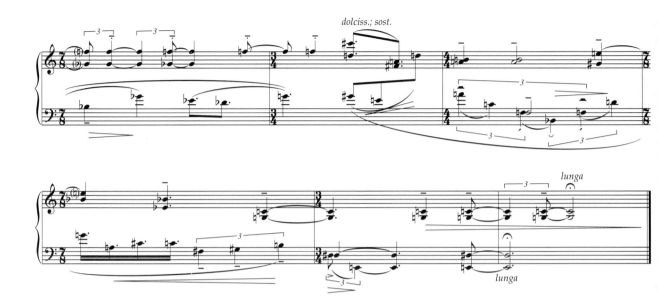

ASSIGNMENT 32.4   EXERCISES FOR COMPOSITION WITH TWELVE-TONE ROWS

EXERCISE 32.10   *Constructing Twelve-Tone Rows*

Create twelve-tone rows with the specified properties. Notate your rows as series of whole notes on the staffs provided. Try to use a variety of intervals between adjacent notes, so that the structural redundancy of the rows is not immediately obvious.

A. All four non-overlapping trichords are members of set class [013], but the row is not R- or RI-symmetrical.

B. All four non-overlapping trichords are members of set class [013], and the row is R-symmetrical.

C. All four non-overlapping trichords are members of set class [013], and the row is RI-symmetrical.

D. All three non-overlapping tetrachords are members of set class [0235].

E. Compose a melody based on a single statement of row A above and emphasizing the trichordal equivalences.

F. Compose a different melody based on a single statement of row A and emphasizing note groupings other than the equivalent non-overlapping trichords.

G. Compose a melody based on a single statement of row B above and emphasizing the trichordal equivalences and symmetrical structure.

H. Compose a melody based on row C above and emphasizing the trichordal equivalences and symmetrical structure. Combine it with an inversional form of the same row in inversional canon.

EXERCISE 32.11   *Twelve-Tone Composition Project*

Use row D above (with the non-overlapping [0235]s) as the basis for a short piano piece. Here are some ideas to get you started:

1. One possibility is to employ a variety of row forms, as in Dallapiccola's "Fregi."
2. Or you might choose to focus just on a small selective group of row forms, as in variations 1 and 7 of Webern's Symphony.
3. The pianists hands can work together to present row forms, as in Schoenberg's op. 33a, or they can present different row forms separately, in counterpoint, as in Dallapiccola's "Fregi."
4. Another possibility is a homophonic texture, in which one hand presents one row form as a series of chords, perhaps in rhythmic ostinato, while the other hand presents a different row form as a single-line melody.
5. Consider ways of both emphasizing and de-emphasizing the row's tetrachordal redundancy.

To help explore your options, make a 12-tone matrix for your row:

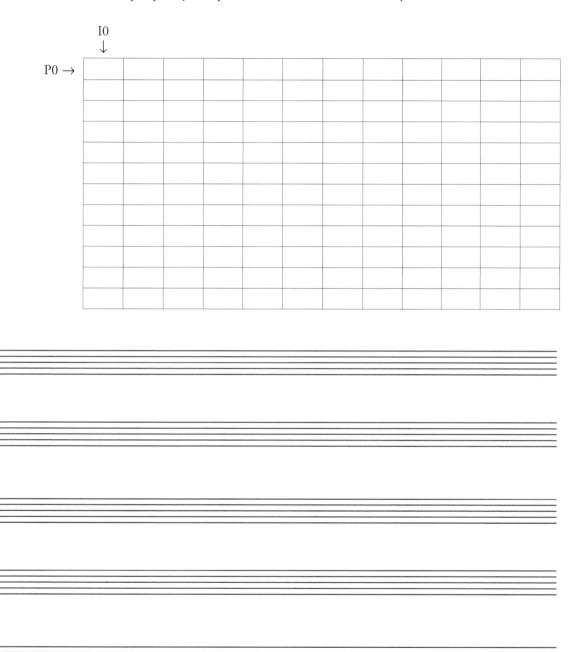

APPENDIX 1

Invertible Counterpoint, Compound Melody, and Implied Harmonies

ASSIGNMENT 1.1
EXERCISES FOR INVERTIBLE COUNTERPOINT

ANALYSIS

EXERCISE 1.1 *Analysis of Invertible Counterpoint*

In the following excerpts, label any invertible counterpoint by using brackets and X and Y for the material in the upper and lower voices, showing how they are exchanged in the repetitions. Do *not* analyze with roman numerals.

A. Handel, Suite no. 7 in G minor, HWV 255, Passacaglia

B. Bach, Two-Part Invention no. 6 in E major, BWV 777

C. Giardini, from *Six Duos for Violin and Cello*, op. 14

WRITING

EXERCISE 1.2   *Writing Chord Progressions That Create Invertible Counterpoint*

From the following models, on a separate sheet of manuscript paper:

1. Provide an outer voice to complement the given voice, such that the voices will produce invertible counterpoint at the octave.
2. Swap the voices to create invertible counterpoint.
3. Determine the contrapuntal/harmonic progression that is implied from the outer-voice counterpoint.
4. Add roman numerals and inner voices.

The first exercise presents one possible solution. Write at least one more for the first exercise and two solutions for B. Play solutions, first the outer voices only and then in four voices.

Optional: In a meter and a rhythmic setting of your choice, string together two or three of the progressions to create a four- to eight-measure piece.

A. Given: bass scale degrees $\hat{1}$–$\hat{2}$–$\hat{3}$–$\hat{4}$–$\hat{3}$

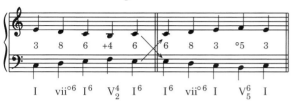

I   vii°⁶   I⁶   V₂⁴   I⁶   I⁶   vii°⁶ I   V₅⁶   I

B. Given: bass scale degrees $\hat{1}$–$\hat{7}$–$\hat{1}$–$\hat{6}$–$\hat{3}$–$\hat{2}$–$\hat{1}$

EXERCISE 1.3   *Analysis of Incomplete Harmonies*

STREAMING AUDIO
www.oup.com/us/laitz

Use roman numerals to analyze the passages based on the harmonic implications of the voices. Label all embellishing tones, including passing and neighboring tones and suspensions. *Note:* You will encounter only the chords we have studied.

A. Bach, Minuet, French Suite no. 3 in B minor, BWV 814

B. Haydn, Piano Sonata no. 30 in D major, Hob XVI.19, *Moderato*

C. Haydn, Piano Sonata no. 5 in G major, Hob XVI.11, *Presto*
   What contrapuntal technique is used in mm. 9–12?

ASSIGNMENT 1.2
EXERCISES FOR INVERTIBLE COUNTERPOINT

ANALYSIS

EXERCISE 1.4   *Analysis of Invertible Counterpoint*

STREAMING AUDIO
www.oup.com/us/laitz

In the following excerpts, label any invertible counterpoint by using brackets and X and Y for the material in the upper and lower voices, showing how they are exchanged in the repetitions. Do *not* analyze with roman numerals.

A. Beethoven, Piano Sonata in E major, op. 109, "Gesangvoll, mit innigster Empfindung," Variation 3

B. Handel, Sonata no. 1 for Flute and Continuo in E minor, op. 1, HWV 359b, *Allegro*

C. Mozart, Piano Concerto in E♭, K. 482

legato

EXERCISE 1.5   *Analysis of Invertible Counterpoint*

Beethoven, like nearly all common-practice musicians, vigorously (if grudgingly) studied theory and counterpoint. Shown is an exercise in invertible counterpoint that he completed under the tutelage of a famous teacher named Albrechtsberger. Study Beethoven's solution and label intervals and suspensions; then on a separate sheet of manuscript paper, recopy his solution in the key of A major so that the counterpoint appears above the cantus firmus. In a sentence or two, remark on the quality of Beethoven's counterpoint.

ASSIGNMENT 1.3
EXERCISES FOR COMPOUND MELODY

EXERCISE 1.6   *Composition*

Complete the following compound-melody excerpt.

1. Determine the appropriate harmonies from the given bass.
2. Add the upper voices. Maintain the basic pattern.
3. Write a new phrase (but one that maintains the general mood and texture of the original phrase) that ends on a half cadence.
4. Play the new phrase, followed by the given phrase. The result is a large antecedent-consequent structure.

EXERCISE 1.7   *Compound Melodies*

STREAMING AUDIO
www.oup.com/us/laitz

1. Analyze the underlying harmonies, circling and labeling all nonharmonic tones. When you encounter a harmony we have not covered, simply write the letter name of the chord's root and its appropriate figured bass.
2. Make a three- or four-voice rhythmic reduction. Maintain good voice leading between the outer voices. It may be difficult to use consistently good voice leading in the inner voices because composers writing compound melody often treat the alto and tenor quite freely, sometimes dropping one of the voices and then having it reenter the texture. Exercise A is completed for you.

A.

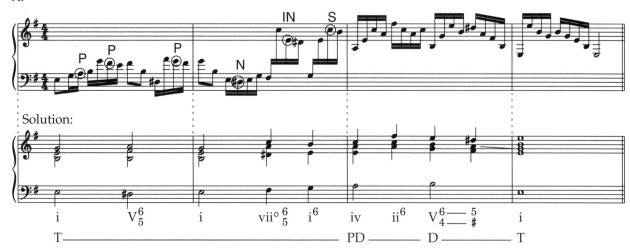

B. Corelli, Violin Sonata in B♭ major, op. 5, no. 2, *Allegro*

C. Bach, Gigue, Partita no. 2 for Solo Violin in D minor, BWV 1004

ASSIGNMENT 1.4
EXERCISES FOR INCOMPLETE HARMONIES

ANALYSIS

EXERCISE 1.8   *Analysis of Incomplete Harmonies*

Use roman numerals to analyze the passages based on the harmonic implications presented by the incomplete chords. Label all embellishing tones, including passing and neighbor tones and suspensions. *Note:* You will encounter only chords we have studied.

EXERCISE 1.9   *Analysis of Compound Melodies*

STREAMING AUDIO
www.oup.com/us/laitz

1. Analyze the underlying harmonies, circling and labeling all nonharmonic tones. When you encounter a harmony we have not covered, simply write the letter name of the chord's root and its appropriate figured bass.
2. Make a voice-leading reduction of the outer voices by using stems for structural notes and unstemmed pitches for passing and neighboring motions.
3. If more than the two outer voices are present, add the inner parts. You need not worry about strict voice leading because inner voices are treated quite freely, sometimes dropping out and reentering the texture.

A. Bach, Prelude, Cello Suite no. 2 in D minor, BWV 1008

B. Bach, Bourrée I, Cello Suite no. 3 in C major, BWV 1009

C. Bach, Allemande, Cello Suite no. 2 in D minor, BWV 1008

D. Bach, Gigue, Cello Suite no. 2 in D minor, BWV 1008

The Motive

ANALYSIS

EXERCISE 2.1 *Motivic Analysis from Bach's Art of the Fugue*

STREAMING AUDIO
www.oup.com/us/laitz

Label the transformation types that you encounter in the given excerpts, each of which is taken from J. S. Bach's *Art of the Fugue*. The main motive is boxed for you. Possible transformations include:

1. embellishment (adding pitches between main notes)
2. reharmonization
3. change of interval
4. transposition
5. sequence
6. inversion
7. retrograde
8. augmentation
9. diminution
10. imitation
11. interpolation
12. fragmentation
13. change of meter

A. Bach, Contrapunctus I

B. Bach, Contrapunctus IV

C. Bach, Contrapunctus V

D. Bach, Contrapunctus VI

E. Bach, Contrapunctus XII

F. Bach, Contrapunctus XVII

ASSIGNMENT 2.2
EXERCISES FOR MOTIVIC ANALYSIS

EXERCISE 2.2 *Motivic Analysis*

STREAMING AUDIO
www.oup.com/us/laitz

Identify the motive and subsequent transformations in the following excerpts.

A. Beethoven, String Quartet in A minor, op. 132, *Assai sostenuto*

B. Corelli, Trio Sonata in C minor, op 1, no. 8, *Vivace*

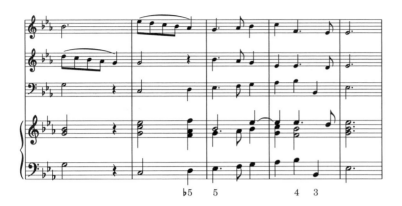

C. Clementi, Sonata in G major, op. 40, no. 1

D. Beethoven, Piano piece, WoO 61a

E. Beethoven, String Quartet in C major, op. 59, no. 3, Menuetto Grazioso

WRITING

EXERCISE 2.3 BASIC MOTIVIC ELABORATION

Given are short, slowly moving melodies and a bass line that implies a harmonic structure. Choose one (or two contrasting) melodic/rhythmic motives and incorporate it or them within the melody. You might want to focus on neighbors, passing, and broken-chord figures, two of which may be combined to form a single longer motive.

ASSIGNMENT 2.3   EXERCISES FOR MOTIVIC REPETITIONS AND OUTER-VOICE ELABORATION

ANALYSIS

EXERCISE 2.4   *Comparison of Motivic Repetitions*

STREAMING AUDIO
www.oup.com/us/laitz

In each of the following examples a motive and one or more repetitions have been boxed. Label the transformation used for each motivic repetition based on the initial statement. Repetitions may be literal (not so common) or transformed (common). Transformations include embellishment (e.g., embellishing tones, interpolation, etc.), transposition, sequence, inversion, retrograde, retrograde inversion, augmentation and diminution, fragmentation, change of interval, imitation, and occasionally, two or more transformations simultaneously.

A. Bach, Gigue, English Suite no. 4 in F major, BWV 809

B. Bach, Organ Fugue in C major, BWV 545

C. Haydn, String Quartet in D major, op. 33, no. 6

D. Bach, Gigue, English Suite no. 4 in F major, BWV 809

WRITING

EXERCISE 2.5   *Outer-Voice Elaboration*

An outer-voice contrapuntal framework is provided, both voices of which you will complete with one or two motives. The result will be a rhythmically interesting and unified composition, one in which the two voices participate equally. Complete the following steps, in order:

1. Based on the harmonic implications of the two voices, analyze, using roman numerals.
2. Choose one or at the most two of the motives given in Appendix Exercise 2.3 (or create your own), adding them in various contexts based on the implied harmonies of the exercise.

ASSIGNMENT 2.4
ANALYSIS

EXERCISE 2.6   *Motivic Analysis*

In each of the following examples one (or in some cases a second) motive has been circled. Identify as many repetitions (transformations) as possible in the rest of each example.

A. Brahms, Capriccio in G minor, op. 116, no. 3

B. Haydn, String Quartet in B♭ major, op. 55, no. 3, *Vivace assai*

1.

2.

ASSIGNMENT 2.5   EXERCISES FOR OUTER-VOICE ELABORATION AND INTERMOVEMENT MOTIVIC RELATIONSHIPS

WRITING

EXERCISE 2.7   *Outer-Voice Elaboration*

Two outer-voice contrapuntal frameworks are provided, both voices of which you will complete with one or two motives. The result will be rhythmically interesting and unified compositions in which the two voices participate equally. Complete the following steps, in order:

1. Based on the harmonic implications of the two voices, analyze, using roman numerals.
2. Choose one or at the most two motives, adding them in various contexts based on the implied harmonies of the exercise.

A.

B.

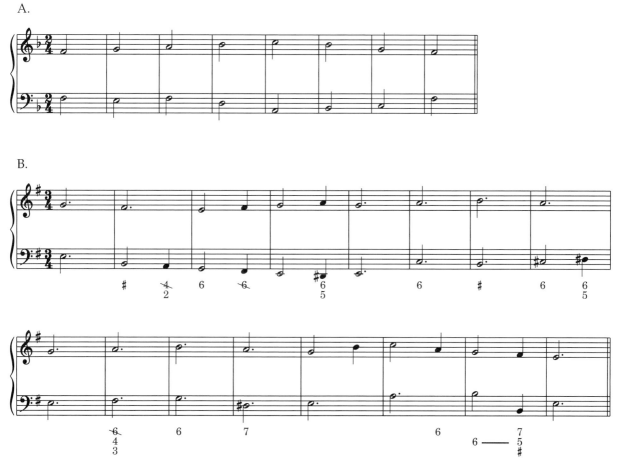

ANALYSIS

EXERCISE 2.8   *Intermovement Motivic Relationships*

STREAMING AUDIO
www.oup.com/us/laitz

Excerpts from two or more movements taken from single works appear next with hints that will lead you to discover motivic relationships that occur between the movements.

A. Mozart, Piano Sonata in C minor, K. 457, *Molto allegro* and *Allegro assai*

These two movements contain numerous relationships, some of which lie directly on the surface, including the rising broken-chord figure that opens the sonata's first movement (Example A1) and its inversion, a falling figure that opens the last movement (Example A2); even the rhythmic figure (long-short-short) reappears in both figures. Other types of relationships occur as well and are somewhat hidden, since they span longer stretches of music, and their members are not stated as adjacent pitches. However, they too are marked by melodic fluency, registral prominence, and musical parallelism (i.e., they are members of a pattern). Identify a single motive that underlies the openings of the first and last movements.

A1.

A2.

B. Corelli, Trio Sonata no. 8 in B minor

    Corelli subtly works in gestures that are not literal transformation, but nonetheless preserve the gestural content of an initial motive.

  B1. Preludio

  B2. Allemanda

  B3. Tempo di Gavotta

C. Corelli, Trio Sonata no. 6 in G minor

The first appearance of the motive is beamed.

C1. Allemanda

C2. Corrente

C3. Giga

ASSIGNMENT 2.6
ANALYSIS

EXERCISE 2.9   *Motivic Saturation: Analysis of Bach's Two-Part Invention in C major, BWV 772*

STREAMING AUDIO
www.oup.com/us/laitz

Listen to and/or play through Bach's invention. On your score, the main theme, called the "subject," is labeled "S." The subject is divided into two smaller motives, a rising step-wise fourth (labeled "x") and a falling third motive (labeled "y"). The highest pitch of the subject, F, belongs to both motives. The "countersubject" (labeled "CS") accompanies the subject. Bach repeats the subject and its motivic components in many ways. On your score, circle all statements of the subject (and its motives x and y) and the countersubject. Answer the questions that follow.

A. In a sentence or two, compare and contrast the contour (melodic shape) of the S and the CS.
B. Is the counterpoint in mm. 1–2 invertible in the strict sense? Explain in a sentence or two.
C. What is the origin of the sequence (right hand) in mm. 3–4?
D. What is the origin of the left hand in the same bars?
E. What is the origin of the sequence (right hand) in mm. 5–6?
F. Compare mm. 7–8 with mm. 1–2.
G. What is the origin of the figure sequenced in mm. 9–10?
H. Compare mm. 15–18 with mm. 9–10. What is the same and what is different?
I. Label all melodic sequences.
J. Use roman numerals to analyze the following measures: 1–3 (downbeat); 7–9 (downbeat).

ASSIGNMENT 2.7
ANALYSIS

EXERCISE 2.10   *Analysis of Implied Harmonies and Motives*

Use roman numerals to analyze the following phrase. Harmonies change usually twice each measure. Then, determine what short pitch/rhythmic event stated at the beginning of the piece may best be labeled a motive. Circle and label it; then trace its repetitions throughout the piece, labeling each according to how it is transformed. Consider that the motive may occur at different levels of the musical structure.

ASSIGNMENT 2.8   EXERCISES FOR MOTIVIC TRANSFORMATIONS

EXERCISE 2.11   *Motivic Transformations*

In each of the following examples a motive and one or more repetitions have been boxed. Label the transformation used for each motivic repetition based on the initial statement. Repetitions may be literal (not so common) or transformed (common). Transformations include embellishment (e.g., embellishing tones, interpolation, etc.), transposition, sequence, inversion, retrograde, retrograde inversion, augmentation and diminution, fragmentation, change of interval, imitation, and occasionally, two or more transformations simultaneously.

A. Haydn, String Quartet in F major, op. 55, no. 2, Finale, *Presto*

B. Haydn, Piano Sonata in D major, Hob XVI.14, Trio

C. Bach, Fugue in C minor, *Well-Tempered Clavier*, Book II, BWV 820

1.

2.

Additional Harmonic-Sequence Topics

WRITING

EXERCISE 3.1   *Figured Bass*

Realize the following figured bass; bracket and label sequences. Provide a roman numeral analysis for all harmonies outside of the sequences. Inverted seventh chords must be complete.

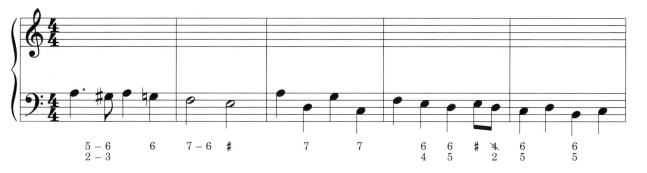

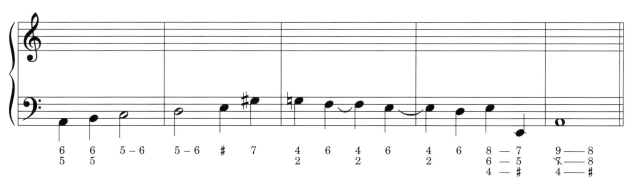

EXERCISE 3.2   *Conversion*

STREAMING AUDIO
www.oup.com/us/laitz

Reduce the following excerpts to homophonic four-voice textures. Then, convert the descending six-three passages into D2 (−5/+4) sequences with seventh chords as shown in the sample solution.

Sample solution:

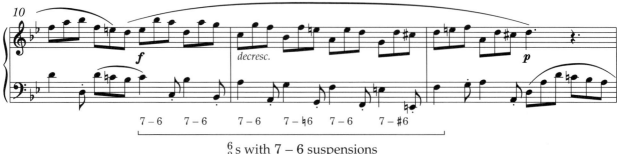

$\frac{6}{3}$ s with 7 − 6 suspensions

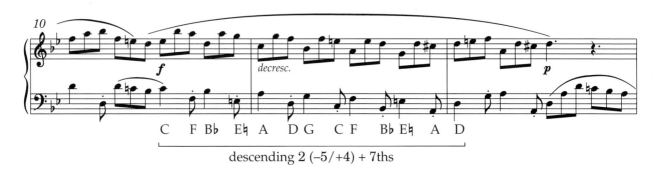

descending 2 (−5/+4) + 7ths

A. Corelli, Concerto Grosso in C major, op. 6, no. 10, Allemande, *Allegro*

B. Corelli, Concerto Grosso in C major, op. 6, no. 10, Corrente

C. Haydn, Piano Sonata no. 37 in E major, Hob XVI.22, Finale, *Tempo di Minuet*

EXERCISE 3.3   *Composition*

On a separate sheet of manuscript paper, complete the following tasks in four-voice chorale style. Each represents compositional guidelines only; you should not restrict your creativity. Use any major or minor key and either $\frac{4}{4}$ or $\frac{6}{8}$ meter. Begin with a compositional plan like the ones discussed so that your sequences fit convincingly into the musical fabric rather than sounding as if they are merely wedged in. Then write the outer voices, making sure that the harmonic rhythm is logical. Finally, write the inner voices.

1. Write a four-measure phrase that contains a sequence: Establish tonic (m. 1)—sequence (mm. 2–3)—cadence.
2. Write an eight-measure interrupted period with a sequence:
    Phrase 1: Establish tonic (mm. 1–2), lead to PD and a HC.
    Phrase 2: Sequence, starting on tonic (mm. 5–6), lead to PD and a PAC.
3. Write an eight-measure period that has a sentence form:
    Phrase 1: Write two two-measure subphrases, the first of which moves from I to IV and the second of which moves from V to I and closes with an IAC.
    Phrase 2: Write a single four-measure gesture that develops the idea in the first subphrase; include a sequence in mm. 2–3 of the phrase.

EXERCISE 3.4   *Embellishing a Homophonic Texture*

Take any of the compositions from the previous exercise and add a florid melody in the soprano voice. This melody will be played by a melody instrument, and the lower three voices will be played by either a small ensemble (strings or winds) or piano. Note that you may have to write parts for transposing instruments. *Optional:* Augment the rhythmic values of each chord by a consistent proportion (e.g., × 2 or × 4), and add more embellishing tones to the melody as well as the inner voices. The resulting 16- or even 32-measure pieces will sound terrific.

ASSIGNMENT 3.2
EXERCISES FOR HARMONIC ANALYSIS

EXERCISE 3.5   *Analysis*

STREAMING AUDIO
www.oup.com/us/laitz

The following examples from the literature present sequences within larger musical contexts. Create a formal diagram for each example (which may include phrases, periods, and sentences). Bracket and label the following in the score: tonic expansion, sequence, and cadence. A sequence may occur at the beginning or at a later point within the tonic prolongation. Circle the bass and soprano pitches of the sequence (one bass note and one soprano note per chord). This outer-voice structure must create good two-voice counterpoint.

A. Mozart, Piano Sonata in C major, K. 545, I

B. Handel, Concerto Grosso in G minor, op. 6, no. 6, HWV 324, *Allegro*

C. Corelli, Concerto Grosso, no. 10 in C major, Corrente

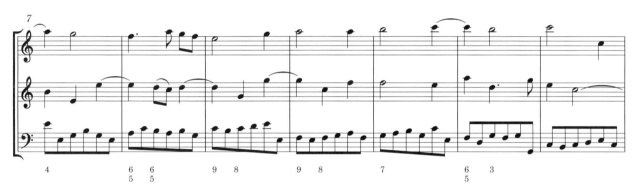

ANALYSIS

EXERCISE 3.6   *Analysis of Sequences Appearing in Compound Melodies*

STREAMING AUDIO
www.oup.com/us/laitz

Determine the sequence type in the following compound melodies and then provide a reductive verticalization of the implied voices (either three or four) as shown in the sample solution.

Sample solution:

A2

A. Bach, Menuet, French Suite no. 3 in B minor, BWV 814

   Bracket subphrases in this example. What type of formal structure occurs?

B. Schumann, *Kreisleriana*, op. 16, no. 5
  While this is not strictly a compound melody, it is possible to create a five-voice structure.

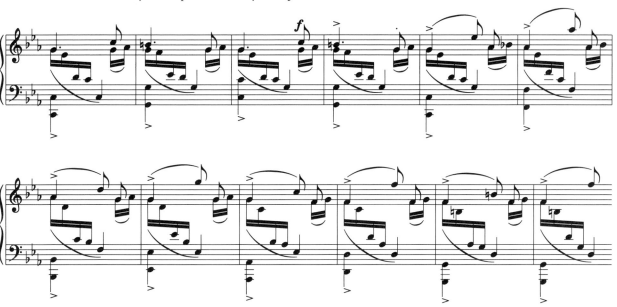

C. Bach, Menuet, French Suite no. 2 in C minor, BWV 813

EXERCISE 3.7 *Analysis of Sequential Progressions and Parallel Six-Three Passages*

STREAMING AUDIO
www.oup.com/us/laitz

Bracket and label sequences, sequential progressions, and parallel six-three chord streams. Label suspensions and determine whether the six-three chords function transitionally or prolongationally.

A. Handel, Gigue, Suite XVI in G minor, HWV 263

Consider this example to be in D minor. Make a 1:1 contrapuntal reduction of the excerpt. What long-range contrapuntal event takes place between the downbeats of mm. 10 and 12?

B. Handel, "But Who May Abide the Day of His Coming?" *Messiah*, HWV 56

What contrapuntal technique is used at the beginning of this excerpt? Compare this example with the previous one.

C. Schubert, German Dance no. 1, *German Dances and Ecossaises*, D. 643

D. Corelli, Concerto Grosso in C major, op. 6, no. 10, Corrente